TOP GRAPHIC DESIGN

TOP GRAPHIC DESIGN

FHK Henrion

Examples of visual communication
by leading graphic designers

Visuelles Kommunikations-Design
an Beispielen führender Grafik-Designer

Le «design» de communication visuelle
illustré par des graphistes de premier plan

ABC Edition Zurich

ABC Verlag Zürich

Editions ABC Zurich

Contents　　　　　　　Inhalt　　　　　　　Sommaire

When I begun the task of compiling the book "Top Graphic Design" I was faced with the inevitability of somehow restricting the range of designers included so that more pages could be devoted to each.

My preference was to show less those whose work has already been substantially exposed in books and magazines. Thus my choice could not be but subjective which I hope, however, is to the good. The book should show the point of view of one who has worked for 45 years in a field which during that time has changed in name from commercial art to graphic design and eventually to visual communication. This change of name is not without significance. Although the activity of graphic design itself has not changed that much, I believe that the approach has altered as we are much more analytical today and as we have a much greater awareness of the process of communication and of visual perception; we also have a greater understanding of the different target publics to whom our messages are addressed. We know more about structure, theory and methodology on the one hand, and the mechanics of intuitive creativity on the other. Modules, grids and systems are all essential ingredients of the design process but they need not be used at the expense of intuition rather than in conjunction with it.

One way of narrowing down the choice of designers likely to be included in the book was to restrict it mainly to members of the Alliance Graphique Internationale, an association to which I have belonged almost from its inception and about which I should say perhaps a few words. Soon after the war, in 1951, three French and two Swiss designers who knew each others work but not each other met in Switzerland and founded the AGI. There is an obvious interest to know the people behind the work personally and try to understand what motivates them. No doubt the AGI is an 'elitist' society and in no way ashamed of it,

Bei der Aufgabe, das Buch «Top Graphic Design» zusammenzustellen, war mein erster Entschluss, die Anzahl der Beiträge zu beschränken, um jedem einzelnen Designer mehr Seiten widmen zu können. Ich entschloss mich daher für eine Anzahl von Kollegen, deren Arbeiten noch nicht in vielen Veröffentlichungen erschienen. Meine Wahl ist sicher subjektiv, was jedoch auch von Vorteil sein kann. Mit dem Buch versuche ich meine Ansichten und Erfahrungen als Grafiker aus den letzten 45 Jahren wiederzugeben. In dieser Zeitspanne hat sich die Bezeichnung unserer Tätigkeit mehrfach geändert, von «Commercial Art» über «Graphic Design» schliesslich zu «Visuelle Kommunikation», und das nicht ohne Bedeutung. Obwohl sich die Aktivität des Grafik-Designs nicht grundlegend geändert hat, benutzen wir heute ganz andere Mittel zur Lösung von Problemen. Wir sind jetzt wesentlich analytischer in unserer Arbeitsmethodik, da wir mit dem Prozess der Kommunikation und der visuellen Wahrnehmung viel vertrauter sind. Wir haben einerseits mehr Kenntnis über die Struktur, Theorie und Methodologie. Andererseits wissen wir aber auch mehr über den Ablauf der intuitiven Kreativität. Modulen, Raster und Systeme gehören zu den wichtigen Bestandteilen des Design-Prozesses. Ihr Einsatz darf jedoch nicht auf Kosten der Intuition geschehen. Beide spielen bei Problemlösungen wichtige, sich gegenseitig unterstützende Rollen.

Bei der Auswahl der Beiträge für dieses Buch habe ich mich entschlossen, mich hauptsächlich auf Mitglieder der Alliance Graphique Internationale zu beschränken. Über diesen Verband, dem ich fast seit seiner Gründungszeit angehöre, möchte ich ein paar Worte sagen. 1951 haben sich drei französische und zwei Schweizer Designer, die zwar die Arbeiten ihrer Kollegen, sich jedoch untereinander nicht kannten, in der Schweiz getroffen und begründeten dort die AGI. Es besteht ein natürliches persönliches Interesse für den Künstler, dessen Arbeiten man zwar kennt, jedoch nicht seine Motivation. Zweifellos ist die AGI ein Eliteverband, ein Be-

Ma réaction spontanée, lorsque j'ai reçu mandat de réaliser le présent ouvrage intitulé «Top Graphic Design», a été de réduire le nombre de graphistes présentés. Mon choix a porté sur des artistes dont les travaux n'ont pas encore été très souvent publiés dans les livres et périodiques. J'ai donc procédé à une sélection nécessairement subjective, ce qui, je l'espère, aura aussi ses bons côtés. Le présent ouvrage devient ainsi le témoignage d'un graphiste ayant travaillé pendant 45 ans dans un domaine qui a évolué de la conception formelle à la communication visuelle, en passant par l'esthétique industrielle. Les changements de désignation de l'activité graphique – «commercial art», «graphic design», «visual communication» – sont révélateurs: s'il est vrai que la création graphique n'a guère beaucoup changé, la manière d'aborder les problèmes est devenue plus analytique: nous sommes en effet beaucoup plus conscients du processus de perception et de communication visuelles. Nous connaissons également davantage le public-cible auquel est destiné notre message. Nous maîtrisons mieux la structure, la théorie et la méthodologie, d'une part, et les mécanismes de la créativité intuitive, d'autre part. Eléments essentiels du processus de conception formelle, les modules, trames et systèmes ne doivent pas être utilisés au détriment de l'intuition, mais bien en conjonction avec elle.

Une manière d'effectuer une sélection des graphistes pour le présent ouvrage consistait à restreindre le choix aux membres de l'Alliance Graphique Internationale (AGI), une association dont je suis membre pratiquement depuis sa fondation et qui mérite bien que j'en dise quelques mots. Peu après la guerre, en 1951, trois créateurs graphiques français et deux suisses qui, sans s'être jamais rencontrés, connaissaient toutefois leurs œuvres respectives, se sont réunis en Suisse et ont fondé l'AGI. Il est toujours fort stimulant de connaître personnellement l'auteur d'une œuvre et de découvrir ce qui l'anime. L'AGI réunit incontestablement

although this word seems to have acquired negative associations of late. In this context, however, it seems to be eminently appropriate to be elitist which means to be elected by ones peers in different countries as one who is internationally known and has made a significant contribution to graphic design. Originally all members were poster designers because in the '50s — as also in the '30s — we lived in the heroic time of the poster. It was the most glamorous, most seen and discussed medium in the wide spectrum of graphic design. Since then the poster has declined and many other facets of visual communication, like packaging, typography, corporate design, book and type design, TV and film animation have become equally and often more important, so that many of the over 200 AGI members in 24 countries are no longer poster designers today. I am convinced that almost without exception the best designers in all the countries are in the AGI. I know most of them from my long involvement with the association. Although less than 10 per cent of all members could be represented in this book it seems a sensible restriction to make this choice mainly from within the AGI membership.

Only two of the designers whose work is shown here are not AGI members. One is Otl Aicher who by conviction is not a joiner of any association. The others are the Grapus team who, because they are a newish group, have not yet been invited.

Why did I chose those eighteen out of many possible colleagues, many no doubt whose work has equal distinction? All of those selected have in my view made a definite contribution to graphic design and without them visual communication would be the poorer.

Rambow, Lienemeyer and van de Sand like the Grapus team are the new phenomena because they work as a co-operative; they share the same values, social involvement and left politics. Whilst the former grew out of the Kassel Academy, where they were students, they have a predilection for the selective eye of the photo-camera or rather their own selective and purposefully biased eyes behind the camera. They found photography a most suitable medium to get their ideas across and perhaps one more convincing than pen, brush and colour. That is why most of their work is in black and white, simple and stark yet powerful, where the use of colour may seem rather sentimental and cosmetic — possibly taking away more than adding to their unmistakable statement. Grapus are no less serious in their objectives but because most of them are French and some of their founders had been trained in the Warsaw Academy by Tomaszewski, their approach is vastly different. Their subjects: theatre, culture and politics are presented with childlike gaiety, originality and even inno-

8

griff, der in letzter Zeit sehr negative Assoziationen hervorruft. In diesem Zusammenhang scheint es jedoch angemessen, «Elitist» zu sein, ohne sich zu schämen. Man wird in den einzelnen Ländern von seinesgleichen innerhalb der Berufsgruppe ausgewählt, als jemand, der auf internationaler Ebene einen entscheidenden Beitrag zum Grafik-Design geleistet hat. Am Anfang waren alle Mitglieder Plakatkünstler, da wir uns in den 50er wie auch zuvor in den 30er Jahren in der heroischen Zeit des Plakats befanden. Das Plakat war innerhalb des breiten Spektrums des Grafik-Designs ein Medium, das am meisten bewundert, gesehen und diskutiert wurde. Es hat jedoch seither an Bedeutung verloren. Andere Bereiche der visuellen Kommunikation, wie Verpackung, Typografie, Corporate Design, Buch- und Schrift-Design, TV und Zeichenfilm, erhielten ähnliche und zum Teil grössere Bedeutung, so dass viele der über 200 AGI-Mitglieder in 24 Ländern heute keine Poster-Designer mehr sind. Ich bin überzeugt, dass fast ohne Ausnahme die besten Grafiker aller Länder Mitglieder der AGI sind. Ich kenne die meisten von ihnen durch mein langjähriges Engagement in dem Verband. Obwohl weniger als ein Zehntel der Mitgliedschaft in diesem Buch vertreten sind, scheint mir die Beschränkung auf den Verband sinnvoll. Ich habe jedoch zwei Ausnahmen gemacht: Otl Aicher, der aus Überzeugung keinem Verband beitritt, wie auch das Grapus-Team, eine Gruppe, die auf Grund ihrer relativ neuen Formierung noch nicht zur AGI-Mitgliedschaft eingeladen oder vorgeschlagen wurde.

Warum traf ich gerade diese 18 in meiner Auswahl unter den vielen möglichen Kollegen, deren Arbeiten den gleichen Qualitätsanspruch erheben? Alle hier ausgewählten Designer haben meiner Ansicht nach eine entscheidende Rolle im Grafik-Design gespielt; ohne ihren Beitrag wäre die visuelle Kommunikation heute wesentlich ärmer.

Rambow, Lienemeyer und van de Sand sowie das Grapus-Team sind in ihrer Form kooperative Neuerscheinungen. Sie haben ähnliche Wert- und Zielsetzungen in ihrer sozialbewussten und linkspolitischen Haltung. Rambow, Lienemeyer und Van de Sand, die alle an der Kasseler Akademie studierten, haben eine Vorliebe für das selektive Auge der Kamera oder gar für ihr eigenes voreingenommenes Auge, das die Kamera bedient. Die Fotografie scheint ihnen das passende Übermittlungsmittel und wahrscheinlich überzeugender als Bleistift, Pinsel und Farbe. Ihre Arbeiten sind daher fast ausschliesslich schwarzweiss, sehr einfach, jedoch besonders ausdrucksvoll. Die Verwendung von Farbe könnte ihren Arbeiten zu leicht einen sentimentalen Charakter verleihen oder gar kosmetisch wirken und damit ihre sehr eindeutigen Aussagen abschwächen. Das Grapus-Team ist eine sozialkritisch genauso stark engagierte Gruppe, die jedoch dadurch, dass sie Franzosen sind und ihre Grün-

une élite, et n'éprouve aucune honte de le faire, même s'il est vrai que ce terme a acquis une connotation négative ces derniers temps. Dans ce contexte, il semble parfaitement approprié d'être qualifié de membre de l'élite, car cela signifie avoir été élu par ses confrères de différents pays en raison de sa notoriété internationale et de sa contribution déterminante à la création graphique. A l'origine, tous les membres étaient des affichistes étant donné que dans les années cinquante – tout comme dans les années trente – nous vivions à l'époque héroïque de l'affiche. Dans la vaste gamme des moyens d'expression graphique, l'affiche était le moyen le plus regardé, admiré et discuté. Depuis lors, l'affiche a perdu de son importance. D'autres secteurs de la communication visuelle, tels que le conditionnement, la typographie, l'image d'identification de l'entreprise, la conception de livres et de caractères, la télévision et les bandes dessinées ont gagné en importance, si bien que de nombreux artistes parmi les plus de 200 membres de l'AGI dans 24 pays ne sont plus guère affichiste de nos jours. Je suis convaincu que, pratiquement sans exception, les meilleurs designers de tous les pays sont membres de l'AGI. Mon engagement au sein de ladite association depuis de très nombreuses années, me permet de connaître la plupart d'entre eux. Bien que le présent ouvrage ne puisse contenir que 10% à peine des membres, il m'a semblé judicieux de restreindre mon choix aux seuls membres de l'AGI. J'ai cependant fait deux exceptions à cette règle: j'ai présenté Otl Aicher, réfractaire systématique à toute affiliation à une association, ainsi que l'atelier Grapus, un groupe d'artistes qui vient de se constituer et qui, pour cette raison, n'a pas encore été invité à adhérer à l'AGI.

Pourquoi mon choix a-t-il porté précisément sur les 18 collègues retenus parmi tant d'autres, pouvant faire état de réalisations de qualité non moins remarquable? J'estime que tous les collègues sélectionnées ont joué un rôle tellement décisif dans le «graphic design» que sans leur contribution la communication visuelle serait sensiblement plus pauvre de nos jours.

Rambow, Lienemeyer et van de Sand, ainsi que l'atelier Grapus, constituent un phénomène nouveau en ce sens que tous ces graphistes se présentent en groupe et réalisent un travail collectif; ils partagent les mêmes valeurs, le même engagement social et la même orientation gauchisante. Les artistes du premier groupe, anciens étudiants de l'Académie de Kassel, ont une prédilection pour l'optique sélective de l'appareil photographique, ou plutôt pour leur propre optique sélective et délibérément préconçue lorsqu'ils utilisent la caméra. La photographie est pour eux le moyen le plus adéquat pour traduire leurs idées, une forme d'expression plus convaincante que le crayon, le pinceau et

cence. To them colour is very important in communicating with a public which has been overfed, spoilt and cajoled by the lures of commercial advertising. It is fascinating to compare the work of these two co-operatives and how they achieve on the whole identical aims in such a different manner.

Roman Cieslewicz, with one foot in Poland and the other in France, also primarily interested in cultural and theatrical subjects seems to be in sympathy with both groups but completely true to himself. He is an artist/designer who could never work as a member of a team. He is experimenting with photographic optics, using the coarse printing screen as an important medium of alienation and abstraction, sometimes restricting himself to black and white only, like the Kassel team, sometimes adding crude, garish, primary colours which arrest and shock and thus create lasting memories. In vivid contrast to this work he also produces by subtle and surrealist blending of full colour images most unlikely but meaningful combinations of heterogeneous elements which, synthesized, express a new idea not contained in either of the component parts (like the Mao-Lisa).

Jacques Richez explores photography and drawing sometimes juxtaposed, sometimes integrated, built into an interactive matrix. His compositions, half drawn and half photographed, are both intriguing and moving. In his Carrara montages two types of photographs fuse into surrealist fantasies of a most compelling nature.

Gert Dumbar and W. Weingart also use photographic ingredients in a novel manner. The former adds designs in papier-mâché as another extension of his graphic palette. The other mixes typefaces, type elements and mechanical tints. These practices in painting were referred to as "faire la cuisine" so that this new graphic cookery hardly comes as a surprise. Predictably the Dutchman and the Swiss use different ingredients but both quite consciously and purposefully upset existing routines and try to break new ground by flouting tradition and conformity. In so doing neither is afraid of occasional failure as this risk must be taken if something new — and therefore not hallowed by precedent — is be achieved.

Both Kieser and Momayez also work with a camera to achieve new graphic effects; the Iranian merely to extend the spectrum of his media which is already enriched by typography and calligraphy. In Kieser's case the implausible is made credible by the use of colour photography. His posters, like the full colour montages by Cieslewicz, seem to emulate Hieronymus Bosch — but in twentieth century terms.

dungsmitglieder bei Tomaszewski in Warschau studierten, eine unterschiedliche Arbeitsweise zeigen. Ihre Hauptthemen, Theater, Kultur und Politik, besitzen eine kindliche Fröhlichkeit, Originalität und eine gewisse Unschuld. Für sie hingegen hat die Benutzung von Farbe eine grosse Bedeutung, denn ihr Zielpublikum ist durch die kommerzielle Werbung in einer listigen Weise verdorben und überfüttert worden. Es ist faszinierend zu beobachten, wie diese beiden Kooperativen bei Verwendung völlig verschiedener Mittel fast die gleichen Ziele erreichen.

Roman Cieslewicz, halb in Polen und halb in Frankreich zu Hause, interessiert sich hauptsächlich für Kultur- und Theaterthemen. Er steht beiden zuvor erwähnten Gruppen nahe, bleibt sich jedoch selbst sehr treu. Er ist ein Künstler und Designer, der nie in einem Team arbeiten könnte. Er experimentiert stark mit der Fotografie und benutzt grobe Raster als Verfremdungsmittel zur Abstrahierung. Auch er beschränkt sich zum Teil wie das Kasseler Team auf Schwarzweiss. Manchmal verwendet er jedoch starke Primärfarben, um durch Schock bleibende Erinnerungen zu schaffen. Darüber hinaus erzielt er zum Teil unter subtilem und surrealistischem Einblenden von vier Farben ganz unerwartete und besonders effektvolle Kombinationen von verschiedenartigen Elementen. Diese erhalten in ihrer neuen Zusammensetzung Aussagen, die keine ihrer Komponenten vorher besass (z. B. Mao-Lisa).

Jacques Richez verwendet Fotografie und Zeichnung zum Teil in einer sehr interessanten, unerwarteten Kombination. Seine halb gezeichneten und halb fotografierten Arbeiten sind für den Betrachter fesselnd und eindrucksvoll. In seinen Carrara-Montagen entsteht unter erfolgreicher Verwendung von zwei verschiedenen Fotografien eine völlig neue, surrealistische Fantasiewelt.

Gert Dumbar und Wolfgang Weingart verwenden Fotografie ebenfalls in einer neuen Weise. Dumbar fügt seiner Palette Papiermaché als Erweiterungselement hinzu. Weingart mischt Schriften, Satzelemente und Farben in einer eigenständigen Weise. Ähnliche Kombinationen sind uns aus der Malerei als «faire la cuisine» bekannt. Vielleicht wundern wir uns deshalb weniger über diesen grafischen Eintopf. Wie zu erwarten, benutzen der Holländer und der Schweizer verschiedene Wege zur Infragestellung existierender Mittel und zum Durchbrechen von Traditionen und Normen. Keiner der beiden fürchtet dabei, gelegentlich einen auf der Suche nach Neuem unvermeidlichen Misserfolg einzugehen.

Auch Kieser und Momayez erreichen mit ihrer Kamera neue grafische Effekte, Momayez nur zur Erweiterung seines bereits durch Typografie und Kalligrafie bereicherten Medienspektrums. Kieser da-

la couleur. Pour cette raison, leurs œuvres sont tenues en noir et blanc et sont tout à la fois simples et expressives. Pour eux, le recours à la couleur équivaudrait à rechercher un effet sentimental et cosmétique, risquerait même d'affaiblir la force d'expression de leur travail. L'engagement des membres de l'atelier Grapus est non moins résolu. Etant donné qu'ils sont Français pour la plupart et que certains de leurs fondateurs ont été formé à Varsovie par Tomazewski, leur approche est fort différente. Leurs principaux sujets, le théâtre, la culture et la politique, frappent par l'expression de gaieté naïve, leur originalité, voire même leur caractère d'innocence. La couleur joue pour eux un rôle important dans la communication avec un public gâté et saturé par les séductions de la publicité commerciale. Il est fascinant de comparer les travaux de ces groupes et de voir comment, avec des moyens foncièrement différents, des objectifs si rapprochés peuvent être atteints.

Roman Cieslewicz, d'un pied en Pologne, de l'autre en France, intéressé lui aussi primairement par les sujets du monde culturel et théâtral, semble sympathiser avec chacun des deux groupes, tout en sachant rester pleinement lui-même. C'est un artiste graphique qui ne pourrait jamais s'accommoder d'un travail en équipe. Il expérimente avec la photographie, utilise des trames grossières comme moyen d'aliénation et d'abstraction. Tantôt il se limite au noir et blanc, à l'instar du groupe de Kassel, tantôt il emploie des couleurs primaires crues et criardes dans le but d'arrêter et de choquer, afin de produire ainsi une impression durable. En vif contraste avec ces réalisations, ses mélanges surréalistes et subtils de couleurs lui permettent de créer des images insolites et des combinaisons significatives d'éléments hétérogènes dont la synthèse aboutit à une idée nouvelle, qui n'est contenue dans aucune des parties composantes (voir p. ex. la Mao-Lisa).

Jacques Richez explore la photographie et le dessin, tantôt en les juxtaposant, tantôt en les intégrant comme éléments constitutifs d'une matrice interactive. Ses compositions, mi-dessinées, mi-photographiées, touchent et séduisent tout à la fois. Dans ses montages «Carrara», deux types de photographies fusionnent en un monde fascinant de fantaisies surréalistes.

Gert Dumbar et W. Weingart utilisent également la photographie de manière inhabituelle. Dumbar élargit ses moyens d'expression graphique en ajoutant des configurations en papier mâché. Weingart produit un mélange de caractères typographiques, éléments de composition et couleurs. «Faire la cuisine» est le terme utilisé pour qualifier ces nouvelles méthodes de travail dans la peinture. Comment s'étonner encore du pot-pourri graphique qui en résulte? Les artistes néerlandais et suisses utili-

9

Monguzzi and de Harak work freely within the self-imposed restrictions of rigorous grids, equally valid whether they work in two or three dimensions. Whether on the printed page or in an exhibition space, they need constraints in order to create freely. The space/time relationship is of the utmost importance irrespective of whether one turns over pages of their books or walks through rooms or corridors of one of their exhibitions.

Alan Fletcher is an individual artist/designer within the Pentagram team working as one of the nine partners within offices comprising over 50 people. He benefits from consultation with his peers in order to be more himself. This seems equally true of the Swiss team of only two, Odermatt + Tissi. They manage to do their own personal work jointly. It is however unlikely that one without the other would produce the same results.

It is difficult to believe that Fukuda produces his amazing and multi-facetted work all by himself — yet he does; he draws, photographs, paints, sculpts, carves, folds, specifies and executes like a team of 50, but he does it all by himself; he carries out each idea personally.

Reisinger is a colour maniac, obsessed by chromatics, paints, pigments and dyes and this obsession gives all his work its distinguishing exhilarating character.

On the other hand Tom Eckersley's and Jacqueline Casey's work has evolved over the years, always consistent, always more polished — their graphic philosophy of maximum simplification finds solutions which they push to the point of perfection. Not unlike Tomaszewski who with very different results refines and eliminates to a point of simplicity beyond which it is almost impossible to persevere. His work is a delicate equation of intellectual problem analysis and of seemingly childlike spontaneity of solution.

Lastly Otl Aicher, a man capable of emotion and sentiment which are, however, constrained and therefore hidden within a framework of a rigid geometrical grid. He is a strong individual creator of systems but often helped by assistants (over 40 for the Munich Olympics). His work on Isny shown in this book proves that his heart and his feelings can find expression within his chosen geometric shackles. Because he felt deeply and warmly about the town, its landscape, its people and animals, he broke through the geometric discipline with — in most cases — very fascinating results.

These critical considerations, all enlarged a little in each introductory section, lead one to recognize in conclusion that there is no general prescription on how to achieve distinguished design solutions. If it

gegen macht durch Farbverwendung Unglaubliches glaubhaft. Seine Plakate, wie auch die Farbmontagen von Cieslewicz, scheinen Hieronymus Bosch nachempfunden, das jedoch unter Verwendung der Mittel des 20. Jahrhunderts.

Monguzzi und de Harak arbeiten innerhalb des von ihnen selbst auferlegten Rasters frei in zwei und drei Dimensionen. Sie benötigen die Einschränkungen, um beim Entwurf einer Textseite oder Ausstellung erfolgreich kreativ sein zu können. Von überwiegender Wichtigkeit ist dabei das Raum-Zeit-Verhältnis. Das wird beim Durchblättern eines Kataloges wie beim Durchschreiten einer Ausstellung oder eines gestalteten Korridors klar.

Alan Fletcher ist ein eigenständiger Partner innerhalb des Pentagram-Teams. Die neun Partner beschäftigen fünfzig Leute in ihrem Büro. Bei Auseinandersetzungen in den Gesprächen mit seinen Partnern findet Alan Fletcher seinen eigenen Stil. Das gleiche trifft für das Schweizer Team Odermatt und Tissi zu, wobei diese gemeinsam ihren persönlichen Stil erreichen und es unwahrscheinlich ist, dass einer ohne den anderen zu gleichen Ergebnissen käme.

Es ist schwer zu glauben, dass Fukuda seine zahllosen, erstaunlichen und vielseitigen Arbeiten alle selbst herstellt. Er zeichnet, fotografiert, malt, modelliert, schnitzt und sitzt völlig allein an Ausführungen, die ein Team von 50 Leuten bewältigen müsste. Doch er arbeitet jede einzelne Idee persönlich aus.

Reisinger ist ein Farb-Fan. Er ist von sämtlichen Farbanwendungsmöglichkeiten sowie Materialverwendungen besessen, was seinen Arbeiten einen besonders hervorstechenden Charakter gibt.

Die Arbeiten von Tom Eckersley und Jacqueline Casey haben sich über mehrere Jahre hin in einer sehr konsequenten Weise entwickelt und verfeinert. Ihre Philosophie der höchsten Vereinfachung im Grafik-Design erzielt Lösungen von hervorragender Perfektion. Auch Tomaszewski, dieser jedoch mit ganz anderen Ergebnissen, verfeinert und eliminiert zu einem Grad von Einfachheit, den man kaum überschreiten kann. Seine Arbeiten zeigen eine sehr delikate Balance zwischen intellektueller Problemanalyse und einer scheinbar kindlichen Spontaneität.

Schliesslich Otl Aicher, ein Mann von Gefühlsemotionen, die jedoch beherrscht und hinter einem strengen geometrischen Rasterrahmen versteckt bleiben. Er ist ein sehr eigenständiger Erfinder von Systemen, oft durch Assistenten unterstützt (über 40 Mitarbeiter bei der Münchner Olympiade). Seine hier gezeigten Arbeiten über Isny beweisen, dass sein Herz und Gemüt auch innerhalb der gewählten

sent, bien entendu, d'autres ingrédients pour s'ériger consciemment et délibérément contre la routine et rompre avec la tradition et le conformisme. Ce faisant, ils n'hésitent pas à encourir, si nécessaire, un échec étant donné que ce risque doit être accepté si quelque chose de nouveau – dérogeant aux usages consacrés – doit être créé par l'artiste.

Kieser et Momayez recherchent de nouveaux effets graphiques par la photographie. Momayez le fait simplement pour élargir sa gamme de moyens graphiques, déjà enrichie par la typographie et la calligraphie. Kieser rend l'incroyable plausible en recourant à la photographie en couleurs. Ses affiches, tout comme les montages en couleurs de Cieslewicz, semblent empruntés à Hiëronymus Bosch, mais dans une interprétation conforme au vingtième siècle.

Monguzzi et de Harak produisent des œuvres bi- et tridimensionnelles en travaillant en toute liberté dans le cadre de la trame rigoureuse qu'ils se sont eux-mêmes imposée. Qu'ils aménagent une page de texte ou une surface d'exposition, ils ont besoin de restrictions pour se sentir pleinement libres. La relation espace – temps est vitale pour eux et ne manque pas de frapper celui qui compulse leurs livres ou déambule à travers les salles et couloirs de leurs expositions.

Alan Fletcher, graphiste indépendant, est un des neuf partenaires composant le groupe Pentagram, dont l'atelier graphique occupe une cinquantaine de personnes. Les contacts et entretiens avec ses confrères lui permettent d'être encore davantage lui-même. Il en va de même pour le groupe Odermatt + Tissi, composé de deux partenaires seulement. Ensemble ils ont su développer un style personnel commun, difficilement réalisable par chacun en marche seule.

Il paraît inimaginable que Fukuda produise tout seul ses étonnantes réalisations, aux facettes si variées: il dessine, photographie, peint, sculpte, grave, plie, spécifie et effectue tout à la fois le travail d'une cinquantaine d'exécutants. Et pourtant, il travaille seul et réalise personnellement chacune de ses idées.

Reisinger est un passionné de la couleur, obsédé par les techniques chromatiques, les peintures, pigments et colorants qu'il utilise pour conférer à ses créations un caractère vivifiant, hors du commun.

Tom Eckersley et Jacqueline Casey ont contamment perfectionné et épuré leurs travaux aux cours de ces dernières années. Leur philosophie, fondée sur un maximum de simplification, engendre des solutions graphiques qui se distinguent par un extrême souci de perfection. Ce même souci anime

were otherwise it would be all too easy. Obviously there are common denominators but everybody is conditioned by his or her different point of departure, by his or her allocation of priorities in terms of media, emphasis and general work philosophy. What they all have in common is the purpose to make an efficient and lasting communication; equally relevant to the subject matter to be conveyed as to the easy comprehension by the public, and to the individual designer and his idiosyncrasies. They all aim to create attention, understanding and memories. This communication must be original, non-conformist and pertinent, yet capable of being understood not only by other designers but by the general public. In my view, each of the eighteen examples give ample proof that these objectives have been achieved.

There is no doubt that the importance of photography, photo-montage and photo-design has grown dramatically. It has evolved considerably since the pioneering efforts of El Lissitzky, Moholy-Nagy, Man Ray and John Heartfield in the early 'twenties. Except for colour photography, which of course did not exist at that time, this evolution owes little to new technology and everything to new conceptual approaches. It is also perhaps a reaction to the use of photography in advertising which overloads our media with euphoric consumer products and male and female sex symbols. It is against this background that the work of the selected eighteen designers can best be evaluated.

To work alone, or alone with assistants, or as a co-operative, or within a large design office organisation with partners, associates, helpers and specialists — there are many ways of designing, but each designer has to create the conditions in which he or she can perform best.

Attempts to be provocative, experimental, sometimes going on purpose beyond the limits of conventional good taste are to be welcomed because they help to create a new visual language which is invigorating and of today. Most of graphic design is ephemeral and it is therefore important that it represents the "Zeitgeist" and is valid and meaningful at the time it is created and shown.

The cliché in graphic design is an important part of its symbol vocabulary and because it has often been seen before it can be assumed to be generally understood. It depends entirely on the context within which it is used and the form in which it is shown. Clichés as well established symbols can play an important part to ensure understanding. There is a constant need to achieve graphic design solutions of a high order which communicate effectively. The swiftly changing world around us obliges us to find ever new solutions at each point in time.

geometrischen Fesseln Ausdruck finden können. Da ihm die Stadt Isny, ihre Umgebung, ihre Menschen und Tiere sehr ans Herz gewachsen waren, durchbrach er die geometrische Disziplin, und das in den meisten Fällen mit faszinierenden Ergebnissen.

Die oben erwähnten kritischen Betrachtungen, die in den jeweiligen individuellen Einführungsabteilungen noch etwas erweitert werden, führen dazu, festzustellen, dass es kein allgemeines Rezept zur Erzielung hervorragender Design-Lösungen gibt, sonst wäre es ja auch zu einfach. Obwohl es gewisse allgemeine Kriterien gibt, so wird doch jeder einzelne von seiner unterschiedlichen Ausgangsbasis bestimmt wie auch durch die Festlegung von Prioritäten in der Wahl der Mittel, Schwergewichtsetzung und seiner allgemeinen Arbeitsphilosophie. Alle streben ein gemeinsames Ziel an, nämlich eine erfolgreiche und bleibende Kommunikation. Dabei versuchen sie, dem Inhalt der Botschaft, dem leichten Verständnis durch das Publikum wie auch ihren eigenen Idiosynkrasien gerecht zu werden. Alle haben eine gemeinsame Absicht, nämlich Aufmerksamkeit, Verständnis sowie bleibende Erinnerung zu erzielen.

Die Kommunikation muss originell, nonkonformistisch und zutreffend sein, sie soll jedoch nicht nur von Design-Kollegen, sondern vom allgemeinen Publikum klar verstanden werden. Meiner Ansicht nach hat jedes der 18 Beispiele bewiesen, dass diese Ziele erreicht wurden.

Es besteht kein Zweifel daran, dass die Bedeutung der Fotografie, der Fotomontage und des Fotodesigns eine dramatische Entwicklung durchgemacht hat. Diese begann ganz entscheidend bei den frühen Versuchen von El Lissitzky, Moholy-Nagy, Man Ray und John Heartfield in den frühen 20er Jahren. Abgesehen von der Farbfotografie, die ja seinerzeit noch nicht existierte, basiert diese Evolution weniger auf der neuen Technik als vielmehr auf den neuen konzeptionellen Arbeitsmethoden. Die Entwicklung ist wahrscheinlich auch eine Reaktion auf den Gebrauch von Fotografie in der Werbung, die unsere Medien mit euphorischen Konsumprodukten sowie männlichen und weiblichen Sexsymbolen überlädt. In diesem Sinn sollten auch die Arbeiten der 18 Designer in diesem Buch bewertet werden.

Jeder Designer muss für sich persönlich entscheiden, unter welchen Bedingungen er die besten Leistungen erzielen kann, sei es allein, mit Assistenten, als Kooperative oder in einer Design-Office-Organisation mit Partnern, Associates, Helfern und Spezialisten.

Versuche, provokativ wie auch experimentell zu sein, wobei manchmal absichtlich die Grenzen des

aussi Tomaszewski qui, avec des résultats foncièrement différents, épure et élague jusqu'à un degré de simplicité quasi impossible à surpasser. Ses œuvres sont l'expression d'un subtil équilibre entre l'analyse intellectuelle des problèmes et la spontanéité apparemment naïve des solutions.

Otl Aicher, enfin, est un homme empreint d'une grande richesse de sentiments et d'émotions; mais parce qu'il les refrène, ils restent dissimulés derrière une trame géométrique rigide. Créateur individuel de systèmes de grande rigueur, Otl Aicher est souvent appuyé par ses assistants (plus de 40 collaborateurs pour les Jeux Olympiques de Munich). Ses travaux sur Isny, montrés dans le présent ouvrage, révèlent que son cœur et ses sentiments peuvent s'exprimer à travers les formes géométriques choisies. L'affection chaleureuse et profonde de l'artiste pour sa ville, avec ses paysages, ses hommes et ses animaux, l'ont amené à faire éclater la discipline géométrique, aboutissant ainsi le plus souvent à des résultats fascinants.

Les considérations critiques présentées jusqu'ici, élargies et précisées encore dans chaque partie introductive, amènent à constater en conclusion qu'il n'existe pas de règles généralement applicables pour parvenir à des réalisations graphiques hors pair. Une telle solution serait d'ailleurs par trop simple. Il existe, certes, des critères communs; mais chaque artiste est conditionné par une base de départ qui lui est propre, par sa manière de fixer les priorités dans le choix des moyens, des accents spécifiques et de la philosophie de travail en général. Ce que tous ces graphistes ont en commun, c'est le désir de créer une communication efficace et durable, qui permette de transmettre avec force le message, d'en assurer une bonne compréhension par le public, et de traduire de manière appropriée la personnalité du graphiste et ses idiosyncrasies. Tous visent à susciter l'attention, la compréhension, l'impression qui dure. La communication doit être originale, non-conformiste et pertinente, tout en étant accessible non seulement à la perception des autres artistes, mais encore à la compréhension du grand public. J'estime que dans chacun des dix-huit exemples présentés, l'artiste a amplement prouvé que ces objectifs ont été atteints.

Il est incontestable que la photographie, le photomontage et le photodesign ont pris un essor considérable. Ce développement est parti des travaux de pionniers de El Lissitzky, Moholy-Nagy, Man Ray et John Heartfield au début des années vingt. Si l'on fait abstraction de la photographie en couleurs qui, comme chacun sait, n'existait pas encore à l'époque, ce développement doit fort peu à la nouvelle technologie et tout aux nouvelles approches conceptionnelles. Il constitue peut-être aussi une réaction à l'usage que la publicité fait de la photo-

In information theory noise is defined as "irregular fluctuations accompanying but not relevant to a transmitted signal". We all suffer from visual pollution today, as we are surrounded by visual noise in our bathroom and kitchen, in the street by the plethora of print, signs, film and TV. To get the message across successfully and in an original manner is no mean challenge for the graphic designer who can and must make a positive contribution to the manmade environment. The illustrations in this book show that this can be done.

konventionellen Geschmacks überschritten werden, sind zu begrüssen. Sie schaffen eine neue visuelle Sprache, die erfrischend ist und der heutigen Zeit entspricht. Das meiste Grafik-Design ist zeitgebunden, und aus diesem Grunde ist es wichtig, dass es den Zeitgeist und die Werte widerspiegelt, die während seiner Entstehung und Verbreitung herrschen.

Das Klischee im Grafik-Design ist ein entscheidender Teil seiner Symbolsprache, denn es ist bekannt und wird daher im allgemeinen verstanden. Es hängt vollkommen vom Zusammenhang und der Form ab, in der es gezeigt wird. Deshalb sind Klischees als gut etablierte Symbole so wichtig, um Verständnis zu garantieren. Es besteht immer Bedarf an Design-Lösungen von hoher Qualität mit klar übermittelten Aussagen. Die sich ständig verändernde Welt zwingt uns, jeweils neue Lösungsmethoden zu entwickeln.

Im Feld der Informationstheorie bezeichnet man sogenannten «Lärm» als «unregelmässige und überflüssige Störungen eines übermittelten Signals». In gleicher Weise wird der Gesamteindruck unserer Umwelt durch visuellen «Lärm» gestört, indem wir in unserer engsten Umgebung und in der Öffentlichkeit durch eine verwirrende Schwemme moderner Kommunikationsmittel überfallen werden. Die Pflicht wie auch die keineswegs leichte Aufgabe des Grafikers besteht darin, diesem Wirrwarr mit nicht nur erfolgreichen, sondern auch originellen Design-Lösungen entgegenzutreten, um dadurch einen positiven Beitrag zu unserem Alltagsleben zu leisten. Die in diesem Buch gezeigten Arbeiten zeigen, dass dieser Anforderung Genüge geleistet werden kann.

graphie, lorsque ce moyen d'expression se trouve submergé de produits de consommation euphoriques et de symboles sexuels masculins et féminins. C'est sur cette toile de fond qu'il convient d'examiner et d'évaluer le travail des dix-huit graphistes sélectionnés.

Parmi les multiples formes et méthodes de travail disponibles, chaque créateur doit décider dans quelles conditions il pourra fournir les meilleures performances: seul ou avec des assistants, sur base collective ou dans le cadre d'une vaste organisation dotée d'un atelier graphique, avec des partenaires, associés, adjoints et spécialistes.

Le désir de provoquer, d'expérimenter, amène à franchir parfois consciemment les limites conventionnelles du bon goût. De telles tentatives doivent cependant être accueillies favorablement car elles contribuent à créer un langage visuel à la fois vivifiant et nouveau. La plupart des réalisations de l'esthétique industrielle sont éphémères. Il est d'autant plus important qu'elles traduisent «l'esprit du temps» et soient valables et significatives pour l'époque à laquelle elles sont créées et diffusées. Le cliché représente un élément essentiel dans le langage des symboles étant donné qu'il est largement connu comme moyen d'expression graphique et, de ce fait, aisément compris. Tout dépend du contexte dans lequel on l'utilise et de sa forme de présentation. En tant que symboles bien établis, les clichés jouent un rôle important pour garantir une bonne compréhension.

Les solutions graphiques de haut niveau, assurant une communication authentique, correspondent à un constant besoin. Le monde en effervescence qui nous entoure, nous contraint à développer à tout moment des solutions nouvelles.

Dans la théorie de l'information, le bruit est défini comme une série de «fluctuations irrégulières qui accompagnent un signal transmi sans toutefois être en relation avec lui». Nous souffrons aujourd'hui tous de la pollution visuelle, nous sommes entourés de «bruits visuels» dans nos salles de bains et cuisines, nous sommes submergés de messages imprimés, signes, films et informations télévisées. Transmettre avec succès un message dans une forme originale n'est pas un défi facile à relever dans un environnement créé par l'homme et auquel le graphiste peut et doit fournir une contribution positive. Les travaux montrés dans le présent ouvrage révèlent que cette exigence peut être valablement remplie.

Otl Aicher

1922	Born in Ulm (Danube)
1946–47	Studied at Akademie der bildenden Künste, München
1943	Self-employed as graphic designer, later to specialise in corporate identity
1957–64	Head of research and development group at the Hochschule für Gestaltung, Ulm
1967	Consultant designer for the corporate identity of the Munich Olympic Games (1972)
1968	Development of a system of pictogrammes

Educational Activities:
1947	Design of first concept for the Hochschule für Gestaltung
1949–54	Member of the founding team of the Hochschule für Gestaltung
1954	Lecturer at the Hochschule für Gestaltung in the department of visual communication
1956–59	Member of the board of governors
1962–64	Director of the Hochschule für Gestaltung, Ulm
1958	Visiting lecturer at Yale University, USA
1958	Speaker at the international seminar of the "Type Directors' Club", New York
1959	Visiting lecturer at the Museo de Arte Moderna, Rio de Janeiro
1960	Delegate at the World Design Congress at Tokio
1954–81	Corporate identity systems for: Braun, Lufthansa, Blohm+Voss, Westdeutsche Landesbank, Bay Wa, Dresdner Bank, Munich Olympic Games, LVA, Erco, EVS, Isny, information system for Frankfurt airport

1922	Geboren in Ulm (Donau)
1946–47	Akademie der bildenden Künste, München
1943	Eigenes Büro, erst Werkgrafik, dann Spezialist für Erscheinungsbilder
1957–64	Leiter einer Entwicklungsgruppe in der Hochschule für Gestaltung, Ulm
1967	Gestaltungsbeauftragter der Olympischen Spiele München (1972)
1968	Entwicklung eines Systems von Piktogrammen

Pädagogische Tätigkeit:
1947	Erstes Konzept einer Hochschule für Gestaltung
1949–54	Mitglied der Aufbaugruppe der Hochschule für Gestaltung
1954	Dozent an der Hochschule für Gestaltung, Abteilung Visuelle Kommunikation
1956–59	Mitglied des Rektoratskollegiums
1962–64	Rektor der Hochschule für Gestaltung
1958	Gastkurs an der Yale University, USA
1958	Sprecher am Internationalen Seminar des «Type Directors' Club», New York
1959	Gastkurs am Museo de Arte Moderna, Rio de Janeiro
1960	Delegierter beim Welt-Design-Kongress in Tokio
1954–81	Erscheinungsbilder für: Braun, Lufthansa, Blohm+Voss, Westdeutsche Landesbank, Bay Wa, Dresdner Bank, Olympische Spiele München, LVA, Erco, EVS, Isny, Informationssystem Flughafen Frankfurt

Ausstellungen:
Beteiligung an zahlreichen internationalen Ausstellungen, One-man-shows in: Yale, Rio de Janeiro, Tokio, Ulm, Sydney

1922	Né à Ulm (Danube)
1946–47	Etudes à l'Académie des beaux-arts de Munich
1943	Ouvre son propre atelier de graphiste et se spécialise ensuite dans la création d'images de marque pour différentes entreprises
1957–64	Préposé au groupe de recherche et de développement de la Hochschule für Gestaltung, Ulm
1967	Graphiste/consultant pour la conception formelle de l'image d'identification des Jeux Olympiques de Munich (1972)
1968	Développement d'un système de pictogrammes

Activités pédagogiques:
1947	Création du premier projet pour la Hochschule für Gestaltung
1949–54	Membre du groupe de fondateurs de la Hochschule für Gestaltung
1954	Enseignement au département de communication visuelle de la Hochschule für Gestaltung
1956–59	Membre du Conseil de l'école
1962–64	Directeur de la Hochschule für Gestaltung, Ulm
1958	Chargé de cours à la Yale University, Etats-Unis
1958	Conférencier au séminaire international du «Type Directors' Club», New York
1959	Chargé de cours au Museo de Arte Moderna, Rio de Janeiro
1960	Délégué au Congrès mondial du design à Tokyo
1954–81	Images de marque pour: Braun, Lufthansa, Blohm+Voss, Westdeutsche Landesbank, Bay Wa, Dresdner Bank, Jeux Olympiques de Munich, LVA, Erco, EVS, Isny, système d'information pour l'aéroport de Francfort

Otl Aicher's pictograms and corporate identity for the Munich Olympics are very well known, as are those of the Frankfurt airport. Some Americans called him the father of geometric man. For many years the head of the Visual Communications dept. of the Hochschule für Gestaltung in Ulm he always favours straight geometrical lines and forms. His detractors sometimes reproached him with lack of humanity and warmth.

When they see his recent work for Isny they will be truly confounded. Isny is a small town of 8,500 inhabitants in the Allgäu, the name for the foot hills of the German Alps. Aicher lives in this region and loves it. When Isny informed him of their need for a new identity to help them attract tourists he decided that the solution was not another symbol, but a series of landscapes and illustrations of people, animals and things, typical of this area. As the town did not dispose of large funds he decided that everything should be reproduced in black and white and his own work (120 images in all) was

Otl Aichers Piktogramme und sein Erscheinungsbild für die Münchner Olympiade, wie auch die des Frankfurter Flughafens, sind besonders bekannt. Einige Amerikaner nannten ihn den Vater des geometrischen Menschen. Als langjähriger Leiter der Abteilung «Visuelle Kommunikation» an der Hochschule für Gestaltung in Ulm bevorzugt er gerade, geometrische Linien und Formen. Seine Kritiker werfen ihm zum Teil Mangel an Humanität und Wärme in seinen Arbeiten vor.

Wenn diese seine kürzlichen Arbeiten für Isny sehen, werden sie staunen. Isny ist eine kleine Stadt von 8500 Einwohnern im Allgäu, einer Gegend in den deutschen Voralpen. Aicher wohnt selbst im Allgäu, das ihm sehr ans Herz gewachsen ist. Als Isny ihn über die Notwendigkeit einer neuen Corporate Identity zur Verbesserung des Fremdenverkehrs informierte, beschloss er, nicht ein weiteres Symbol zu entwerfen. Er gestaltete vielmehr eine Reihe von Landschaften und Darstellungen von Menschen, Tieren und dieser Gegend eigenen Din-

Les pictogrammes et images d'identification créés par Otl Aicher pour les Jeux Olympiques de Munich, tout comme ceux de l'aéroport de Francfort, ont acquis une notoriété internationale. Certains Américains ont appelé Aicher le «père de l'homme géométrique». Préposé pendant de longues années à la «section de communication visuelle» de la Hochschule für Gestaltung à Ulm, il a toujours eu une préférence marquée pour les lignes et formes géométriques. Ses détracteurs lui ont parfois reproché de manquer de chaleur humaine.

En voyant ses récents travaux pour Isny, ses critiques ne manqueront pas de s'étonner. Isny est une petite ville allemande de 8500 habitants dans l'Allgäu, région typique des Préalpes. Aicher habite lui-même cette région qu'il aime beaucoup. Lorsque Isny lui a fait connaître son désir d'avoir une nouvelle image d'identification pour attirer le tourisme, Aicher décida de ne pas refaire simplement un nouveau symbole. Il a créé une série de paysages et d'illustrations des hommes, animaux et objets

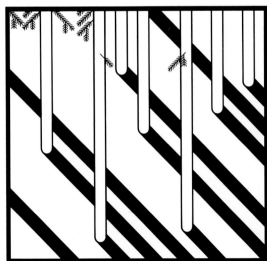
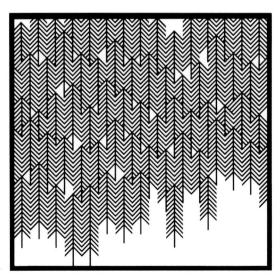

largely a labour of love. But this is the reason why it is so good. He hardly ever compromised on his very geometric style, yet he caught the visual spirit of each item perfectly. The degree of alienation is applied similarly to tree, mountain, village, animals and people, yet it is the abstraction which makes them all so endearing and unique. Some are used as posters and the black and white colour stands out most effectively against the conformity of the surrounding traditionally garish Tourist Posters with blue sky and lake and yellow sun; they are all used in a number of standard smaller sizes, but equally effective. Never has the abstract pictogram language been so successfully applied to original nature and has an artist's selective eye converted it into rigid designs with — dare I say it — true romantic content. This new identity concept seems to work well as it attracts the special tourist who, made curious and inspired by Aicher's drawing, leaves his car behind and explores and perceives new details of nature, men and man-made things.

gen. Da der Stadt wenig Mittel zur Verfügung stehen, beschloss Aicher, dass sämtliche Reproduktionen nur in Schwarzweiss zu machen seien. Seine Arbeiten – er machte insgesamt 120 Bilddarstellungen – waren grösstenteils ein Liebeswerk für Isny und deshalb wohl auch so besonders gut. Fast ohne Kompromisse an seinen geometrischen Stil zu machen, traf er den visuellen Eindruck jedes einzelnen Gegenstandes in hervorragender Weise. Der gleiche Grad von Verfremdung wird regelmässig durchgeführt, ob es sich um einen Baum, einen Berg, ein Dorf, um Tiere oder Menschen handelt. Aber gerade diese Abstrahierung macht die Arbeiten so einmalig und liebenswert. Manche erscheinen als Plakate, deren Schwarzweiss sich besonders erfolgreich gegenüber den traditionellen Touristenplakaten, meistens mit grellblauem Himmel, Meer und der Sonne abhebt. Die gleichen Abbildungen werden auch in einer Anzahl von standardisierten kleineren Grössen ebenso erfolgreich verwendet. Noch nie wurde die abstrakte Piktogrammsprache so erfolgreich eingesetzt, um Naturgegenstände so getreu wiederzugeben. Kein Künstler hat zuvor bei der sehr bewussten und strengen Darstellung der Naturobjekte soviel romantischen Inhalt erzielt. Dieses Identity-Konzept scheint besonders erfolgreich, denn es zieht die Touristen an, die, durch Aichers Zeichnungen inspiriert und neugierig geworden, ihr Auto zurücklassen, um neue Einzeleindrücke der Natur, der Menschen und ihrer Produkte zu sammeln.

typiques de la région. Etant donné que la ville ne disposait pas de moyens financiers illimités, Aicher a opté pour la reproduction en noir et blanc. Ses travaux, 120 images au total, sont le reflet de son profond attachement à Isny. C'est aussi ce qui explique leur haute qualité. Bien qu'il n'ai pratiquement jamais accepté de compromis dans son style géométrique, Aicher a su admirablement saisir l'impression visuelle de chaque objet. Le même degré d'aliénation est appliqué partout, qu'il s'agisse d'un arbre, d'une montagne, d'un village, d'hommes ou d'animaux. Mais c'est précisément cette abstraction qui confère à ses œuvres leur caractère unique et attachant. Certains de ces travaux sont utilisés sous forme d'affiches, dont le noir et blanc forme un heureux contraste avec l'affiche touristique traditionnelle au ciel invariablement bleu. Les mêmes images sont aussi utilisées avec succès pour un certain nombre de formats plus petits.
Jamais encore le langage des pictogrammes avait-il été appliqué avec autant de force aux objets de la nature, transformés par le regard sélectif de l'artiste en abstractions empreintes – si je puis dire – de beaucoup de romantisme.

Isny, a new identity approach for a town. Instead of the usual symbol Aicher produced 120 black and white, mostly geometric images of the architecture, people, animals, things and specially landscapes of the area. They are used as posters, labels and on every kind of printed matter, inviting the tourist to visit the town and surroundings in the foot-hills of the German Alps.

Isny ist ein neuer Versuch für ein Stadterscheinungsbild. An Stelle des üblichen Symbols entwarf Aicher 120 Schwarzweiss-Bildmotive, die meisten von ihnen in sehr geometrischer Art, um Menschen, Tiere, Gegenstände und besondere Landschaftseigenschaften der Gegend wiederzugeben. Sie werden auf Plakaten, Aufklebern und jeglicher Art von Drucksachen verwendet, um Touristen aufzufordern, die Stadt und ihre Umgebung im Voralpengebiet zu besuchen.

Isny, symbole d'une nouvelle approche pour créer l'image d'identification d'une ville.
Renonçant aux symboles traditionnels, Aicher a produit 120 motifs en noir et blanc, avant tout géométriques, pour donner une idée des hommes, objets et animaux, ainsi que des paysages typiques de la région. Ces motifs sont utilisés sur des affiches, étiquettes et tous genres d'imprimés pour inviter le touriste à visiter la ville et ses environs dans cette région allemande des Préalpes.

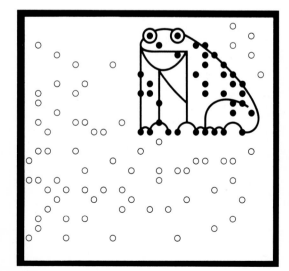

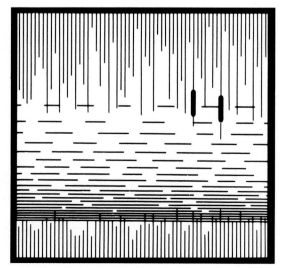

  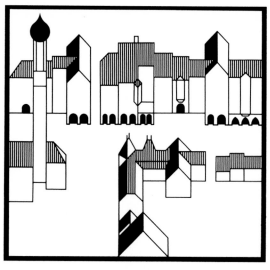

 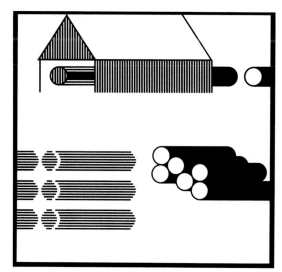 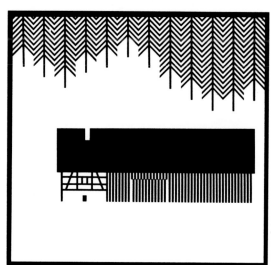

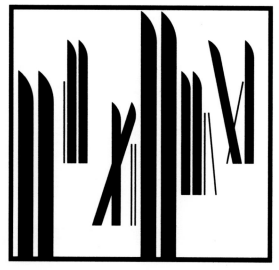 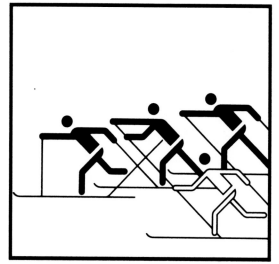 

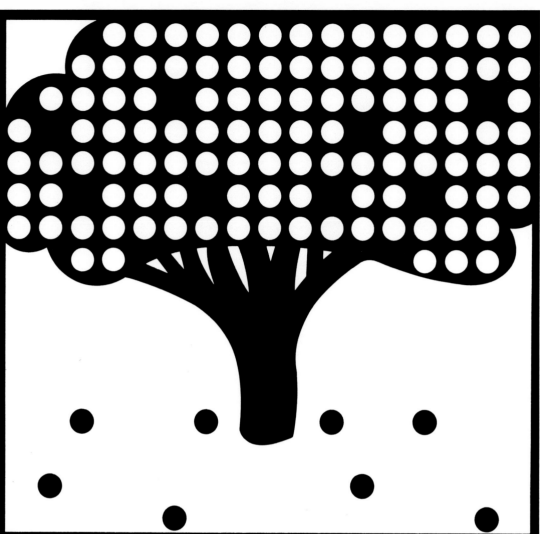

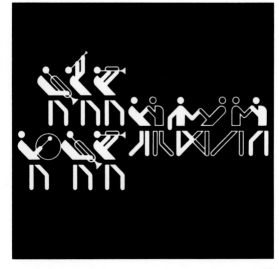

The corporate identity for EVS, an energy-supply of Baden-Württemberg, one of the West-German states:
The EVS corporate identity — very different to that of Isny — is based on a 90° and 45° grid. It constitutes a very methodically conceived and applied system, particularly appropriate for an energy-supply utility. (Symptomatically in the English language grid applies equally to electricity and typography — an additional semantic nicety.)
The whole system is based on a specially designed grid which consists of orthogonals and diagonals which accommodate geographic maps and electric supply areas as well as computer-generated electric circuitplans and their variable loads.
The logotype is also based on the grid which forms the structure for all applications.
The three house colours are silver, grey and black.

Das Erscheinungsbild für EVS, einen Energieverteiler in Baden-Württemberg:
Die EVS Corporate Identity, sehr anders als die von Isny, basiert auf einem 90°- und 45°-Raster. Daraus entsteht ein sehr methodisch entwickeltes System, das in seiner konsequenten Anwendung besonders passend ist für einen Energielieferanten. (Im englischen Sprachbereich wird das Wort Raster sowohl im elektrischen Bereich wie auch in der Typografie benutzt, was ihm im Falle von EVS eine zusätzliche semantische Bedeutung verleiht.)
Das ganze System basiert auf einem speziell entworfenen Raster aus Orthogonalen und Diagonalen, der die Unterbringung von geographischen Karten, Stromverteilungsplänen, computerbetriebenen Stromkreisleitungen und deren unterschiedliche Ladung ermöglicht.
Die Logotype basiert auch auf dem Raster, das die Struktur für sämtliche Anwendungsmöglichkeiten bildet.
Die drei Hausfarben sind Silber, Grau und Schwarz.

L'image d'identification pour EVS, entreprise de distribution d'énergie en Bade-Wurtemberg, Allemagne fédérale:
L'image d'identification EVS, très différente de celle d'Isny, se fonde sur une trame de 90° et 45°. Elle constitue un système méthodiquement conçu et appliqué, parfaitement approprié au secteur de l'approvisionnement en énergie. (En anglais, le terme de «grid» [trame, grille] s'emploie à la fois en électricité et en typographie, ce qui confère à l'image EVS une note sémantique intéressante.)
L'ensemble du système se fonde sur une trame spécialement conçue, formée de lignes orthogonales et de diagonales et permettant d'établir des cartes géographiques, des zones d'approvisionnement électrique, ainsi que des schémas de circuits électriques réalisés sur ordinateur, avec leurs charges variables.
Le logotype est également fondé sur la trame qui constitue la structure de base pour toutes les applications.
Les trois couleurs de l'entreprise: argent, gris et noir.

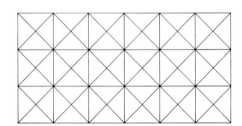

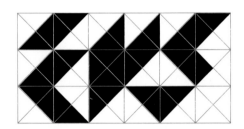

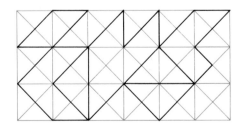

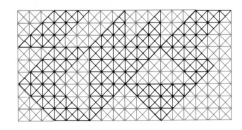

All technical drawings are standardised as to angle of vision and thickness of line.

Alle technischen Zeichnungen sind standardisiert, was den Blickwinkel und die Liniendicke anbelangt.

Tous les dessins techniques sont normalisés: même angle de vision et même épaisseur de ligne.

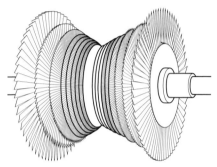

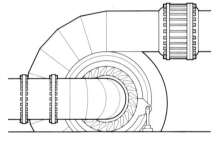

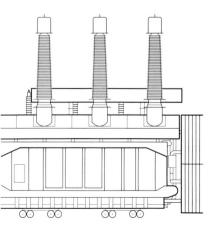

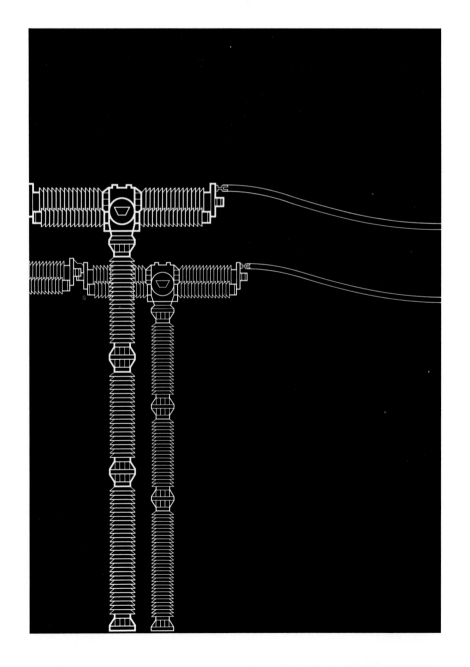

Jacqueline S. Casey

Born in Massachusetts.
Certificate in Fashion Design and Illustration;
Bachelor of Fine Arts Degree from the Massachusetts College of Art.
Worked in fashion illustration, advertising, interior decorating, and trade publication.
Since 1955 design director of Design Services of Massachusetts Institute of Technology, Cambridge/Boston.
Examples of her work in the permanent collections of the Museum of Modern Art, New York, the Cooper-Hewitt Museum, New York, the ICA and the Library of Congress.
Guest lecturer at the Massachusetts College of Art, Yale University, Carnegie-Mellon University, Simmons College.
Jury member of several national exhibitions.
Presently a panel member reviewing government graphics for the Visual Communications Section of the National Endowment for the Arts in Washington.
Member of the AGI (Alliance Graphique Internationale).

Included in "Who's Who in American Art", "The World Who's Who of Women", "The Dictionary of International Biography", and "Who's Who of American Women".

Work appeared in the following magazines and annuals:
Idea Magazine, Important US Graphic Designers of the Last Twenty-Five Years, Graphis, Graphis Annual, Photographis, Publicité, Novum Gebrauchsgrafik, Typographische Monatsblätter, International Poster Annual, Modern Publicity, CA Magazine, CA Annual, Print, Art Direction, Idea, World Graphic Design.

Geboren in Massachusetts.
Abschluss in Fashion-Design und Illustration; Examen als Bachelor of Fine Art am Massachusetts College of Art.
Arbeiten in Modezeichnen, Werbung und Innenarchitektur sowie Handelspublikationen.
Seit 1955 Design-Direktor der Design Services des Massachusetts Institute of Technology, Cambridge/Boston.
Beispiele ihrer Arbeiten in den permanenten Sammlungen des Museum of Modern Art, New York, des Cooper-Hewitt Museum, New York, bei ICA und der Library of Congress.
Gastvorlesungen am Massachusetts College of Art, Yale University, Carnegie-Mellon University, Simmons College.
Jury-Mitglied für verschiedene nationale Ausstellungen.
Zur Zeit Mitglied des Ausschusses der Überarbeitung der Regierungs-Grafiken für die Visual Communications Section der National Endowment for the Arts in Washington.
Mitglied der AGI (Alliance Graphique Internationale).

In den folgenden Veröffentlichungen erwähnt:
«Who's Who in American Art», «The World Who's Who of Women», «The Dictionary of International Biography» und «Who's Who of American Women».

Veröffentlichungen:
Idea Magazine, Important US Graphic Designers of the Last Twenty-Five Years, Graphis, Graphis Annual, Photographis, Publicité, Novum Gebrauchsgrafik, Typographische Monatsblätter, International Poster Annual, Modern Publicity, CA Magazine, CA Annual, Print, Art Direction, Idea, World Graphic Design.

Née dans l'Etat de Massachusetts.
Certificats en Fashion Design et Illustration; Bachelor of Fine Arts du Massachusetts College of Art.
Activité dans le dessin de mode, la publicité, la décoration intérieure et l'édition commerciale.
Depuis 1955, directeur artistique de Design Services du Massachusetts Institute of Technology, Cambridge/Boston.
Exemples de travaux dans les collections permanentes du Museum of Modern Art, New York, du Cooper-Hewitt Museum, New York, de l'ICA et de la Library of Congress.
Chargé de cours au Massachusetts College of Art, Yale University, Carnegie-Mellon University, Simmons College.
Membre du jury de diverses expositions nationales.
Actuellement membre de la commission chargée de revoir le graphisme gouvernemental pour la Section de la communication visuelle du National Endowment for the Arts à Washington.
Membre de l'AGI (Alliance Graphique Internationale).

Mentionnée dans «Who's Who in American Art», «The World Who's Who of Women», «The Dictionary of International Biography» et «Who's Who of American Women».

Ses travaux ont paru dans:
Idea Magazine, Important US Graphic Designers of the Last Twenty-Five Years, Graphis, Graphis Annual, Photographis, Publicité, Novum Gebrauchsgrafik, Typographische Monatsblätter, International Post Annual, Modern Publicity, CA Magazine, CA Annual, Print, Art Direction, Idea, World Graphic Design.

Jacqueline Casey, the other US designer whose work is shown here, has been working at the MIT Press in Boston for almost 30 years during which she developed a highly individualistic graphic style consistent in itself yet capable of the greatest variety.

Her control of all visual communication material of MIT has created a powerful, appropriate and well-known image for that University. She says about herself: "Being a graphic designer at MIT continues to be a fascinating experience for me. My job is a constant learning experience. While MIT has its roots in tradition, the University represents all that is experimental, exciting and future-oriented. For me designing is highly personal and private. I object to others commenting on my work before I have decided it is complete. In the beginning I collect information from clients, libraries, museums, laboratories and so on. Before I start designing, I research the subject so that my work will be representative of it. I always try to use colours and materials which relate to the subject, and the typeface must fit into the whole design. Then I decide what I will use from the collected material. I sketch for all my ideas and sift through them for the strongest solution. I often work through more than one solution, compare, then discard.

Quite simply, my objective is to design a product with an accurate visual and verbal message that can be understood by the audience. It has to make sense to me and my client. I am deeply gratified

Jacqueline Casey, die zweite der amerikanischen Designer, deren Arbeiten hier gezeigt werden, arbeitete fast 30 Jahre lang an der MIT Press in Boston. Während dieser Zeit hat sie einen sehr persönlichen grafischen Stil von grosser Konsequenz entwickelt, und gleichzeitig zeigen ihre Arbeiten besondere Vielseitigkeit.

Ihre Kontrolle über die visuellen Kommunikationsmittel von MIT liess ein starkes und besonders passendes Image für die Universität entstehen. Sie sagt über sich selbst: «Bei MIT als Grafik-Designer zu arbeiten, ist immer wieder neu eine faszinierende Erfahrung für mich. Meine Aufgabe ist ein ständiger Lernprozess. Während die Wurzeln von MIT in seiner Tradition liegen, vertritt die Universität auch alle experimentellen, anregenden und zukunftsorientierten Aspekte. Für mich ist Design etwas sehr Persönliches und Privates. Ich lehne es ab, dass andere zu meiner Arbeit Stellung nehmen, bevor ich sie nicht selbst als abgeschlossen ansehe. Anfangs sammle ich Material beim Kunden, in Bibliotheken, Museen und Laboratorien usw. Bevor ich mit der Designarbeit beginne, untersuche ich die Aufgabe gründlich, damit meine Arbeiten die Haupteigenschaften widerspiegeln. Ich versuche immer, dem Problem entsprechende Farben und Materialien zu wählen, wie auch die Schrift im Charakter zum gesamten Design passen muss. Dann erst entscheide ich, welche von den gesammelten Unterlagen ich für meine Gestaltungsarbeiten benutzen werde. Ich skizziere mehrere Rich-

Jacqueline Casey, deuxième graphiste américain dont les travaux sont exposés dans le présent ouvrage, a travaillé pendant près de 30 ans pour MIT Press à Boston. Durant cette période, elle a développé un style graphique très personnel, qui s'exprime par des œuvres à la fois conséquentes et d'une riche variété.

L'ampleur du matériel de communication visuelle du MIT dont elle pouvait disposer, lui a permis de créer une image suggestive et percutante pour cette université. Parlant d'elle-même, elle dit: «Etre graphiste du MIT est une expérience fascinante qui ne cesse de me passionner. Mon travail est un processus d'apprentissage continu. Tout en étant parfaitement enraciné dans la tradition, MIT représente tout ce qui est expérimental, stimulant et orienté vers l'avenir. Pour moi, la conception graphique est un travail strictement personnel et privé. Je m'oppose aux avis que d'autres portent sur mon travail avant que je ne le considère moi-même comme achevé. Au départ, je recueille des informations auprès des clients, bibliothèques, musées, laboratoires, etc. Avant de commencer, j'étudie soigneusement le sujet afin de pouvoir en exprimer les aspects les plus représentatifs. J'essaie toujours de choisir des couleurs et matériaux appropriés, ainsi que des caractères typographiques bien adaptés à la conception d'ensemble. Alors seulement, en présence de tout ce que j'ai collectionné, je décide ce que je vais utiliser. J'esquisse toutes mes idées, pour retenir ensuite la plus ex-

1

2

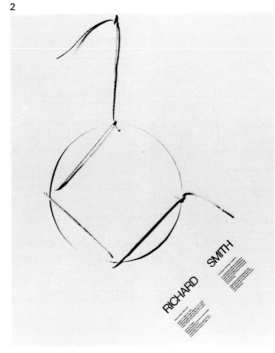

3

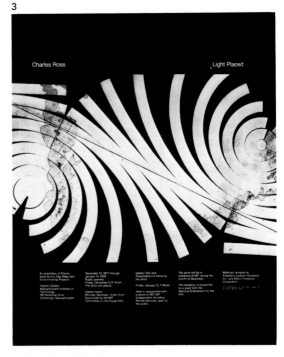

1 4 Painters exhibition
2 "Richard Smith" exhibition
3 "Charles Ross" exhibition

1 Ausstellung von 4 Malern
2 Ausstellung «Richard Smith»
3 Ausstellung «Charles Ross»

1 Exposition de 4 peintres
2 Exposition «Richard Smith»
3 Exposition «Charles Ross»

when this form of advertising stimulates people to enroll for a course or programme, or to attend a concert or exhibition. I measure my succes as a designer when the work is displayed in offices and dormitories on and off the campus when the event is a memory.''

tungsversuche und entscheide mich dann für die stärkste Lösung. Manchmal arbeite ich mehrere Lösungen aus, vergleiche sie und entscheide mich erst dann für die endgültige.

Mein Hauptanliegen ist es, etwas zu entwerfen, das die richtige visuelle und verbale Aussage besitzt und vom Publikum verstanden wird; es muss für mich wie auch für den Kunden eine sinnvolle Lösung sein. Ich bin besonders zufrieden, wenn diese Art der Werbung Leute stimuliert, sich für einen Kursus anzumelden oder ein Konzert oder Ausstellung zu besuchen. Ich messe meinen Erfolg als Designer, wenn ich meine Arbeiten – lange, nachdem das Ereignis vorüber ist – in Büros oder Schlafräumen innerhalb und ausserhalb des Universitätsgeländes finde.»

pressive. Souvent je mets au point plusieurs solutions intéressantes, je les compare et je procède à un tri.

En terme très simples, mon objectif est de créer un message visuel et verbal percutant, qui soit aisément compris par le public et constitue une solution pertinente pour moi et pour le client. Je suis toujours profondément heureuse lorsque ce genre de publicité incite les gens à s'inscrire à un cours ou à venir à un concert ou une exposition. J'estime avoir réussi dans mon travail de graphiste si, longtemps après un événement donné, mes créations continuent d'être accrochées dans les bureaux et chambres de la cité universitaire et en dehors.»

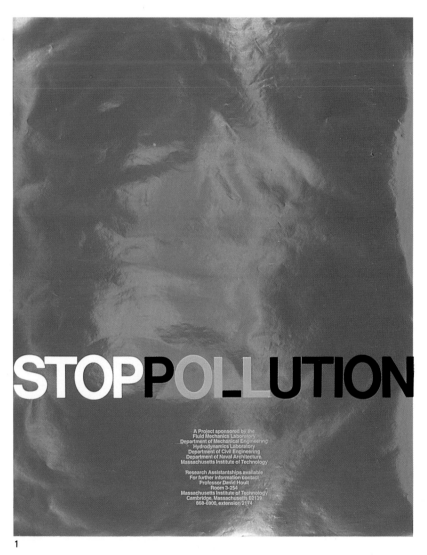

1

2

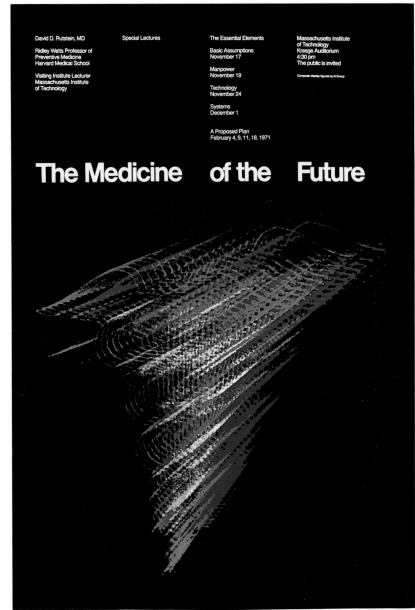

David D. Rutstein, MD

Ridley Watts Professor of
Preventive Medicine
Harvard Medical School

Visiting Institute Lecturer
Massachusetts Institute
of Technology

Special Lectures

The Essential Elements

Basic Assumptions
November 17

Manpower
November 19

Technology
November 24

Systems
December 1

A Proposed Plan
February 4, 9, 11, 18, 1971

Massachusetts Institute
of Technology
Kresge Auditorium
4:30 pm
The public is invited

Computer display figures by AI Group

The Medicine of the Future

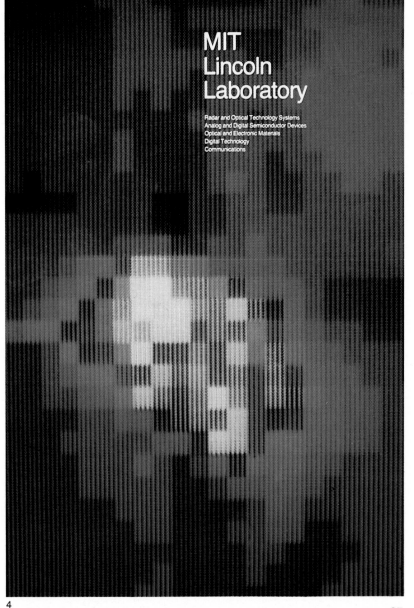

MIT
Lincoln
Laboratory

Radar and Optical Technology Systems
Analog and Digital Semiconductor Devices
Optical and Electronic Materials
Digital Technology
Communications

3

4

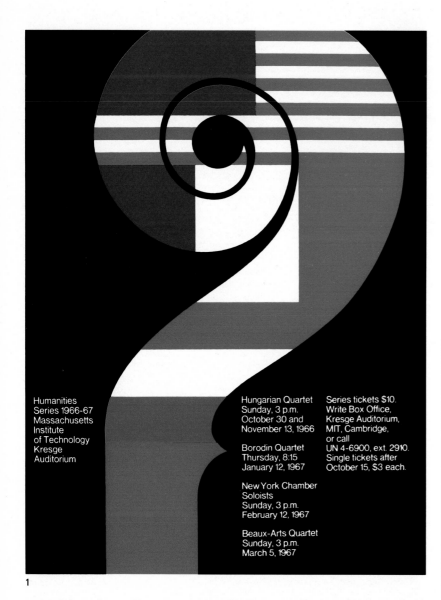

1

2

CORNERS

PAINTERLY AND
SCULPTURAL WORK

HAYDEN GALLERY
MASSACHUSETTS INSTITUTE
OF TECHNOLOGY

HAYDEN MEMORIAL
LIBRARY BUILDING
160 MEMORIAL DRIVE
CAMBRIDGE,
MASSACHUSETTS 02139

RICHARD ARTSCHWAGER
JENNIFER BARTLETT
ANTHONY CARO
DON DUDLEY
JAMES FORD
BRYAN HUNT
PATRICK IRELAND
MARILYN LENKOWSKY
JOHN AVERY NEWMAN

SEPTEMBER 29
NOVEMBER 4, 1979
PUBLIC PREVIEW
FRIDAY, SEPTEMBER 28
5-7 PM

GALLERY HOURS
10-4 DAILY
6-9 WEDNESDAY EVENING

TELEPHONE
GALLERY 253-4680
OFFICE 253-4400

ORGANIZED BY THE
MIT COMMITTEE ON THE
VISUAL ARTS

3

Art for Public Transit Spaces

An Exhibition Documenting Artists'
Proposals and Architects' Designs for the
MBTA Red Line Northwest Extension
Harvard Square Station
Porter Square Station
Davis Square Station
Alewife Station

Hayden Gallery and Hayden Corridor Gallery
Massachusetts Institute of Technology
Hayden Library Memorial Building
160 Memorial Drive
Cambridge, Massachusetts 02139

Public Reception February 8, 6 to 8 pm
Artists and Architects Will Attend

February 9 through March 16, 1980
Gallery Hours 10 to 4 Daily
Wednesday Evening 6 to 9
Telephone
Gallery 253-4680, Office 253-4400

Illustrated Catalogue and Videotaped Critique
"Conversations on Public Art" Available

Organized by the MIT Committee on the
Visual Arts in Collaboration with
The Cambridge Arts Council Arts on the Line
is a Pilot Project of the United States
Department of Transportation
through the Urban Mass Transportation
Administration and the Massachusetts Bay
Transportation Authority

ARTS ON THE LINE

4

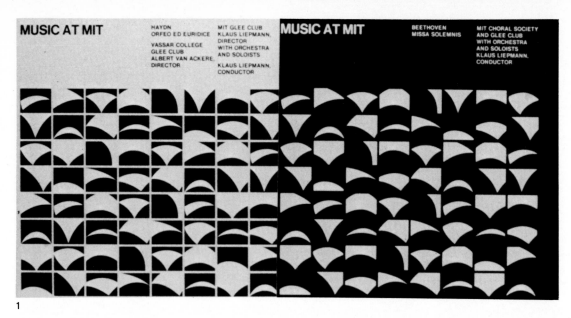

MUSIC AT MIT

HAYDN
ORFEO ED EURIDICE

VASSAR COLLEGE
GLEE CLUB
ALBERT VAN ACKERE,
DIRECTOR

MIT GLEE CLUB
KLAUS LIEPMANN,
DIRECTOR
WITH ORCHESTRA
AND SOLOISTS

KLAUS LIEPMANN,
CONDUCTOR

MUSIC AT MIT

BEETHOVEN
MISSA SOLEMNIS

MIT CHORAL SOCIETY
AND GLEE CLUB
WITH ORCHESTRA
AND SOLOISTS
KLAUS LIEPMANN,
CONDUCTOR

1 Music at MIT
2 Bartók Concert
3 "TSAI" exhibition

1 Musik an der MIT
2 Bartók-Konzert
3 Ausstellung «TSAI»

1 Musique au MIT
2 Concert Bartók
3 Exposition «TSAI»

1

2

Bartok

The Enchanted Stags

MIT Choral Society
Sixty-three members of the
Boston Symphony Orchestra
Klaus Liepmann, conducting
Jack Litten, tenor
Francis Hester, bass

Stravinsky

Symphony of Psalms

May 5, 1968, at 8.30 pm
Kresge Auditorium
Massachusetts Institute
of Technology

Bruckner

Mass in E minor

Tickets:
$2.00 (unreserved seats)
$3.00 (reserved seats)
Available in Building 10 lobby
or call
UN 4-6900, extension 2910

3

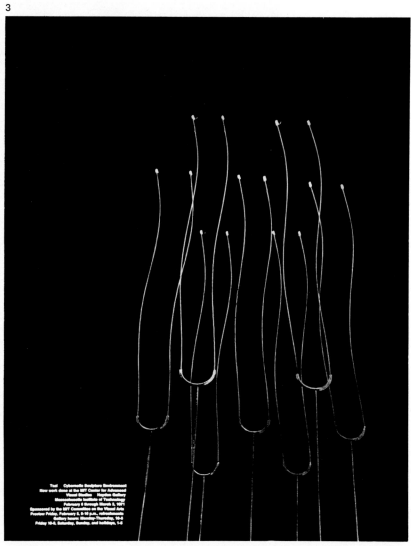

Tsai   Cybernetic Sculpture Environment
New work done at the MIT Center for Advanced
Visual Studies   Hayden Gallery
Massachusetts Institute of Technology
February 6 through March 3, 1971
Sponsored by the MIT Committee on the Visual Arts
Preview Friday, February 5, 5-10 p.m., refreshments
Gallery hours: Monday-Thursday, 10-5
Friday 10-9, Saturday, Sunday, and holidays, 1-5

President's Ball
Präsidenten-Ball
Bal présidentiel

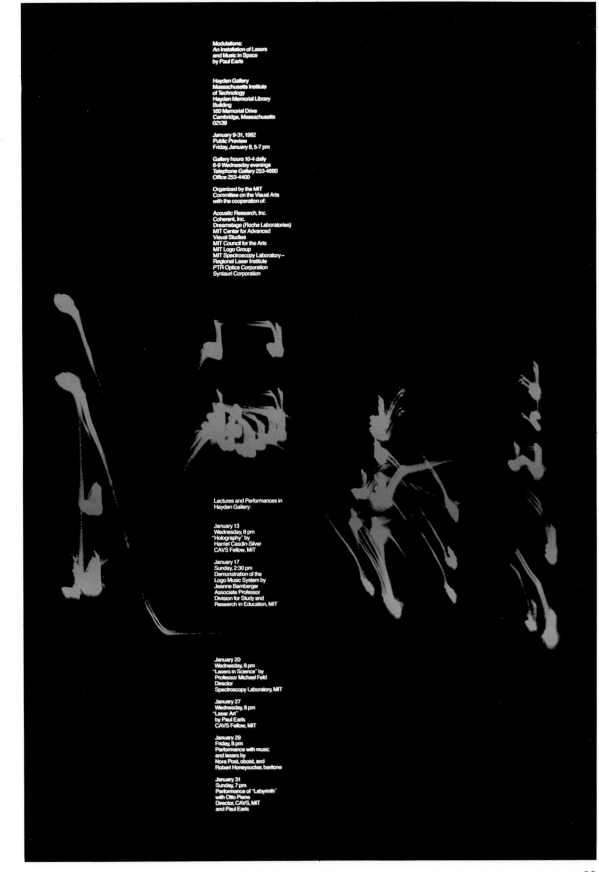

Modulations:
An Installation of Lasers
and Music in Space
by Paul Earls

Hayden Gallery
Massachusetts Institute
of Technology
Hayden Memorial Library
Building
160 Memorial Drive
Cambridge, Massachusetts
02139

January 9-31, 1982
Public Preview
Friday, January 8, 5-7 pm

Gallery hours 10-4 daily
6-9 Wednesday evenings
Telephone Gallery 253-4680
Office 253-4400

Organized by the MIT
Committee on the Visual Arts
with the cooperation of:

Acoustic Research, Inc.
Coherent, Inc.
Dreamstage (Roche Laboratories)
MIT Center for Advanced
Visual Studies
MIT Council for the Arts
MIT Logo Group
MIT Spectroscopy Laboratory—
Regional Laser Institute
PTR Optics Corporation
Syntauri Corporation

Lectures and Performances in
Hayden Gallery:

January 13
Wednesday, 8 pm
"Holography" by
Harriet Casdin-Silver
CAVS Fellow, MIT

January 17
Sunday, 2:30 pm
Demonstration of the
Logo Music System by
Jeanne Bamberger
Associate Professor
Division for Study and
Research in Education, MIT

January 20
Wednesday, 8 pm
"Lasers in Science" by
Professor Michael Feld
Director
Spectroscopy Laboratory, MIT

January 27
Wednesday, 8 pm
"Laser Art"
by Paul Earls
CAVS Fellow, MIT

January 29
Friday, 8 pm
Performance with music
and lasers by
Nora Post, oboist, and
Robert Honeysucker, baritone

January 31
Sunday, 7 pm
Performance of "Labyrinth"
with Otto Piene
Director, CAVS, MIT
and Paul Earls

Roman Cieslewicz

1930	Born at Lwow, Poland
1954	Received Diploma from the Academy of Arts in Cracow; has received many prizes
1972	Gold medal at the Poster Biennale, Warsaw
	He had over 60 one-man shows
	His posters were exhibited at Museums in Amsterdam, Paris, Warsaw, Poznan and New York; he works mostly for advertising agencies and publishing houses
1971	Obtained French nationality
1975–	Teaching at the Ecole Supérieure d'Arts Graphiques at Paris
	Member of the Alliance Graphique Internationale

1930	Geboren in Lwow, Polen
1954	Diplom an der Kunstakademie in Krakau; erhielt viele Preise
1972	Goldmedaille der Poster-Biennale, Warschau
	Hatte über 60 Einzelausstellungen
	Seine Plakate wurden in folgenden Museen gezeigt: Amsterdam, Paris, Warschau, Posen und New York; er arbeitete hauptsächlich für Werbeagenturen und Verlage
1971	Erhielt die französische Nationalität
1975–	Lehrer an der Ecole Supérieure d'Arts Graphiques in Paris
	Mitglied der Alliance Graphique Internationale

1930	Né à Lwow, Pologne
1954	Diplôme de l'Académie des beaux-arts de Cracovie; a reçu de nombreux prix
1972	Médaille d'or de la Biennale internationale de l'affiche, Varsovie
	Il a eu plus de 60 expositions individuelles
	Ses affiches ont été exposées dans les musées de: Amsterdam, Paris, Varsovie, Poznan et New York; il a surtout travaillé pour des agences de publicité et des maisons d'édition
1971	Acquiert la nationalité française
1975–	Enseignement à l'Ecole Supérieure d'Arts Graphiques à Paris
	Membre de l'Alliance Graphique Internationale

Roman Cieslewicz, originally a Pole, has been living and teaching for over twenty years in Paris. His tool is the camera and his studio the darkroom. Through montage and superimposition of photo negatives and through the use of coarse photographic screens he has achieved a style of his own in poster design. The expressionist posters dating back to the '50s and '60s have obviously influenced him as well as Paris, which always acts as an inspiring hothouse for foreigners who visit or settle there. He proves that photography is not necessarily objective and that it can be used as a maleable medium which has substantially enlarged the available design vocabulary. Photo surrealism and photo expressionism have developed in new directions since Man Ray and the early montages of Max Ernst. At first his posters were largely black and white and his use of screens in conjunction with solid black and white areas seemed to make the use of colour unnecessary but lately he has made most successful experiments in colour photo montage and colour printing, achieving a most successful marriage of artistic sensibility, photo technology and a strong sense of design.

Roman Cieslewicz, ursprünglich Pole, lebt und unterrichtet jedoch seit über 20 Jahren in Paris. Sein Werkzeug ist seine Kamera und die Dunkelkammer sein Studio. Durch Montagen und Übereinanderlegen von Negativen wie auch durch die Verwendung von groben fotografischen Rastern hat er seinen eigenen Plakat-Designstil entwickelt. Die expressionistischen Plakate aus den fünfziger und sechziger Jahren haben ihn stark beeinflusst, wie aber auch Paris, das auf viele Fremde, die sich dort niederlassen, wie ein Treibhaus wirkt. Cieslewicz beweist, dass Fotografie nicht immer objektiv ist, dass sie aber als ein zusätzliches Arbeits- und Ausdrucksmittel das Design-Feld besonders bereichert. Fotosurrealismus und -expressionismus haben seit Man Ray und den frühen Montagen von Max Ernst neue Richtungen eingeschlagen. Ursprünglich entwarf Cieslewicz fast nur Schwarzweiss-Plakate, und seine Verwendung von Rastern im Zusammenhang mit vollen Schwarzweiss-Feldern schienen Farbe überflüssig zu machen. In der letzten Zeit jedoch hat er besonders erfolgreiche Experimente in der Farbfotomontage wie auch im Farbdruck gemacht. Hier zeigt er eine wunderbare

Roman Cieslewicz, d'origine polonaise, vit et enseigne cependant depuis plus de 20 années à Paris. Son instrument de travail est l'appareil photographique et son studio, la chambre noire. Le montage et la superposition de négatifs, ainsi que le recours à des trames photographiques grossières, lui ont permis de développer un style personnel dans la conception formelle de l'affiche. Les affiches expressionnistes des années cinquante et soixante l'ont fortement marqué, de même que la ville de Paris, qui produit toujours l'effet d'une serre sur les étrangers qui viennent la visiter ou s'y établir. Cieslewicz prouve que la photographie n'est pas nécessairement objective et qu'elle constitue un instrument flexible et enrichissant dans la vaste gamme des moyens d'expression graphique. Le photosurréalisme et le photoexpressionnisme ont pris des orientations nouvelles depuis Man Ray et les premiers montages de Max Ernst.
A l'origine, les affiches de Cieslewicz étaient primairement en noir et blanc. L'utilisation de trames en conjonction avec des aires complètement tenues en noir et blanc, semblait rendre toute couleur superflue. Récemment, Cieslewicz a effectué

He says about himself: "In my profession creative pleasure is always the major argument. For that reason I can't remember any time when my work has been conditioned by a client's requirements at the expense of my own personal research. It makes no difference to me whether I do so-called 'studio work' or so-called 'commercial work'. I am trying to concentrate on what is essential. I have never done a design for an object or an action in which I do not believe. I have therefore a small group of clients and I work mostly in the cultural sector. I try to continue working believing in the principles of Bosch,

Verbindung von künstlerischer Sensibilität, Fototechnik und einem starken Gespür für Design.
Er sagt über sich selbst: «In meinem Beruf ist die kreative Freude immer der wichtigste Punkt. Ich kann mich daher an keinen Fall erinnern, in dem meine Arbeit durch Bedingungen des Kunden zum Verzicht meiner eigenen persönlichen Recherchen führte. Es ist für mich gleichgültig, ob ich an sogenannter Studioarbeit oder kommerzieller Arbeit sitze. Ich versuche mich jeweils auf das Wichtigste zu konzentrieren. Jedoch habe ich noch nie an einem Design gearbeitet, das einem Objekt oder

des expériences fort intéressantes avec le photomontage en couleurs et l'impression polychrome, réalisant ainsi une association harmonieuse entre la sensibilité artistique, la phototechnique et son flair très marqué pour la conception formelle.
Il dit de lui-même: «Dans ma profession, le plaisir de créer constitue toujours un des éléments essentiels. Je ne puis, en fait, me rappeler d'aucun cas où mon travail aurait été conditionné par les seules exigences du client, au détriment de mes recherches personnelles. Peu importe si j'effectue un simple ‹travail de studio› ou un ‹travail commer-

1 Poster "La Joconde"
2 "La nature morte à quatre pattes", collage

1 Plakat «La Joconde»
2 «La nature morte à quatre pattes», Collage

1 Affiche «La Joconde»
2 «La nature morte à quatre pattes», collage

1

2

1

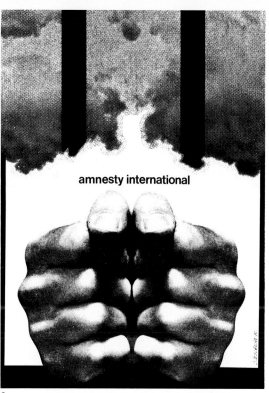

Capiello, Marcel Duchamps, Rodshenko (and many others!) which says that an image which does not shock is not worth anything."

amnesty international

einer Handlung galt, an die ich nicht glaubte. Daher habe ich eine kleine Anzahl von Kunden und arbeite meistens an Aufgaben für den kulturellen Sektor. Ich versuche weiterzuarbeiten, indem ich an das Prinzip von Bosch, Capiello, Marcel Duchamps, Rodschenko und vieler anderer glaube, nämlich dass ein Image, das nicht schockiert, nichts wert ist.»

cial). Je m'applique à retenir chaque fois l'essentiel. Je n'ai encore jamais réalisé un travail de conception formelle pour un objet ou une action sans y croire véritablement. De ce fait, j'ai un petit groupe de clients et je me concentre avant tout sur le secteur culturel. J'essaie de poursuivre mon travail en croyant aux principes de Bosch, Capiello, Marcel Duchamps, Rodtchenko et de beaucoup d'autres, à savoir qu'une image qui ne choque pas, ne vaut rien.»

3

un autre regard pour   d'autres rapports

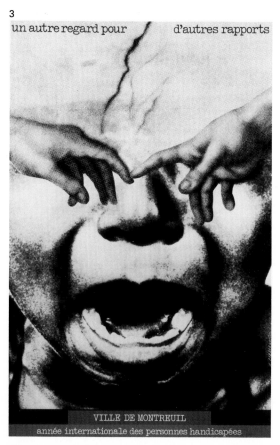

4

AVEC L'ENFANT

VILLE DE MONTREUIL
année internationale des personnes handicapées

1 "Corps diplomatique", collage
2 Political poster for Amnesty International
3 Poster for "The International Year of Handicapped People"
4 Poster for "The Year of the Child" in Montreuil

1 «Corps diplomatique», Collage
2 Politisches Plakat für Amnesty International
3 Plakat für das Internationale Jahr für Körperbehinderte
4 Plakat für das «Jahr des Kindes» in Montreuil

1 «Corps diplomatique», collage
2 Affiche politique pour Amnesty International
3 Affiche pour «L'année internationale des Handicapés»
4 Affiche pour «L'année de l'Enfant», Montreuil

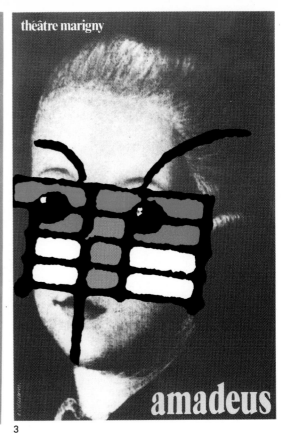

1 Theatre poster "Arrabal"
2 Poster for a play "The Process"
3 Theatre poster "Amadeus"
4 Poster "Les Demoiselles de Wilko"
5 Poster "Karl Dedecius"

1 Theaterplakat «Arrabal»
2 Theaterplakat «Der Prozess»
3 Theaterplakat «Amadeus»
4 Plakat «Les Demoiselles de Wilko»
5 Plakat «Karl Dedecius»

1 Affiche de théâtre «Arrabal»
2 Affiche pour la pièce «Le procès»
3 Affiche de théâtre «Amadeus»
4 Affiche «Les Demoiselles de Wilko»
5 Affiche «Karl Dedecius»

1 Poster for a play "The Shoemaker"
2 Zoom against visual pollution

1 Theaterplakat «Der Schuhmacher»
2 Gegen visuelle Verunreinigung

1 Affiche pour la pièce «Le cordonnier»
2 Campagne contre la pollution visuelle

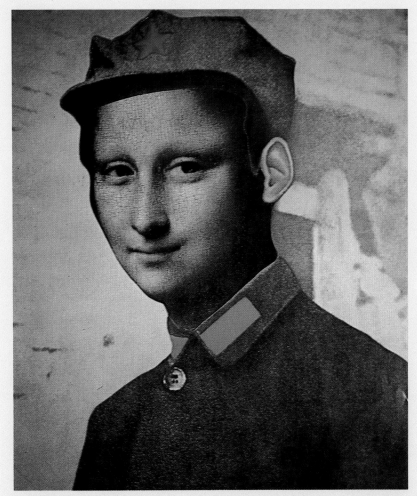

MAISON DU TOURISME 6 JUILLET · 30 SEPTEMBRE 1979 EXPOSITION OUVERTE
1·2 QUAI DE LA REPUBLIQUE TOUS LES JOURS DE 10 A 12 H
AUXERRE 14 H A 18 H 30

roman cieslewicz
PHOTOMONTAGES

1

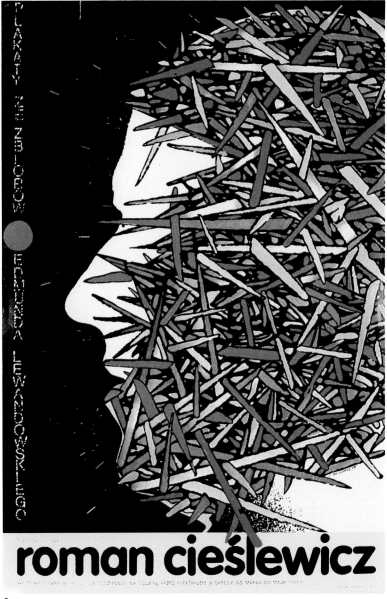

roman cieślewicz

2

1 Poster "Mona-Tse-Tung" 1 Plakat «Mona-Tse-Tung» 1 Affiche «Mona-Tse-Tung»
2 Poster "R.C. Exhibition" 2 Plakat «R.C. Exhibition» 2 Affiche «Exposition R.C.»

1

2

3

4

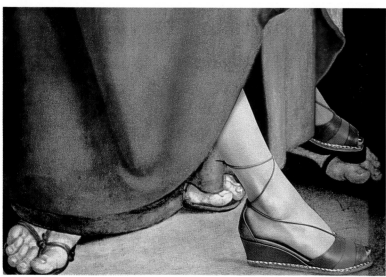

5

6

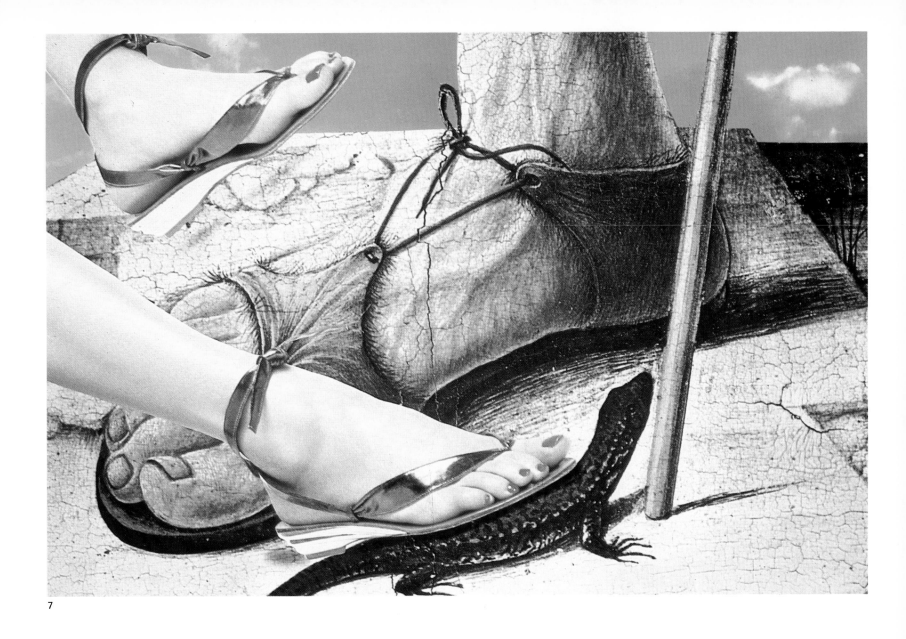

7

Gert Dumbar

1940	Born in Jakarta, Indonesia
1959–63	Royal Academy of Fine Arts, The Hague
1964–67	Royal College of Art, London
1967	Founded the graphic design department of "Tel Design Associates" at The Hague. Contributed to the realization of two- and three-dimensional projects.
1968	Became and still is involved with the two-dimensional design for the Dutch railways: complete house-style, railway guides, time-tables, pictograms, signage plans on railway stations, logotype, colour-system and railway station interiors.
1970–77	Projects completed for C & A International, Dutch ministry of cultural affairs, Simon de Wit (supermarkets), Dutch dairy bureau, Hollandse Beton Groep (building company).
1977	Breaks ties with Tel Design and sets up for himself as "Studio Dumbar".
1978	Design for a travelling exhibition on Dutch design for the public sector.
1979	Guest-lecturer for 7 weeks at the University of Jakarta (Indonesia).
1979–80	Design for a hospital's signage system, house-style and pictograms, design of the complete house-style for the Dutch postal services in collaboration with Total Design, Amsterdam.
1981–82	Design of the new visual presentation for the Dutch National Museum in Amsterdam.

Past chairman of the professional organization of Dutch Designers (GVN), member of AGI.

1940	Geboren in Jakarta, Indonesien
1959–63	Royal Academy of Fine Arts, Den Haag
1964–67	Royal College of Art, London
1967	Gründete die Graphik-Design-Abteilung bei «Tel Design Associates» in Den Haag. Arbeitete an der Durchführung zwei- und dreidimensionaler Projekte.
1968	Begann das zweidimensionale Design für die holländische Eisenbahn, für die er immer noch arbeitet. Es wurden unter anderem folgende Arbeiten erstellt: kompletter Hausstil, Eisenbahnführer, Fahrpläne, Piktogramme, Zeichensystem für Eisenbahnstationen, Logotype, Farbsystem sowie die Innenausstattung der Eisenbahnstationen.
1970–77	Projekte abgeschlossen für C&A International, das holländische Kultusministerium, Simon de Wit-Supermärkte, das holländische Molkerei-Büro, Hollandse Beton Groep (Bauunternehmen).
1977	Trennt sich von Tel Design, um sich als «Studio Dumbar» selbständig zu machen.
1978	Design für Wanderausstellung über holländisches Design für den öffentlichen Dienst.
1979	Gastdozent für 7 Wochen an der Universität Jakarta, Indonesien.
1979–80	Design für ein Krankenhaus-Zeichen-System, Hausstil und Piktogramme; Design eines kompletten Hausstils für die holländische Post in Zusammenarbeit mit Total Design, Amsterdam.
1981–82	Design der neuen visuellen Aufmachung des holländischen National Museum in Amsterdam.

Ehemaliger Chairman des Berufsverbandes der holländischen Designer (GVN), Mitglied der AGI.

1940	Né à Jakarta, Indonésie
1959–63	Académie royale des beaux-arts, La Haye
1964–67	Royal College of Art, Londres
1967	Fondation du Département d'art graphique de la Société «Tel Design Associates» à La Haye. Contribution à la réalisation de projets bi- et tridimensionnels.
1968	Travail de création formelle à deux dimensions pour les Chemins de fer néerlandais: style d'entreprise global, guides, horaires, pictogrammes, signalisation des stations, logotype, système de couleurs et aménagement des stations d'arrêt.
1970–77	Projets complets pour le Ministère néerlandais des affaires culturelles, C & A International, Simon de Wit (supermarchés), la Centrale laitière néerlandaise, Hollandse Beton Groep (entreprise du bâtiment), etc.
1977	Se sépare de Tel Design et ouvre son propre atelier, le «Studio Dumbar».
1978	Projet pour une exposition itinérante sur le design néerlandais pour les services publics.
1979	Chargé de cours pendant 7 semaines à l'université de Jakarta (Indonésie).
1979–80	Création d'un système de signalisation pour un hôpital, style de l'établissement et pictogrammes, conception du style d'entreprise global pour les services postaux néerlandais en collaboration avec Total Design, Amsterdam.
1981–82	Conception de la nouvelle présentation visuelle du Musée national des Pays-Bas à Amsterdam.

Ancien président de l'Association professionnelle des graphistes néerlandais (GVN), membre de l'AGI.

Gert Dumbar is an important designer from Holland who, first through Tel Design, was responsible for the wellknown corporate identity and sign system of the Dutch railways.

In 1977 he started his own design group in The Hague and restricted its size purposely to not more than ten people — large enough to tackle major assignments and small enough not to lose control nor to be overburdened with management worries. His work is particularly interesting as he is capable of doing superb typography as that for the Dutch railway timetables, showing a clear, rational and methodical approach in the Swiss-German tradition. However, this is never enough for him as he also feels the deep need to introduce emotion, humour, in short: humanity. These two trends however are often in conflict with each other when juxtaposed but he sees it as a challenge to reconcile and integrate them. Thus he developed a special papier-mâché technique to introduce mostly humorous figures. They appear on the cover and from time to time in the railway timetable to provide relief to the rigid and cold typography; one of them is prominent in his poster "Perfidia". Sometimes they take over as in a signage scheme of the Scheveningen Hotel, where they enrich and humanize the visual environment.

This environmental approach is perhaps most pronounced in the ball motive which identifies the 16 floors of the Westeinde Hospital. In the three exhibition posters for Mondrian, De Stijl and Piet Zwart he achieved complete integration of the personality of the artists and typical elements of their work although he could not resist endowing Van Doesburg with papier-mâché arms.

This marriage of the rational and irrational is admirable as it attempts to reconcile two polarities, which if not reconciled impoverish most design

Gert Dumbar ist ein bedeutender Designer aus Holland, der, ursprünglich durch Tel Design, für das so bekannte Corporate Identity und Zeichensystem der holländischen Eisenbahn verantwortlich war. 1977 begründete er seine eigene Design-Gruppe in Den Haag, deren Mitgliedzahl er bewusst nicht über zehn wachsen lässt. Sein Büro ist gross genug, um grössere Aufträge zu bearbeiten, und klein genug, um nicht die Kontrolle zu verlieren und nicht mit zu viel Managementsorgen belastet zu sein.

Seine Arbeiten sind besonders interessant, wie die hervorragende Typografie für die Fahrpläne der holländischen Eisenbahn zeigt. Sie verraten eine klare, rationelle und methodische Arbeitsweise in der deutschschweizerischen Tradition. Diese Seite allein genügt ihm jedoch nicht, denn er verspürt eine starke Notwendigkeit, auch Emotion, Humor, kurz gesagt Menschlichkeit in seine Arbeiten einzubeziehen. Diese beiden Trends stehen jedoch oft bei Gegenüberstellung in Konflikt miteinander. Es ist aber eine besonders reizvolle Aufgabe für Dumbar, sie so zu integrieren, dass sie in Einklang miteinander stehen. Er hat aus diesem Grund eine besondere Papiermaché-Technik entwickelt, um humorvolle Figuren in seine Arbeiten einzubeziehen. Diese erscheinen auf dem Umschlag oder teilweise innerhalb des Fahrplans, um eine Auflockerung der etwas strengen, kühlen Typografie herbeizuführen. Ein sehr prominentes Beispiel ist auf seinem Plakat «Perfidia» zu sehen. Manchmal übernehmen sie eine führende Rolle, wie zum Beispiel im Fall des Hotels Scheveningen, wo sie der Umgebung eine besonders menschliche Ausstrahlung geben, in diesem Fall auf Glas graviert.

Diese Behandlung der Umgebung drückt sich besonders stark im Ball-Motiv aus, das die 16 Stockwerke des Westeinde Hospital kennzeichnet. In

Gert Dumbar, graphiste néerlandais reconnu, a développé – tout d'abord pour la Société Tel Design – l'image de marque et le système de symboles bien connus pour les Chemins de fer des Pays-Bas.

En 1977, il a fondé son propre atelier de graphistes à La Haye, dont il a délibérément restreint le nombre de collaborateurs à dix au maximum. Cet ordre de grandeur lui suffit pour accepter des mandats importants, sans lui faire perdre le contrôle d'ensemble et le surcharger de travaux d'organisation et de gestion.

Ses travaux sont particulièrement intéressants du point de vue de leur excellente qualité typographique, comme le montrent les horaires des chemins de fer néerlandais, et révèlent une approche rationnelle et méthodique dans le respect des meilleures traditions suisses allemandes. Ce seul aspect ne lui suffit cependant pas, car il éprouve le besoin impératif d'intégrer à ses travaux l'émotion, l'humour, bref, le côté humain. Ces deux tendances entrent souvent en conflit l'une avec l'autre lorsqu'elles sont juxtaposées. Dumbar, acceptant le défi, réussit à les reconcilier et à les harmoniser. Pour cette raison, il a développé une technique spéciale qui lui permet d'intégrer à son travail des figures en papier mâché, le plus souvent de caractère humoristique. Ces figures apparaissent sur la couverture, parfois à l'intérieur de l'horaire, et viennent animer la typographie froide et rigide. L'une d'elles apparaît en grand format sur l'affiche «Perfidia». Parfois elles jouent un rôle prédominant, comme dans le cas de l'hôtel Scheveningen, où elles enrichissent et humanisent l'environnement visuel par un système de signes gravés sur verre. Cette conception formelle de l'environnement devient particulièrement expressive dans le motif de la balle, qui permet d'identifier les 16 étages de l'hôpital Westeinde. Dans les trois affiches d'expo-

1, 2
Exhibition "Dutch design for the public sector" (for touring in Europe). Structure made of light and economical industrial tubing, panels of transparent plexiglass.

1, 2
Ausstellung «Holländisches Design für den öffentlichen Dienst» (Wanderausstellung für Europa). Struktur aus leichten, preiswerten Industrierohren, Wände aus transparentem Plexiglas.

1, 2
Exposition «Design néerlandais pour les services publics» (exposition itinérante pour l'Europe). Structure en tubes industriels légers et peu chers, panneaux en plexiglas transparent.

solutions. Most designers renounce one at the expense of the other and thereby win easy victories. Gert's struggle to use both together often succeeds — not by any means always — in creating original, worthwhile and humorous solutions which satisfy equally mind and heart.

The bouncing ball seems to work well with patients and staff at the hospital — but I am not sure whether from ward through corridor and lift to the operating theatre the pursuit of this ball would give more comfort than irritation to a patient about to be operated. However, if in doubt I think it is better to err on the side of humanity, risk occasional defeat in order to win greater victories.

seinen 3 Ausstellungsplakaten für Mondrian, De Stijl und Piet Zwart erreicht er eine völlige Integrierung der Künstlerpersönlichkeit und den jeweiligen typischen Elementen ihrer Arbeiten. Zwar konnte er nicht widerstehen, Van Doesburg mit einem Papiermaché-Arm darzustellen, was starke Kritik auslöste.

Diese Verbindung von Rationalem und Irrationalem ist bewundernswert, da sie versucht, die Polarität von Gegensätzen auszugleichen, ohne deren Einklang meistens weniger erfolgreiche Designlösungen entstehen. Die meisten Designer verzichten auf eine Seite, zwar auf Kosten der anderen, und machen sich ihren Erfolg dadurch etwas leicht. Gerts Kampf um eine glückliche Verbindung beider Seiten gelingt oft – zwar nicht unbedingt immer –, indem er originelle, gelungene, humorvolle Lösungen bringt, die Herz und Verstand erfreuen.

Der herumspringende Ball scheint bei Patienten und Hospitalpersonal gut anzukommen. Ich bin mir zwar nicht sicher, ob diese Ballverfolgung auf dem Weg vom Krankenzimmer durch den Korridor und Lift zum Operationssaal einem Patienten kurz vor der Operation mehr Trost oder Ärger bringt. Doch im Zweifel lohnt es sich, im Interesse des Menschlichen, Fehler zu machen und Misserfolge in Kauf zu nehmen, um manchmal grössere Siege zu erringen.

sition pour Mondrian, De Stijl et Piet Zwart, il a réalisé une intégration totale de la personnalité de chaque artiste et des éléments typiques de leurs travaux. Il n'a toutefois pas pu résister à la tentation de présenter Van Doesburg avec des bras en papier mâché, ce qui n'a pas manqué de déclencher de violentes critiques.

Cette alliance du rationnel et de l'irrationnel est remarquable, car elle traduit la tentative de réconcilier deux extrêmes. Or c'est précisément cette harmonisation qui permet souvent d'aboutir à de meilleures solutions. De nombreux artistes sacrifient un aspect au détriment de l'effet général et préfèrent la solution de facilité à l'effort conscient d'harmonisation. Sa lutte pour concilier les deux aspects réussit souvent en aboutissant à des solutions originales et pleines d'humour qui emportent l'adhésion spontanée à la fois du cœur et de la raison.

La balle qui rebondit semble être bien accueillie par les patients et le personnel de l'hôpital. Je ne suis cependant pas sûr si la poursuite de cette balle depuis la chambre de malade, par le corridor et l'ascenseur, jusqu'à la salle d'opération constitue pour le malade sur le point de se faire opérer une source d'irritation ou de réconfort. En cas de doute, je crois qu'il est préférable d'opter pour la solution plus humaine et d'accepter le risque d'une défaite pour remporter de plus grandes victoires.

1–3
Exhibition "Dutch design for the public sector" (for overseas touring). Panels made of industrial building board, signs fixed with wing nuts. Human figures cut out in plexiglass sheet, repeated throughout exhibition provide the human element in contrast to the geometry of the panels. The figures fixed to solid metal bases are wholly transparent and show only as a ghost-like profile. The lively mixture of background grid, wing nut screws and diagonal and horizontal typography are typical of Dumbar's work; also the fact that 150 m² of Exhibition took four men 50 minutes for complete assembly.

1–3
Ausstellung «Holländisches Design für den öffentlichen Dienst» (Wanderausstellung für Übersee). Wände aus Industriebaubrettern, Zeichen mit Flügelschrauben befestigt. Aus Plexiglas ausgeschnittene Figuren, die sich durch die Ausstellung hindurch als menschliche Kontrastelemente zu den geometrischen Wänden wiederholen. Die Figuren, die auf soliden Metallplatten stehen, sind völlig durchsichtig und haben geisterähnliche Profile. Das lebendige Gemisch von Hintergrundraster, Flügelschrauben sowie diagonaler und horizontaler Typografie sind typisch für Dumbars Arbeiten, wie auch die Tatsache, dass der Aufbau der Ausstellung mit 150 m² nur 50 Minuten in Anspruch nahm.

1–3
Exposition «Design néerlandais pour les services publics» (exposition itinérante pour les pays d'outre-mer). Cloisons en panneaux de construction industriels, signes fixés avec des écrous à ailettes. Figures humaines découpées en plexiglas et répétées à travers toute l'exposition pour lui conférer un aspect humain, contrastant avec la géométrie rigoureuse des panneaux. Les silhouettes fixées sur des plaques métalliques solides sont entièrement transparentes, ce qui leur donne l'air de surgir d'un monde irréel. Le judicieux mélange de la trame de fond avec les écrous à ailettes et la typographie horizontale et diagonale est typique pour le travail de Dumbar.

1

2

3

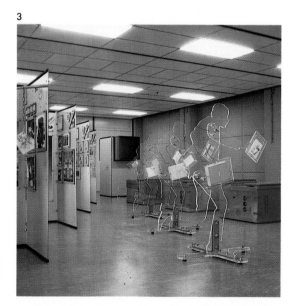

1

2

3

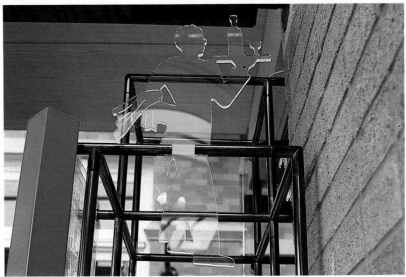

4

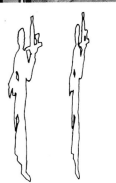

1–4
Sign scheme, combined with figures as environmental decoration for a hotel in Scheveningen. Figures, cut out of acrylic sheets or etched on glass point the way to restaurant (cook), to coffee bar (waiter), etc. These figures are profiles reduced in width through photographic rotation (see diagram).

1–4
Zeichenschema in Kombination mit Figuren als Umweltdekoration für ein Hotel in Scheveningen. Aus Acrylplatten ausgeschnittene oder auf Glas geätzte Figuren weisen den Weg zum Restaurant (ein Koch), zur Kaffeebar (ein Kellner) usw. Diese Figuren sind Profile, die durch fotografische Rotation (siehe Diagramm) in ihrer Breite reduziert werden.

1–4
Schéma de signes, en combinaison avec différentes figures, comme éléments décoratifs destinés à agrémenter les environs d'un hôtel à Scheveningen. Les figures découpées dans des panneaux en verre acrylique ou gravées sur verre indiquent le chemin du restaurant (cuisinier), du bar à café (sommelier), etc. Ces figures sont des silhouettes réduites dans le sens de la largeur par effet de rotation photographique (voir diagramme).

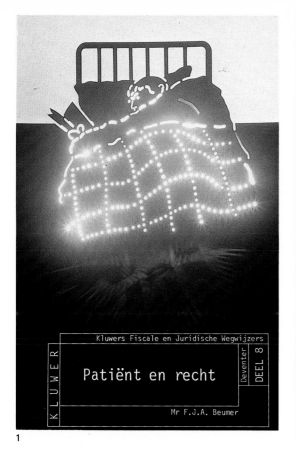

1

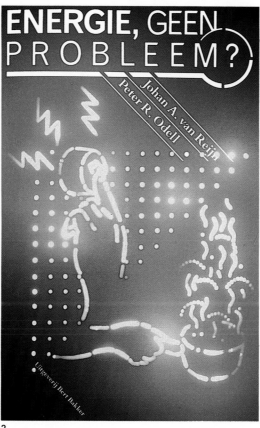

2

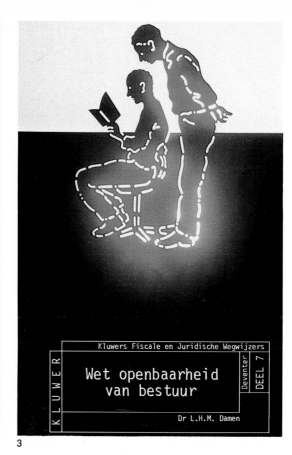

3

4

1–3
Book covers using a novel technique. The design is created by paper perforations, lit from behind and photographed, thus achieving a high-tech image.
4
Invitation card to a party

1–3
Buchumschlag unter Verwendung einer neuartigen Technik. Das Design, ein High-Tech Image, wurde durch Perforierung erreicht, die von hinten beleuchtet und fotografiert wurde.
4
Einladungskarte für eine Party

1–3
Couvertures de livres réalisées selon une nouvelle technique. Des perforations sur papier, éclairées depuis l'arrière, sont photographiées pour produire une image à caractère hautement technique.
4
Carte d'invitation pour une surprise-party

Poster for book "Perfidia" using a papier-mâché figure

Plakat für das Buch «Perfidia» mit einer Papiermaché-Figur

Affiche pour le livre «Perfidia» avec une figure en papier mâché

1–3
Posters for Exhibition by Mondrian, De Stijl and Piet Zwart. In each case the artist is surrounded by elements of his work in a surreal graphic space. An entirely new approach when compared with traditional exhibition posters.

1–3
Plakate für eine Ausstellung von Mondrian, de Stijl und Piet Zwart. In jedem Fall ist der Künstler in einem surrealistischen, grafischen Raum von Elementen seiner Arbeit umgeben, verglichen mit anderen Ausstellungsplakaten ein völlig neuer Stil.

1–3
Affiches pour une exposition de Mondrian, De Stijl et Piet Zwart. L'artiste est chaque fois entouré d'éléments typiques de son travail dans un environnement graphique surréaliste. Comparé aux affiches traditionnelles, le style créé par Dumbar est foncièrement nouveau.

2

1

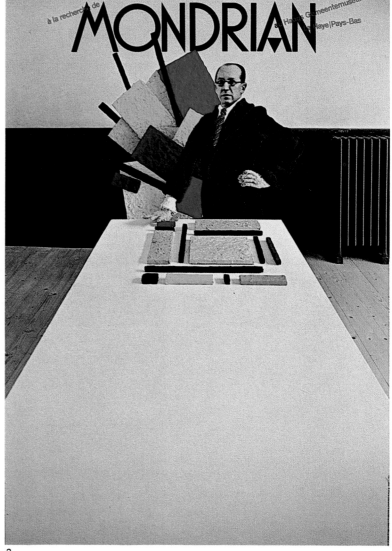

3

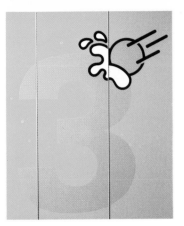

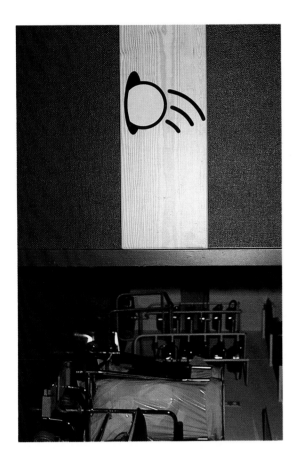

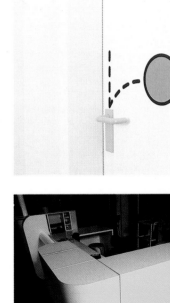

Personnel and patients were confused on which of the 16 floors of the Westeinde hospital they found themselves so that it became necessary to develop a clearly differentiated identity for each floor. The bouncing ball motif — different for each floor — did the trick. It was applied everywhere from doors, walls to furniture, ceilings and floors to connect and identify all items on the same floor. Each ball bounced on and off objects along an implied yet invisible connecting path; collaborator: Ko Sliggers.

Um sowohl für Patienten wie auch für Angestellte die Orientierung der 16 Stockwerke des Westeinde-Hospitals zu erleichtern, wurde ein System entwickelt, das jeden einzelnen Stock besonders kennzeichnet. Der tanzende Ball, der auf jedem Stock variiert, war die Lösung. Er wurde überall verwendet von Türen zu Wänden, Möbeln, Decken, Böden, um alles auf einem bestimmten Stockwerk zu identifizieren und in Einklang zu bringen. Der Ball, der auf die Gegenstände zu und wieder wegspringt, formt eine unsichtbare Verbindungslinie als Wegweiser; Mitarbeiter: Ko Sliggers.

Le personnel et les patients ayant eu de la peine à s'orienter dans l'hôpital à 16 étages de Westeinde, il a fallu trouver un système d'identification clair pour chaque niveau. Le motif de la balle rebondissante, différent d'un étage à l'autre, apporta la solution. Il a été appliqué partout, sur les portes et les murs, le mobilier, les plafonds et les sols, pour identifier et harmoniser tout ce qui se trouve sur un même étage. Chaque balle bondissante et rebondissante trace un chemin invisible, mais bien déterminé; collaborateur: Ko Sliggers.

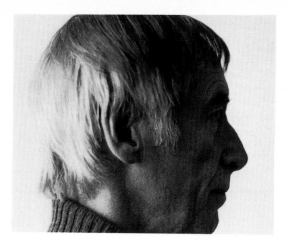

Tom Eckersley

1914	Born at Newton-le-Willows, Lancashire
1930–34	Studied at Salford College of Art
1934	Awarded Heywood medal of merit
1934–39	Moved to London and worked in partnership with Eric Lombers
1937–39	Visiting lecturer at Westminster School of Art
1940–45	Served in the Royal Air Force as a cartographer while also designing posters for the Ministry of Information, General Post Office and Royal Society for the Prevention of Accidents
1945	Freelance poster designer
1948	Awarded the OBE for services to British poster design
1951	Member of the AGI
1954	Published "Poster Design" at "The Studio Publications"
1957–77	Head of Graphic Design Department, London College of Printing
1961	Appointed Fellow of the Society of Artists and Designers, Fellow of the Society of Typographic Designers, Honorary Fellow of Manchester College of Art and Design
1963	Appointed Royal Designer of Industry
1981	Visiting lecturer at Yale, USA

Exhibitions:
London, Washington D.C., Stockholm, New York, California, Kassel, Warsaw, Brno, Yale, USA

Public Collections:
Museum of Modern Art, New York; Imperial War Museum and Victoria and Albert Museum, London; Australia National Gallery

1914	Geboren in Newton-le-Willows, Lancashire
1930–34	Studium am Salford College of Art
1934	Empfängt die «Heywood medal of merit»
1934–39	Umzug nach London und Partnerschaft mit Eric Lombers
1937–39	Gastdozent an der Westminster School of Art
1940–45	Mitglied der Royal Air Force, für die er als Kartograf tätig war, gleichzeitig arbeitete er als Plakatkünstler für das «Ministry of Information», «General Post Office» und die «Royal Society for the Prevention of Accidents»
1945	Freischaffender Plakatkünstler
1948	Erteilung des «OBE Award» für seine englischen Plakate
1951	Mitglied der AGI
1954	Veröffentlichung von «Poster Design» bei «The Studio Publications»
1957–77	Leiter der Graphik-Design-Abteilung des Londoner College of Printing
1961	Fellow der Society of Artists and Designers, Fellow der Society of Typographic Designers, Honorary Fellow des Manchester College of Art and Design
1963	Ernennung zum «Royal Designer for Industry»
1981	Gastdozent in Yale, USA

Ausstellungen:
London, Washington DC, Stockholm, New York, Kalifornien, Kassel, Warschau, Brno, Yale, USA

In folgenden Sammlungen vertreten: Museum of Modern Art, New York; Imperial War Museum und Victoria and Albert Museum, London; Australia National Gallery

1914	Né à Newton-le-Willows, Lancashire
1930–34	Etudes au Salford College of Art
1934	Reçoit la «Heywood medal of merit»
1934–39	S'installe à Londres et travaille avec son partenaire Eric Lombers
1937–39	Chargé de cours à la «Westminster School of Art»
1940–45	Membre de la Royal Air Force où il est responsable de la cartographie; en même temps, travail comme affichiste pour le ministère de l'Information, les PTT britanniques et la Société royale de prévention des accidents
1945	Affichiste indépendant
1948	L'«OBE Award» lui est décerné pour ses affiches britanniques
1951	Membre de l'AGI
1954	Publication de «Poster Design» aux Editions «The Studio Publications»
1957–77	Directeur du département «Graphic Design» du «London College of Printing»
1961	Fellow de la «Society of Artists and Designers», fellow de la «Society of Typographic Designers», Honorary Fellow du «Manchester College of Art and Design»
1963	Nommé «Royal Designer for Industry»
1981	Chargé de cours à Yale, Etats-Unis

Expositions:
Londres, Washington DC, Stockholm, New York, Californie, Kassel, Varsovie, Brno, Yale, USA

Collections publiques:
Museum of Modern Art, New York; Imperial War Museum et Victoria and Albert Museum, Londres; Australia National Gallery

Tom Eckersley started designing posters in 1934 and has done so ever since. His development as a poster designer has been always consistent in choosing colours carefully, sensibly and sparingly just as in his constant refinement of form. The result has been a continuous evolution during which his last poster is always better, simpler and more direct than previous ones. He always achieves 'doing more with less' following Mies van der Rohe's dictum.

He comments himself: "The graphic field as we know it today had its roots in the twenties and thirties. Certain designers began to realize the many exciting visual possibilities that could be derived from the major art movements currently taking place. Supported by enlightened clients they made possible a new dimension of visual imagery in graphic work which has continued to influence graphic designers through the following decades to this day.

The early thirties made a strong and lasting impression on me, helping to shape my attitude to graphic work. At that time the poster was perhaps the most significant form of publicity. The great Cassandre and other French designers produced avant-garde posters, as well as McKnight-Kauffer in England. This greatly influenced me and I soon became seriously involved in poster design. For me the poster has always had immense appeal and my

Tom Eckersley ist seit 1934 ein Plakat-Designer. Seine Entwicklung als Plakat-Entwerfer zeigt eine ständige und intensive Evolution. Seine sorgfältige und sparsame Farbwahl wie auch die Verfeinerung seiner Form beweisen eine besondere und rare Sensibilität. Jedes weitere Plakat ist besser, einfacher und direkter als das vorhergehende. Er erreicht es tatsächlich, nach Mies van der Rohes Wahlspruch zu arbeiten, nämlich «mehr mit weniger zu erreichen».

Er sagt über sich selbst: Der Bereich Grafik, wie wir ihn heute kennen, hatte seine Wurzeln in den 20er und 30er Jahren. Gewisse Designer fingen an, sich darüber klarzuwerden, wie viele visuelle Möglichkeiten aus den derzeitigen grossen Kunstbewegungen abgeleitet werden können. Unterstützt durch vorurteilsfreie Kunden erreichten sie neue Dimensionen von visuellen Ausdrucksmitteln in der Grafik, die andere Designer während der weiteren Dekaden bis heute beeinflusst haben.

Auf mich haben die frühen 20er Jahre einen starken, bleibenden Eindruck hinterlassen, der mir half, meine eigene Arbeitsweise zu finden. In der Zeit war das Plakat vielleicht eine der wichtigsten Werbeformen. Der grossartige Cassandre und andere französische Designer entwarfen Avantgarde-Plakate, wie auch McKnight-Kauffer in England. Das hat mich stark beeinflusst und bald ernsthaft im Plakat-Design engagiert. Für mich haben Plakate

Tom Eckersley dessine des affiches depuis 1934. Sa carrière montre une évolution constante et intense. Le choix soigneux et parcimonieux des couleurs, tout comme le raffinement des formes trahissent une sensibilité rare et particulière. Chaque affiche, sans exception, est meilleure, plus simple et plus directe que la précédente. Il réussit vraiment à travailler selon le mot d'ordre de Mies van der Rohe, «atteindre plus avec moins».

De lui-même, il affirme: «Les arts graphiques, comme nous les connaissons aujourd'hui, plongent leurs racines dans les années 20 et 30. Certains graphistes ont commencé à découvrir combien de possibilités visuelles pouvaient naître des grands courants artistiques de l'époque. Encouragés par des clients sans préjugés, ils ont atteint de nouvelles dimensions dans l'art graphique et ses moyens d'expression visuels; leurs découvertes influenceront les décennies suivantes jusqu'à nos jours.

Les années 20 ont exercé sur moi une influence forte et durable, qui m'a aidé à trouver ma propre voie. A ce moment-là, l'affiche était peut-être l'une des principales formes de publicité. Le formidable Cassandre et d'autres artistes français ont conçu des affiches d'avant-garde, tout comme l'Anglais McKnight-Kauffer. C'est ce qui a provoqué mon engagement résolu dans le monde de l'affiche. Les affiches ont toujours eu sur moi un immense po-

1

2

1 Exhibition Poster
2 Seminar Poster

1 Ausstellungsplakat
2 Plakat für ein Seminar

1 Affiche pour une exposition
2 Affiche pour séminaire

main output of work has been in this area.
I enjoy the personal statement as well as the satisfaction of solving the particular communication problem involved. The fact that you are on your own, in a sense similar to the painter, has always been in tune with my own approach to my work which is a very private one.
I contend that any careful examination of the development of graphic design up to the present time reveals that a larger part of the finest work has a personal quality identified with the individual designer. It also has a visual quality combined successfully with clarity of idea and purpose.''

immer eine immense Anziehungskraft besessen, und meine hauptsächlichen Arbeiten liegen in diesem Bereich.
Mir macht die persönliche Aussage ebenso viel Spass, wie ein spezielles Kommunikationsproblem mit Zufriedenheit zu lösen. Die Tatsache, dass ich alleine arbeite, vielleicht ähnlich wie ein Maler, entspricht mir sehr als persönliche Arbeitsweise, die ich als sehr privat empfinde.
Ich bin der Meinung, dass man bei genauer Betrachtung der Entwicklung des Grafik-Designs bis heute feststellt, dass die besten Arbeiten eine persönliche Qualität besitzen, die dem individuellen Designer eigen ist. Sie zeigen gleichzeitig eine visuelle Qualität sowie Klarheit der Aussage und Absicht.»

voir d'attraction et mes travaux principaux se placent dans ce domaine.
Le message personnel me donne autant de satisfaction que la solution d'un problème précis de communication. Le fait de travailler seul, peut-être comme un peintre, répond à une méthode très personnelle, très privée.
J'estime, à bien considérer l'évolution des arts graphiques jusqu'à nos jours, que les meilleures œuvres ont une qualité personnelle propre à chaque graphiste. Elles présentent en même temps une valeur visuelle et une clarté expressive qui rend l'intention transparente.»

1

2

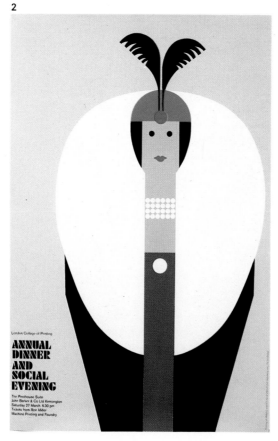

3

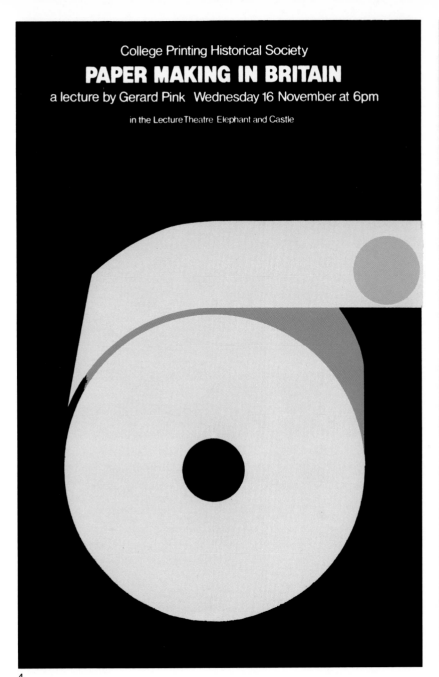

College Printing Historical Society
PAPER MAKING IN BRITAIN
a lecture by Gerard Pink   Wednesday 16 November at 6pm

in the Lecture Theatre Elephant and Castle

4

Open Week

London College of Printing
28 January-1 February 1974
9.30-12.30 1.30-4.30 5.30-8.30

See the college at work
Meet students and staff
See the range of advanced equipment
Visits can be arranged
for individuals or parties
at the Elephant and Castle
or Clerkenwell building
A visit can be for a full day
part of a day or an evening

Visit the following departments
Bookbinding and Print Finishing
Composing
Graphic Design
Graphic Reproduction
Library and Learning Resources Centre
Machine Printing and Foundry
Management Studies
Photography
Science and Technology
General Studies

For further particulars
please write or telephone
Assistant Principal
and Director of Studies
London College of Printing
Elephant and Castle
London SE1 6SB
Telephones 01-735 8484
01-735 9100

5

1–5
Posters for "London College of Printing"

1–5
Plakate für «London College of Printing»

1–5
Affiche pour le «London College of Printing»

working for the survival of the living world

1 Poster "Working for the Survival of the Living World"
2 Theatre Poster "Equus"
3 Design for woven rug

1 Plakat für «Working for the Survival of the Living World»
2 Theaterplakat «Equus»
3 Entwurf für einen Teppich

1 Affiche «Working for the Survival of the Living World»
2 Affiche de théâtre «Equus»
3 Projet pour un tapis tissé

6

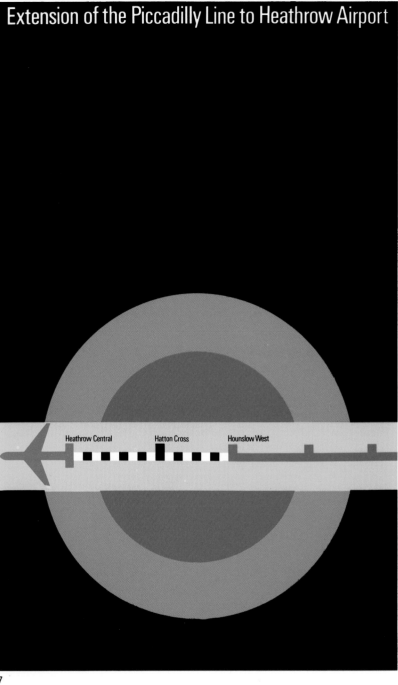

Extension of the Piccadilly Line to Heathrow Airport

Heathrow Central · Hatton Cross · Hounslow West

7

4–7
Posters for "London Transport"

4–7
Plakate für «London Transport»

4–7
Affiches pour les services de transport londoniens

1

2

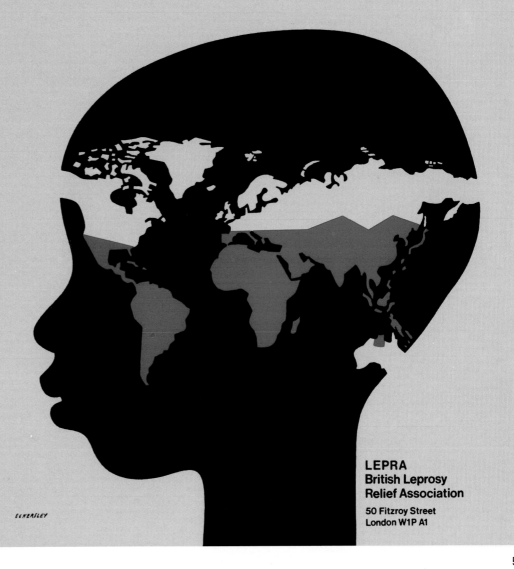

Poster "Help Lepra fight Leprosy"
Plakat für «Help Lepra fight Leprosy»
Affiche «Help Lepra fight Leprosy»

Alan Fletcher

1931   Born in Nairobi, Kenya
Training at the Central School of Arts and Crafts, the Royal College of Art, the School for Architecture and Design, Yale University
1958–59   Fortune Magazine, New York
1959–62   Freelance practice, London
1962–65   Partner of Fletcher/Forbes/Gill
1965–72   Partner of Crosby/Fletcher/Forbes
1972   Partner of Pentagram

Membership and appointments:
Associate of the Royal College of Art; M.A. Yale University; Fellow of the Society of Industrial Artists and Designers; Royal Designer for Industry; International President of AGI 1983; President of Designers' and Art Directors' Association 1973

Awards:
Designers and Art Directors' Association, Gold Award for Design 1974; "One Show" New York, Gold Award 1974; Designers' and Art Directors' Association, Presidents Award 1977; SIAD Medal for 1982

Publications:
Co-author of the following books:
"Graphic Design: A visual comparison"; "A Sign Systems Manual"; "Identity Kits", all Studio Vista; "Living by Design", Lund Humphries, Watson Guptill; Author and illustrator of "Was ich sah", Oetinger

1931   Geboren in Nairobi, Kenia
Ausbildung an der Central School of Arts and Crafts, am Royal College of Art und an der School for Architecture and Design, Yale University
1958–59   Fortune Magazine, New York
1959–62   Freischaffender Designer, London
1962–65   Partner von Fletcher/Forbes/Gill
1965–72   Partner von Crosby/Fletcher/Forbes
1972   Partner von Pentagram

Mitgliedschaften und Ernennungen:
Associate of the Royal College of Art; M.A. Yale University; Fellow of the Society of Industrial Artists and Designers; Royal Designer for Industry; Internationaler Präsident der AGI 1983; Präsident der Designers and Art Directors Association 1973

Auszeichnungen:
Designers and Art Directors Association, Gold Award for Design 1974; «One Show» New York, Gold Award 1974; Designers and Art Directors Association, Presidents Award 1977; SIAD-Medaille 1982

Veröffentlichungen:
Mitverfasser folgender Bücher: «Graphic Design: A visual comparison»; «A Sign Systems Manual»; «Identity Kits», alle Studio Vista; «Living by Design», Lund Humphries, Watson Guptill; Autor und Illustrator von «Was ich sah», Oetinger

1931   Né à Nairobi, Kenya
Etudes à la Central School of Arts and Crafts et au Royal College of Art et School for Architecture & Design, Yale University
1958–59   Graphiste pour Fortune Magazine, New York
1959–62   Travail comme graphiste indépendant, Londres
1962–65   Partenaire de Fletcher/Forbes/Gill
1965–72   Partenaire de Crosby/Fletcher/Forbes
1972   Partenaire du Pentagram

Nominations et affiliations:
Associate of the Royal College of Art; M.A. Yale University; Fellow of the Society of Industrial Artists and Designers; Royal Designer for Industry; Président international de l'AGI 1983; Président de la Designers and Art Directors Association 1973

Prix et distinctions spéciales:
Médaille d'or de la Designers and Art Directors Association 1974; «One Show» New York, médaille d'or 1974; Presidents Award de la Designers and Art Directors Association 1977; médaille de la SIAD 1982

Publications:
Co-auteur des ouvrages suivants: «Graphic Design: A visual comparison»; «A Sign Systems Manual»; «Identity Kits», tous Studio Vista; «Living by Design», Lund Humphries, Watson Guptill; auteur et illustrateur de «Was ich sah», Oetinger

A graduate of the Royal College of Art in London and the School of Architecture and Design, Yale University, Alan Fletcher began his professional career working in New York during the late fifties. At that time New York had the greatest concentration of graphic talent in the world and he openly acknowledges the debt to that experience.

On his return to London he joined Bob Gill and Colin Forbes to form the graphic partnership of Fletcher/Forbes/Gill in the early sixties. The natural development of the partnership grew and changed eventually resulting in the formation of Pentagram in the early seventies, of which he is a founder partner.

As a designer, he is intrigued by visual ambiguities and paradoxes for their own sake, as well as in the practical design problems posed by clients.

To quote some of his own observations: "Designers have the opportunity if not also the obligation to offer a smack of connection between the objects we use, and the human gift for artful extremes. Function is fine but designers as the artists of our system must, as it were, provide the spice as well as the nutrition.

Much of the work I do is in conjunction with my partners in Pentagram. Ideas are mutually exchanged, stood on their head, elaborated or simplified, but the process of translation from notion into image is an individual interpretation.

Thus solving a problem is not the problem. The problem is adding value, investing solutions with visual surprise and above all with wit. To misquote the axiom: 'A smile is worth a thousand pictures.'"

Nach Abschluss am Royal College of Art in London und der School of Architecture and Design an der Yale-Universität begann Alan Fletcher Ende der 50er Jahre seine Berufskarriere in New York. Zu der Zeit kamen in New York die grössten Talente in der Grafik zusammen. Alan Fletcher gibt auch ganz offen zu, wieviel er ihnen an Erfahrung verdankt. Nach seiner Rückkehr nach London, Anfang der 60er Jahre, gründete er mit Bob Gill und Colin Forbes die Partnerschaft Fletcher/Forbes/Gill. Die natürliche Entwicklung dieser Partnerschaft wuchs, und sie formierte sich schliesslich in den frühen 70er Jahren um zu Pentagram, zu deren Gründungsmitgliedern Alan Fletcher zählt.

Als Designer ziehen ihn immer wieder visuelle Ambiguitäten und Paradoxe an, sowohl um ihrer selbst willen wie auch in praktischen Design-Problemen für seine Kunden.

Hier einige seiner eigenen Beobachtungen: «Designer haben die Möglichkeit, wenn nicht sogar die Verpflichtung, Gebrauchsgegenstände mit Fantasie zu bereichern, ohne dabei die Funktionalität zu beeinträchtigen. Als Künstler müssen sie den Produkten ausser Nahrung auch die nötige Würze verleihen.

Die meisten Probleme werden in Zusammenarbeit mit meinen Partnern bei Pentagram gelöst, durch gegenseitigen Gedankenaustausch sowie Hinzufügen und Vereinfachen. Die Übertragung in das endgültige visuelle Bild jedoch ist die individuelle Interpretation des einzelnen Partners, der mit der Aufgabe betraut ist.

Ein Problem zu lösen ist nicht das Wichtigste. Die Hauptaufgabe ist es, Werte hinzuzufügen und Lösungen mit visuellen Überraschungen und vor allem mit Witz zu finden. Um das Axiom falsch zu zitieren: ‹Ein Lächeln ist 1000 Bilder wert.›»

Après des études au Royal College of Art à Londres et à la School of Architecture and Design de la Yale University, Alan Fletcher commença sa carrière professionnelle à New York à la fin des années cinquante. A cette époque, les plus grands noms du graphisme international se retrouvaient à New York, et Alan Fletcher reconnaît ouvertement avoir largement profité de tous ces talents et expériences réunis.

Après son retour à Londres, vers la fin des années soixante, il s'est associé comme partenaire avec Bob Gill et Colin Forbes pour former le groupe Fletcher/Forbes/Gill. Cette collaboration fonctionna bien et aboutit, au début des années soixante-dix, au groupe Pentagram, dont Fletcher est un des membres fondateurs.

En tant que graphiste, il se sent constamment attiré par les ambiguïtés et paradoxes visuels, tant sous forme de questions qui l'intriguent comme telles que de problèmes que lui confient ses clients.

Voici comment il exprime ses propres observations: «Les graphistes ont la faculté, voire même l'obligation d'établir un certain rapport entre les objets que nous utilisons et le penchant naturel de l'homme à la fantaisie. Le caractère fonctionnel, c'est très bien; mais en tant qu'artiste, le graphiste doit ajouter à notre nourriture quotidienne le sel de sa fantaisie.

J'effectue mon travail en majeure partie en collaboration avec mes partenaires du Pentagram. Nous échangeons des idées, nous les retournons dans tous les sens, nous complétons et simplifions. Le passage de l'idée à l'image visuelle définitive relève cependant de l'interprétation individuelle de chacun des partenaires.

Résoudre un problème n'est pas le problème essentiel. La tâche principale constitue dans la recherche de nouvelles valeurs et dans la découverte de solutions riches en surprises visuelles et, surtout, pleines d'esprit. En variant l'adage bien connu, on pourrait dire: «Un sourire vaut bien mille images.»

The Pirelli Presenter is a "tyreman" and unique to Pirelli. He is a geometric figure and not a cartoon or a caricature, nevertheless he is an individual with character, wit and style (collaborating designer: Jessica Strang).

Die Pirelli-Figur ist ein Reifenmann und ein besonderes Unikum für Pirelli. Er ist eine geometrische Gestalt und weder Cartoon noch Karikatur, jedoch von individuellem Charakter, Witz und Stil.

Le présentoir à pneus Pirelli est une figure géométrique unique en son genre. Sans relever ni de la caricature, ni du dessin animé, le fameux personnage Pirelli possède son caractère très individuel, plein de charme et d'esprit.

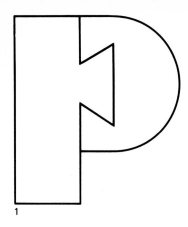

1

2

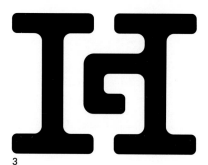

3

4

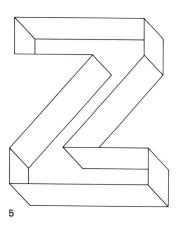

5

MICHĒLE

6

1

Mr. Purser was a joiner who put up the shelves in our first studio and didn't understand what we did — so we designed him a trademark.

2

This symbol was part of a corporate graphic programme developed for the Conference of Islamic Solidarity in Saudi Arabia. Alternate white and green crescents represented six Islamic countries.

3

Gebrüder Heinemann are a German company who retail duty free goods. The brief was for a monogram based on GH, in which the letter H needed to be dominant.

1

Herr Purser hat in unserem ersten Studio als Schreiner Regale angebracht. Es war ihm nicht klar, was wir machen, so entwarfen wir ihm ein Warenzeichen.

2

Dieses Symbol war Teil eines «Corporate Graphic Programme». Es wurde für die Konferenz der Islamischen Solidarität in Saudi-Arabien entwickelt. Die abwechselnden weiss-grünen Halbmonde repräsentierten sechs islamische Länder.

3

Gebrüder Heinemann ist ein deutsches Unternehmen, das zollfreie Waren vertreibt. Der Auftrag war, ein Monogramm herzustellen, das auf GH basiert, der Buchstabe H jedoch dominiert.

1

M. Purser est un menuisier qui était venu monter des rayonnages dans notre premier atelier. Comme il ne comprenait pas en quoi consiste notre travail, nous avons créé pour lui une image de marque.

2

Le présent symbole fait partie du programme graphique développé pour la Conférence sur la solidarité islamique en Arabie Saoudite. Les croissants de lune blancs et verts qui alternent représentent six pays islamiques.

3

Gebrüder Heinemann est une entreprise de distribution de produits en franchise. Il s'agissait de créer un monogramme avec GH dans lequel la lettre H était prédominante.

4

The symbol of a star for "The Commercial Bank of Kuwait" is constructed on the Arabic words for "Commercial" and "Bank" (calligrapher: Jamil Majid, collaborating designer: Paul Anthony).

5

This impossible figure with curious three dimensional properties expresses not only the initial letter, but also the die casting businesses represented by the Zinc Association.

6

Logotype for a brand of cosmetics sold by Marks and Spencer. Cutting and raising the bar of the letter E created the necessary accent for the French name "Michèle" (collaborating designer: Kati Durrer).

4

Das Symbol eines Sternes für die Commercial Bank of Kuwait ist auf den arabischen Worten für kommerziell und Bank aufgebaut.

5

Dieser Buchstabe mit merkwürdigen dreidimensionalen Eigenschaften enthält nicht nur den Anfangsbuchstaben des Unternehmens, sondern weist auch auf den Spritzgussverkauf der Firma hin.

6

Logotype für eine Kosmetikreihe, die bei Marks and Spencer verkauft wird. Der Schnitt und das Anheben des Balkens vom Buchstaben E liess den für den französischen Namen «Michèle» nötigen Akzent entstehen.

4

Le symbole de l'étoile pour la «Commercial Bank of Kuwait» est créé à partir des mots arabes pour «commercial» et «banque» (calligraphie: Jamil Majid, collaboration: Paul Anthony).

5

Cette figure impossible, aux étranges propriétés tridimensionnelles, ne représente pas seulement la lettre initiale de l'association, mais encore les produits de moulage sous pression qu'elle diffuse.

6

Logotype pour une gamme de produits cosmétiques vendus chez «Marks and Spencer». La manière de couper et de renforcer la barre de la lettre E a permis de mettre en valeur le nom français «Michèle» (collaboration: Kati Durrer).

The intention of this calendar, published in a limited edition by Olivetti, was to regularly change an environment by twelve number paintings. It was not conceived to be legible or even practical, but evocative, stimulating and colourful. Hand printed in fluorescent inks, mismatched to produce sensational optical sensations... even the printer had to wear sunglasses. The ink company thought it the most vulgar calendar they had ever seen. It is in the collection of the Museum of Modern Art in New York and the Stedelijk Museum in Amsterdam.

Die Absicht dieses Kalenders, der in einer begrenzten Auflage von Olivetti herausgegeben wird, war, die Umgebung durch 12 Nummernbilder zu verändern. Es war nicht beabsichtigt, dass er praktische Anwendung besass oder lesbar war, jedoch auffällig, stimulierend und bunt. Er wurde handgedruckt in fluoreszierenden Farben. Diese erschienen in so ungewöhnlichen Zusammenstellungen, dass sie sensationelle optische Effekte erbrachten; sogar der Drucker brauchte Sonnenbrillen. Die Farbenhersteller hielten ihn für den vulgärsten Kalender. Folgende Sammlungen führen ihn: Museum of Modern Art und das Stedelijk-Museum in Amsterdam.

Ce calendrier, publié par Olivetti en un tirage limité, avait pour but de transformer régulièrement l'environnement par ses douze images numérotées. Il n'avait pas été conçu pour être lisible, voire même pratique, mais évocateur, stimulant et coloré. Imprimé à la main, en des combinaisons inhabituelles d'encres fluorescentes, il visait à produire des effets insolites, obligeant même l'imprimeur à porter des lunettes de soleil. Le fabricant des encres à imprimer le considéra comme le calendrier le plus horrible jamais produit. Le calendrier figure dans la collection du Museum of Modern Art à New York, ainsi qu'au Musée Stedelijk à Amsterdam.

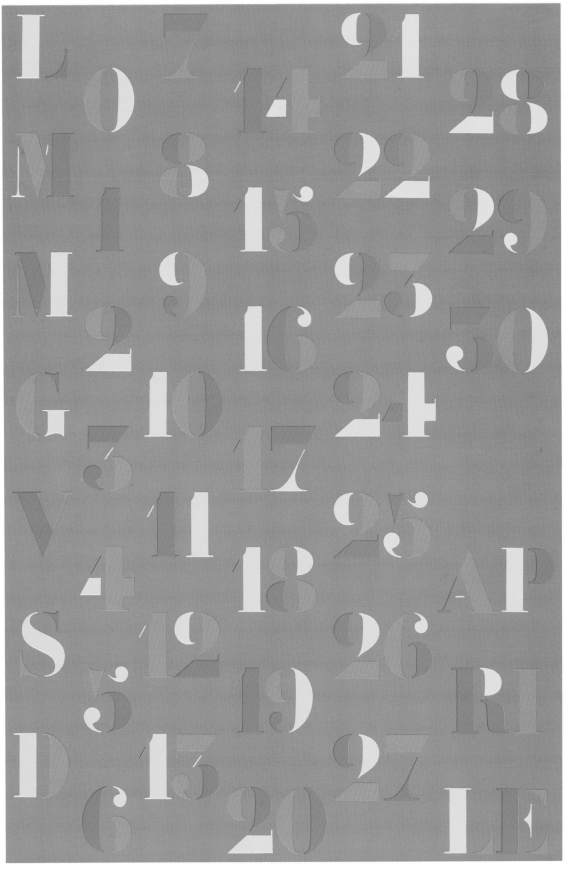

British Painting '74 Hayward Gallery
Arts Council of Great Britain 26 September to 17 November 1974
Monday to Friday 10 to 8/Saturdays 10 to 6/Sundays 12 to 6
Admission 30p/Children, students and pensioners 15p
10p all day Monday and between 6 to 8 Tuesdays to Fridays

1

2

1
An ambiguous visual configuration was designed as the mark for an advertising agency, Manton, Woodyer, Ketley and Partners. The device is used graphically for print as well as in reality in the reception, where it undergoes a daily floral change! (collaborating designer: Julia Alldridge).
2
The concept was to redraw conventional letterforms and take them to the boundaries of illegibility, and so convert them into abstract symbols interpreting typography as painting.

1
Eine zweideutige visuelle Konfiguration, das Zeichen für die Werbeagentur Manton, Woodyer, Ketley and Partners. Es wird grafisch im Druck verwendet und ebenfalls in Wirklichkeit am Empfang des Unternehmens als täglich frisches Blumenarrangement (Mitarbeiter: Julia Alldridge).
2
Das Konzept war, Buchstabenformen immer wieder zu zeichnen und an die Grenze der Lesbarkeit zu führen, damit sie zu abstrakten Symbolen für die Interpretation von Typografie und Malerei wurden.

1
Configuration visuelle ambiguë, symbole de l'agence de publicité Manton, Woodyer, Ketley et Partners. Elle est utilisée graphiquement pour les imprimés et apparaît à la réception de l'agence sous forme d'arrangement floral, renouvelé tous les jours (collaboration: Julia Alldridge).
2
Le concept consiste à retracer continuellement les formes conventionnelles des caractères et à les amener jusqu'à l'extrême limite de la lisibilité afin de les convertir en symboles abstraits, permettant d'interpréter la typographie en tant que peinture.

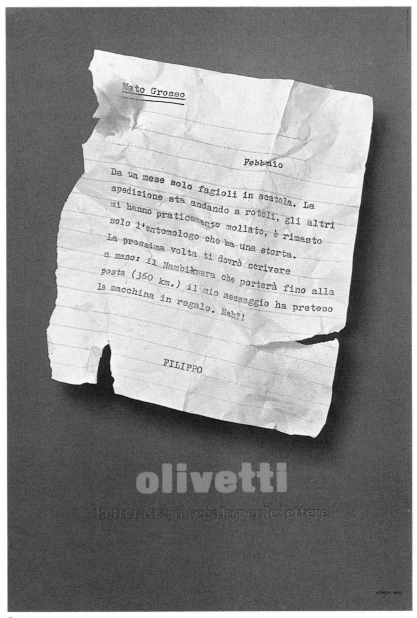

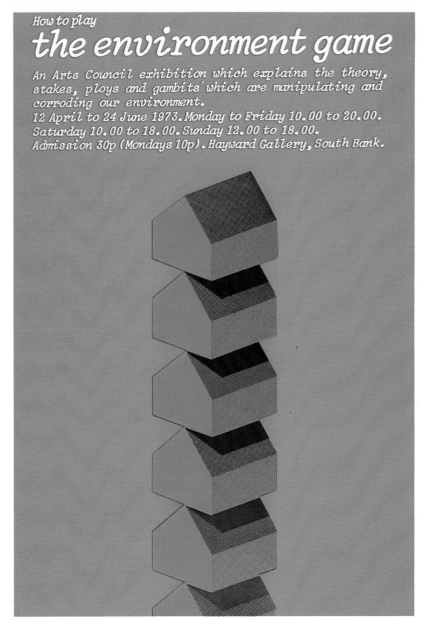

3

4

3

A poster campaign was designed to promote the Lettera 32 typewriter in Italy. The message was put across in a series of amusing letters, apparently typewritten by jilted lovers, grateful nieces and job seekers.

4

A poster produced for an exhibition about the urban environment. The graphic image of the exhibition and the poster was based on the green houses used as pieces in the game of "Monopoly".

3

Eine Plakat-Kampagne, die zur Werbung für die Schreibmaschine Lettera 32 in Italien entworfen wurde. Die Botschaft wurde in einer Serie amüsanter Briefe übermittelt, die anscheinend von sitzengelassenen Verliebten, dankbaren Nichten und Arbeitsuchenden geschrieben waren.

4

Plakat für eine Ausstellung über städtische Umwelt. Das grafische Bild der Ausstellung und des Plakates stammen von den grünen Häusern aus dem Spiel «Monopoly».

3

Campagne publicitaire avec affiche pour lancer la machine à écrire Lettera 32 en Italie. Le message se dégage d'une série de lettres amusantes, soi-disant écrites par des amoureux éconduits, ou par des nièces reconnaissantes ou des personnes en quête de travail.

4

Affiche pour une exposition sur l'environnement urbain. L'image graphique de l'exposition et de l'affiche est empruntée aux maisons vertes du jeu de «Monopoly».

An ashtray, nicely named the Clam, was produced in a range of bright coloured melamine and in an expensive version of chromed brass. The identical halves made from a single mould not only provide two ashtrays but also a lid, and teeth to grip the cigarette. The design was pirated and copied in four countries within a month of production (collaborating designer: Jessica Strang).

Ein Aschenbecher mit dem passenden Namen «Muschel». Er wurde in einer Anzahl von kräftigen Farben in Melamine und in einer teureren Ausführung «in verchromtem Messing» hergestellt. Die identischen Hälften machten aus einem Guss nicht nur zwei Aschenbecher, sondern auch einen Deckel und Zacken als Zigarettenhalter. Das Design war innerhalb eines Monats nach Produktionsbeginn in vier Ländern kopiert (Mitarbeiter: Jessica Strang).

Un cendrier, portant le joli nom de «Coquille», a été réalisé en mélamine aux couleurs vives, ainsi qu'en une exécution plus chère, en laiton chromé. Les deux moitiés identiques, produites avec un seul moule, forment non seulement un cendrier, mais encore un couvercle ou des dents pour retenir une cigarette. Le sujet a été imité et copié dans quatre pays en l'espace d'un mois après la production (collaboration: Jessica Strang).

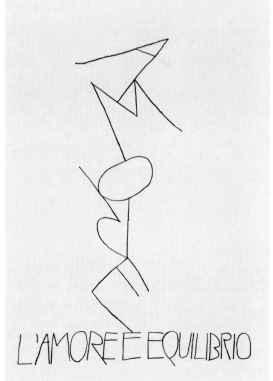

An alphabetic whimsy of an Italian aphorism.
Ein alfabetischer Witz eines italienischen Aphorismus.
Boutade alphabétique sur un aphorisme italien.

Best of British Authors

TWENTY OF OUR GREATEST LIVING BRITISH WRITERS

BERYL BAINBRIDGE · JOHN BETJEMAN · MALCOLM BRADBURY · ANTHONY BURGESS

MARGARET DRABBLE · LAWRENCE DURRELL · JOHN FOWLES · LEON GARFIELD

WILLIAM GOLDING · GRAHAM GREENE · TED HUGHES · JOHN LE CARRÉ · LAURIE LEE

ROSAMOND LEHMANN · IRIS MURDOCH · V S NAIPAUL · V S PRITCHETT

ROSEMARY SUTCLIFF · LAURENS VAN DER POST · REBECCA WEST

THE BOOK MARKETING COUNCIL

The caricature was used as a symbol and the major graphic element on a poster.

Die Karikatur diente als Symbol und wichtigstes grafisches Element auf einem Plakat.

La caricature a été utilisée comme symbole et élément graphique déterminant sur une affiche.

Shigeo Fukuda

1932	Born in Tokyo, Japan	1932	Geboren in Tokio, Japan	1932	Né à Tokyo, Japon
1956	Graduated from Tokyo National University of Art and Music	1956	Abschluss an der National University of Art and Music in Tokio	1956	Diplôme de la Tokyo National University of Art and Music
1967	One-man Show "Toys and Things", IBM Gallery, USA	1967	Einzelausstellung «Toys and Things» in der IBM Gallery, USA	1967	Exposition individuelle «Toys and Things», IBM Gallery, Etats-Unis
1968/70/72/ 74/76/78/80	Exhibited at Graphic Art Biennale Brno, Czechoslovakia	1968/70/72/ 74/76/78 und 80	Teilnahme an der Ausstellung der Graphic Art Biennale Brno, Tschechoslowakei	1968/70/72/ 74/76/78 et 80	Participe à la Biennale de l'art graphique Brno en Tchécoslovaquie
1970	Exhibited at "Design and Children", Paris	1970	Ausstellungsteilnahme bei «Design and Children», Paris	1970	Participation à l'exposition «Design and Children», Paris
1971	Exhibited at "Japon Joconda", Paris One-man Show "The World of Shigeo Fukuda" at De Young Memorial Museum, Santa Barbara Museum, USA	1971	Ausstellungsteilnahme bei «Japon Joconda», Paris Ein-Mann-Ausstellung bei «The World of Shigeo Fukuda» bei De Young Memorial Museum, Santa Barbara Museum, USA	1971	Participation à l'exposition «Japon Joconda», Paris Exposition individuelle «The World of Shigeo Fukuda» au Musée De Young Memorial, Musée de Santa Barbara, Etats-Unis
1972	Awarded Gold Medal "Fourth International Poster Biennale", Poland	1972	Goldmedaille der vierten Internationalen Plakat-Biennale in Polen	1972	Médaille d'or à la 4e Biennale internationale de l'affiche en Pologne
1974	Awarded prize "The ninth Japan Art Festival", Japan	1974	Preis des «The Ninth Japan Art Festival», Japan	1974	Prix du 9e Festival d'art japonais, Japon
1974/76/78 and 80	Exhibited at "International Poster Biennale", Poland	1974/76/78 und 80	Ausstellungsteilnahme an der Internationalen Plakat-Biennale in Polen	1974/76/78 et 80	Participation à la Biennale internationale de l'affiche en Pologne
1975	Awarded First Prize "international competition for a Poster", commemorating the 30th Anniversary of victory Awarded First Prize international competition for a coin design 21st Olympic Games Montreal Awarded Prize "Second International Biennale of Cartoon and Small Satirical Sculpture", Bulgaria	1975	Erster Preis des Internationalen Plakat-Wettbewerbs zum 30-Jahr-Siegesgedenktag Erster Preis des internationalen Wettbewerbs für ein Münzen-Design der 21. Olympischen Spiele in Montreal, Preisverleihung an der «Second International Biennale of cartoon and small satirical sculpture», Bulgarien	1975	Premier prix au Concours international de l'affiche pour son travail sur la commémoration du 30e anniversaire de la victoire Premier prix au Concours international de médailles pour les 21es Jeux Olympiques à Montréal Prix à la «2e Biennale internationale des dessins animés et petites sculptures satiriques», Bulgarie
1977	Exhibited at "Deception in Art, Nature and Play", Canada	1977	Ausstellungsteilnahme bei «Deception in Art, Nature and Play», Kanada	1977	Participation à l'exposition «Deception in Art, Nature and Play», Canada
1978	Awarded Prize "International Poster Exhibition", USA	1978	Preisverleihung der «International Poster Exhibition», USA	1978	Prix de l'«Exposition internationale de l'affiche», Etats-Unis
1982	Invited as a guest lecturer for four weeks at Yale University, USA Member of AGI	1982	Gastdozent für einen Monat an der Yale-Universität, USA, Mitglied der AGI	1982	Invité pour un mois comme chargé de cours à la Yale University, Etats-Unis, membre de l'AGI

Each of Fukuda's new concepts is methodically developed in all possible alternatives, applications and variations until it is fully exploited in every way. It is then abandonned to make room for a completely new and unlikely idea which in turn is again systematically conjugated through all tenses, all declinations and possible inflexions and so on. Each series is an example of subjective leaps of fantasy, objectively controlled and structured. He imposes a rational order and sequence on his irrational visual joy rides.

Paul Rand writes in an introduction to a book on Fukuda's work: ''Acclaimed by his colleagues in Europe, US and his native Japan as a design genius, he is equally at ease whether he designs in two or three dimensions, in Japanese tradition or in perception psychology. Functional, fanciful, bewilderingly intricate, or disarmingly simple, the work of this artist is always flavoured with that pinch of mischievous humor which we have come to recognize as his mark. Whether he is cutting out paper dolls, solving problems in combinatorial geometry or optical illusions, making simple drawings, or figuring out some highly complex sculptural puzzle, this same whimsical spirit prevails. Designing toys or posters, books or trademarks, Fukuda is always involved in the pleasures of exploration.''

Jedes von Fukudas neuen Konzepten ist in einer ganz methodischen Arbeitsweise auf sämtliche alternativen Anwendungsmöglichkeiten und Variationen bis zum letzten Punkt ausgearbeitet. Nachdem das Konzept völlig ausgewertet ist, greift er dann einen völlig neuen Gedanken auf, den er wieder in systematischer und gründlicher Weise auf alle Möglichkeiten durchexerziert. Jede Serie ist eine Reihe von sehr subjektiven Fantasiesprüngen, die jedoch objektiv kontrolliert und durchstrukturiert sind. Seine irrationalen visuellen Fantasieausflüge unterliegen jedoch einer rationalen und logischen Ordnung.

In der Einführung zu einem Buch über Fukudas Arbeiten schreibt Paul Rand: «Fukuda, von seinen Kollegen in Europa, in den USA und in Japan als Design-Genie anerkannt, versteht sich auf Design jeder Art, ob zwei- oder dreidimensional, im traditionellen japanischen Stil oder auf erkennungspsychologischer Grundlage. Ob funktionell, verspielt, höchst kompliziert oder entwaffnend einfach, die Arbeit dieses Künstlers hat immer einen gewissen frechen Humor, den wir als seine ganz persönliche Note kennengelernt haben. Ob er nun Papierfiguren ausschneidet, sich mit Problemen kombinatorischer Geometrie oder optischer Illusionen befasst, einfache Zeichnungen anfertigt oder ein höchst kompliziertes skulpturelles Puzzle zu lösen versucht, immer herrscht dieselbe Originalität. Ob er Spielsachen oder Poster, Bücher oder Warenzeichen entwirft, Fukuda hat stets seine Freude an der Erforschung neuer Möglichkeiten.»

Chacun des nouveaux concepts de Fukuda est développé systématiquement dans toutes ses variantes et formes d'application, jusqu'à épuisement total de toutes les possibilités. Il est ensuite abandonné pour céder la place à une idée foncièrement nouvelle et invraisemblable qui, à son tour, est exploitée sous tous ses aspects et dans toutes ses implications. Chaque série est un exemple des bonds subjectifs de l'imagination artistique, contrôlés et structurés en toute objectivité. Les envols dans le monde irrationnel de l'imaginaire sont toujours soumis à un ordre rationnel et logique. Dans son introduction à un livre sur le travail de Fukuda, Paul Rand écrit: «Salué par ses collègues en Europe, aux Etats-Unis et das son pays natal, le Japon, comme un génie du design, Shigeo Fukuda possède la même aisance, qu'il travaille en deux ou trois dimensions, dans la tradition japonaise ou dans le domaine de la psychologie de perception. Fonctionnelles, imaginatives, d'une complexité impénétrable ou d'une simplicité désarmante, les créations de cet artiste sont toujours assaisonnées d'une pincée d'humour espiègle qui est devenue pour nous sa signature. Qu'il découpe des poupées en papier, résolve des problèmes de géométrie combinatoire ou d'illusion optique, brosse de simples croquis ou s'attaque à des puzzles tridimensionnels hautement complexes, le même esprit de fantaisie prévaut. Qu'il crée des jouets, des affiches, des livres ou des logos, Fukuda s'adonne toujours aux plaisirs de l'exploration.»

1
2

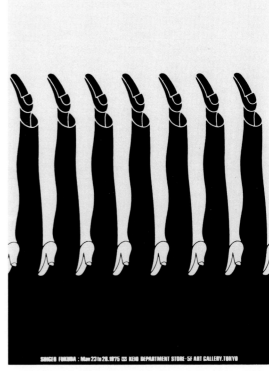

1 Group
2 Illusions

1 Gruppe
2 Illusionen

1 Groupe
2 Illusions

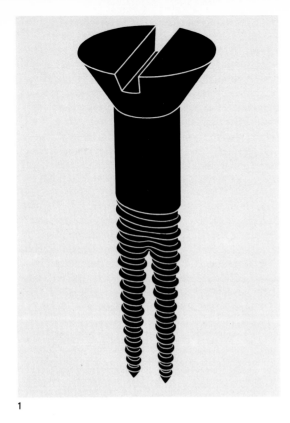

1

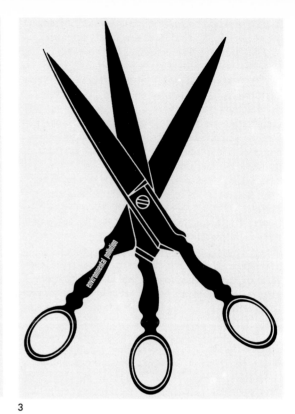

2

3

1–3 Impossible objects

1–3 Unmögliche Objekte

1–3 Objets impossibles

4–6 Coffee-cup phantasies

4–6 Kaffeetassen-Phantasien

4–6 Fantaisies de tasses de café

4

5

6

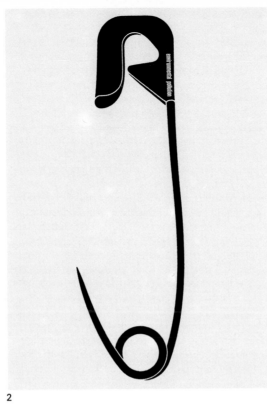

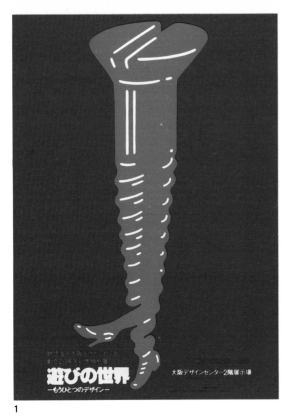

1

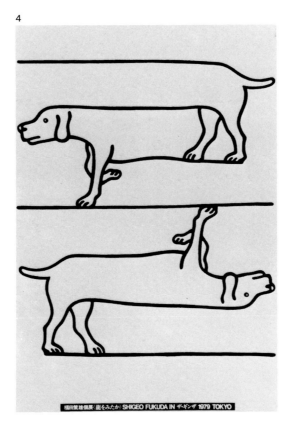

2

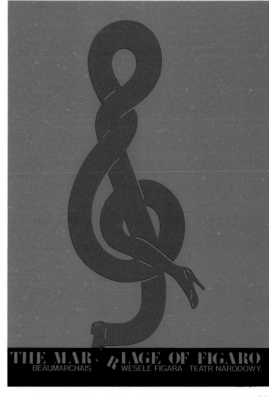

3

4

5

1 Poster for Exhibition "Museum of Humour"
2 Poster Private Exhibition "Ceramic"
3 Poster Kymogen (Japanese Traditional Accomplishments)
4 Poster Private Exhibition (Illustrations for Newspaper Novel)
5 Poster "Marriage of Figaro"

1 Ausstellungsplakat «Museum of Humor»
2 Plakat für Privatausstellung «Ceramic»
3 Plakat Kymogen (japanische Bräuche)
4 Plakat für private Ausstellung, Illustration für einen Zeitungsroman
5 Plakat «Hochzeit des Figaro»

1 Affiche pour l'exposition «Le musée de l'humour»
2 Affiche pour une exposition privée «La céramique»
3 Affiche Kymogen (réalisations dans la tradition japonaise)
4 Affiche pour une exposition privée (illustration d'un récit de journal)
5 Affiche «Le mariage de Figaro»

1

2

3

4

5

6

7

8

1–8
Space objects for department store
(the figure is fixed to the wall, animals move along fence)

1–8
Raumobjekt für ein Warenhaus
(die sitzende Figur ist an der Mauer befestigt, die Tiere laufen
im Vordergrund am Zaun entlang)

1–8
Objet spécial pour un grand magazine
(l'homme assis est fixé sur un mur en arrière, les animaux pas-
sent devant la palissade)

1

2

3

4

5

1
Lincoln on the floor of a big store
2–5
Lincoln as line, as rainbow, as butterfly and as chair

1
Lincoln, Bodendekoration für ein Warenhaus
2–5
Lincoln als Stock, als Regenbogen, als Schmetterling und als Stuhl

1
Lincoln sur le plancher d'un grand magasin
2–5
Lincoln comme ligne, comme arc-en-ciel, comme papillon et comme chaise

3

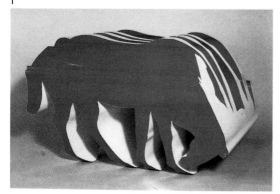

1

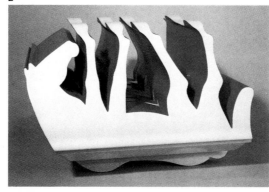

2

1, 2
Horse with profile in reverse

1, 2
Pferd mit umgekehrtem Profil

1, 2
Cheval au profil à l'envers

3
Mural for rehabilitation center
4
Monument of rehabilitation center

3
Wanddekoration für ein Rehabilitations-Zentrum
4
Monument für ein Rehabilitations-Zentrum

3
Dessin mural pour un centre de réhabilitation
4
Monument pour un centre de réhabilitation

4

Grapus

1970   Formation of the Grapus Studio by Pierre Bernard, François Miehe, Gerard Paris-Clavel with the aim of producing social, political and cultural images as a design co-operative and under a joint signature
The following have been members of the Grapus team: Geneviève Bentolila, Gerard Delafosse, Evelyne Deltombe, François Fabrizi, Jean-Louis Gigue, Patricia Lemorvan, Martine Loyau, François Miehe, Annick Poulet, Claire Prebois, Marjolaine Preiss, Michel Quarez, Michel Robledo, Jean-Luc Soulier, Thierry Sarfis, Chantal Sueur, Joseph Balette

1980   Present team members:
Jean-Paul Bachollet, Pierre Bernard, Alexander Jordan, Gerard Paris-Clavel and

1981   Marc Dumas joins the team

Exhibitions:
1979   Quimper and Grenoble, France
1980   Düsseldorf, Germany
1981   Athens, Amsterdam, Zagreb, Mons
1982   Pecs, Budapest, Zurich, Paris

Prizes and medals:
1978   Silver medal, Warsaw
Grand Prix, Brno
1980   Gold and silver medals, Warsaw
Gold, silver and bronze medals, Brno
1981   1st prize, Lahti, Finland

1970   Gründung des Grapus-Studios von Pierre Bernard, François Miehe, Gerard Paris-Clavel für sozialpolitische und kulturelle Designarbeiten in Form einer Kooperative
Folgende Designer waren Mitglied des Grapus-Teams: Geneviève Bentolila, Gerard Delafosse, Evelyne Deltombe, François Fabrizi, Jean-Louis Gigue, Patricia Lemorvan, Martine Loyau, François Miehe, Annick Poulet, Claire Prebois, Marjolaine Preiss, Michel Quarez, Michel Robledo, Jean-Luc Soulier, Thierry Sarfis, Chantal Sueur, Joseph Balette

1980   Jetzige Mitglieder des Grapus-Teams:
Jean-Paul Bachollet, Pierre Bernard, Alexander Jordan, Gerard Paris-Clavel und

1981   Marc Dumas

Ausstellungen:
1979   Quimper und Grenoble, Frankreich
1980   Düsseldorf, BRD
1981   Athen, Amsterdam, Zagreb, Mons
1982   Pecs, Budapest, Zürich, Paris

Preise und Auszeichnungen:
1978   Silbermedaille, Warschau
Grosser Preis, Brno
1980   Gold- und Silbermedaille, Warschau
Gold-, Silber- und Bronzemedaille, Brno
1981   1. Preis, Lahti, Finnland

1970   Formation de l'atelier Grapus par Pierre Bernard, François Miehe, Gérard Paris-Clavel ayant pour objectif de réaliser par un travail collectif, sous une signature collective, Grapus, des images sociales, politiques et culturelles

Ont participé à Grapus: Geneviève Bentolila, Gérard Delafosse, Evelyne Deltombe, François Fabrizi, Jean-Louis Gigue, Patricia Lemorvan, Martine Loyau, François Miehe, Annick Poulet, Claire Prébois, Marjolaine Preiss, Michel Quarez, Michel Robledo, Jean-Luc Soulier, Thierry Sarfis, Chantal Sueur, Joseph Balette

1980   Depuis le printemps, Grapus se compose de Jean-Paul Bachollet, Pierre Bernard, Alexander Jordan, Gérard Paris-Clavel et

1981   Marc Dumas

Expositions:
1979   Quimper et Grenoble
1980   Düsseldorf, Allemagne fédérale
1981   Athènes, Amsterdam, Zagreb, Mons
1982   Pecs, Budapest, Zurich, Paris

Distinctions et médailles:
1978   Médaille d'argent, Varsovie
Grand Prix, Brno
1980   Médailles d'or et d'argent, Varsovie
Médailles d'or, d'argent et de bronze, Brno
1981   1er prix, Lahti, Finlande

Tomaszewski's influence can still be seen in the work of Grapus, a design team which was formed by three graphic designers in the wake of the events of 1968. The three worked and discussed future involvement in the Institute of the Environment, founded by some former students from the Ulm design school, with psychologists and architects on a multi-disciplinary basis. They deliberated how they and their colleagues could make an optimal contribution towards establishing and educating such a new society.

The spontaneous posters appearing on the walls of Paris at this time were almost all done by non-professionals, by ordinary people who felt strongly about the issues of these events. These posters were extraordinarily powerful and compelling, simple and direct. A professional design approach seemed almost suspect because known techniques of typography, composition and aesthetic considerations rather diminished the power of the message both in words and visualisation. It would have seemed as disingeneous as asking a professionally trained actor to address a political meeting. The difference between communication to sell products and merchandise (advertising) and one that attempts to inform, enlighten and enthuse about social and cultural issues became ever more apparent. The language of publicity, which aims at

Der Einfluss von Tomaszewski ist immer noch in den Arbeiten von Grapus zu erkennen, einem Design-Team, das von drei engagierten Grafik-Designern nach den Ereignissen von 1968 gegründet wurde. Diese drei arbeiteten und diskutierten zukünftiges Engagement im Umweltinstitut, das von einigen ehemaligen Studenten der Ulmer Design-Schule zusammen mit Psychologen und Architekten auf einer multidisziplinären Ebene gegründet wurde. Sie überlegten, wie sie und ihre Kollegen einen optimalen Beitrag zur Formierung und Erziehung einer neuen Gesellschaft leisten konnten.

Die spontanen Plakate, die zu dieser Zeit an den Pariser Wänden erschienen, wurden fast ausschliesslich von Laien gemacht, von einfachen Leuten, die aber sehr intensiv hinter den jeweiligen Aussagen und Ereignissen standen. Diese Plakate waren besonders wirksam, zwingend, einfach und direkt. Eine professionelle Design-Methode schien fast suspekt, da die bekannten Techniken der Typografie, Komposition und ästhetischen Betrachtungen, sowohl in Worten wie auch visuell, die Kraft der Aussage reduziert hätten. Es wäre genauso unaufrichtig gewesen, einen ausgebildeten Schauspieler zu bitten, auf einer politischen Versammlung eine Ansprache zu halten. Der Unterschied zwischen Kommunikation zum Ver-

L'influence de Tomaszewski se retrouve encore dans les travaux de Grapus, une équipe constituée par trois graphistes, au début des événements de 1968. Ils travaillaient et discutaient leur engagement futur à l'Institut de l'Environnement (que d'anciens élèves de l'Ecole de design d'Ulm avaient fondé avec des psychologues et des architectes, à un niveau multidisciplinaire). Ils réfléchissaient à la meilleure contribution possible en vue de former et d'éduquer une nouvelle société.

Les affiches spontanées qui fleurissaient à l'époque sur les murs parisiens sont presque toutes l'œuvre d'amateurs, c'est-à-dire de gens simples qui s'identifiaient fortement aux messages et aux événements. Elles étaient très efficaces, percutantes, simples et directes. Toute approche professionnelle paraissait presque suspecte, puisque les techniques connues de la typographie et de la composition et les considérations esthétiques auraient réduit l'impact des mots et des images et diminué la force du message. Il aurait été tout aussi peu authentique de prier un acteur professionnel de tenir un discours devant une assemblée politique. La différence se creusait entre la communication visant à vendre des produits et des marchandises (publicité) et celle qui tâche d'informer, d'expliquer, de susciter l'enthousiasme pour les préoccupations socio-culturelles. Le langage de

Political poster "No Neutrons Mr. Reagan"
Politisches Plakat «Nein zur Neutronenbombe»
Affiche politique «Relais de la paix»

maximising profits and thus creating demands could not be the same one which aims at satisfying needs.

Aware of these seemingly irreconcilable contradictions, the three founder members of Grapus determined to work together as a design co-operative rather than as individual artists. They went to Poland to study graphic design under Henryk Tomaszewski at the Warsaw Academy of Arts. When they returned to Paris and started to work as Grapus design co-operative they felt that the Polish experience and the previous environmental studies had given them the required strength and self-confidence of how to go about their work in their chosen sphere. "The beautiful image which we discovered in Poland made us devote ourselves to changing the world." They did not want to create ideas to sell more margarine, soups or cigarettes but to create images and texts in the spirit of 1968, publicising freedom of expression, progressive town councils, community centres, experimental theatres, exhibitions, etc.

During an interview at that time they stated: "To us a good image is one that conveys a message with maximal clarity and with the largest possible subjective dimension (poetry, pleasure, invention and humour)."

Instead they use symbols and signs which are generally understood like suns, moons, stars, fireworks. Photography and photomontage, postcards, stickers, badges and simple and sometimes infantile handwriting, and graffiti, are the elements which on their own or superimposed try to achieve the required clarity of message. Their posters conceived in constant dialogue are the result of teamwork — always with the same aim: to be understood, enjoyed and acted upon. The result is a complete integration of word and image, leading often to visual and verbal ambiguity or puns. But never at the expense of the directness of the message. Who contributes to what does not matter, as long as the jointly agreed objectives are achieved.

kauf von Produkten und Waren (Werbung) und derjenigen, die versucht zu informieren, aufzuklären und Begeisterung für soziale und kulturelle Anliegen wachzurufen, wurde immer auffälliger. Die Sprache der Werbung, die eine Maximierung der Profite anstrebt und daher eine Nachfrage kreiert, konnte nicht die gleiche sein wie diejenige, die versucht, bestehende Notwendigkeiten zu befriedigen.

Im vollen Bewusstsein dieser unüberbrückbaren Gegensätze entschlossen sich die drei Gründungsmitglieder von Grapus, als eine Design-Kooperative zusammenzuarbeiten und nicht als individuelle Künstler. Zwei von ihnen studierten Grafik-Design in Polen bei Henryk Tomaszewski an der Warschauer Kunstakademie. Nach ihrer Rückkehr nach Paris begannen sie ihre Zusammenarbeit als Grapus-Design-Kooperative in der Überzeugung, aus ihren polnischen Erfahrungen und ihren vorhergehenden Umweltstudien genügend Kraft und Selbstsicherheit gewonnen zu haben, um Aufgaben auf dem von ihnen gewählten Gebiet richtig anzufassen. «Die herrlichen Bilder, die wir in Polen sahen, veranlassten uns, unsere Kräfte einzusetzen, die Welt zu ändern.» Sie wollten keine Ideenhilfe zum Verkauf von Margarine, Suppen oder Zigaretten geben, sondern Bilder und Texte entwerfen, im Geiste von 1968 für freie Meinungsäusserung, für progressive Stadtverwaltungen, Gemeindezentren, experimentelle Theater, Ausstellungen usw.

In einem Interview zu der Zeit sagten sie über sich selbst: «Für uns ist ein Bild nur gut als eine Aussage mit maximaler Klarheit und der grösstmöglichen subjektiven Dimension (Dichtung, Vergnügen, Fantasie, Humor).»

Deshalb verwenden sie Symbole und Zeichen, die allgemein verstanden werden, z. B. Sonne, Mond, Sterne, Feuerwerk. Fotografie und Fotomontage, Postkarten, Aufkleber, Abzeichen und einfache, manchmal kindliche Handschriften und Graffiti sind die Elemente, die sie sowohl allein oder hinzugefügt verwenden, um die angestrebte Klarheit ihrer Botschaft zu erzielen. Ihre Plakate entstehen im ständigen Dialog und sind das Ergebnis von Teamarbeit, immer mit der gleichen Absicht: verstanden zu werden, zu unterhalten und Handlung hervorzurufen. Das Ergebnis ist eine völlige Integrierung von Wort und Bild, die oft zu visuellen oder verbalen Ambiguitäten oder Wortspielen führt, das jedoch nie auf Kosten der angestrebten direkten klaren Aussage. Es ist nicht wichtig, wer dabei welchen Teil übernimmt, solange die gemeinsam gesetzten Ziele im Resultat erreicht werden.

la publicité, visant à maximiser les profits et à créer une demande à cette fin, ne pouvait convenir à la satisfaction des nécessités existantes.

Pleinement conscients de ce fossé infranchissable, les trois fondateurs de Grapus ont décidé de travailler en coopérative, et non plus en tant qu'artistes isolés. Deux d'entre eux avaient suivi à l'Académie des Beaux-Arts de Varsovie les cours d'Henryk Tomaszewski. A leur retour à Paris, ils ont commencé à travailler sous le nom collectif de Grapus, convaincus d'avoir tiré de leurs expériences polonaises et de leur étude antérieure de l'environnement suffisamment de force et d'assurance pour aborder convenablement les tâches appartenant au domaine qu'ils avaient choisi. «Les merveilleuses images que nous avions vues en Pologne nous poussaient à employer nos forces à changer le monde.» Ils ne voulaient pas fournir des idées pour vendre des magazines, des potages ou des cigarettes, mais bien concevoir des images et des textes dans l'esprit de 1968, pour la liberté d'expression, pour des municipalités progressistes, pour des centres communaux, des théâtres et des expositions de recherche, etc.

Dans une interview à cette époque, ils ont déclaré: «Pour nous, une image n'est bonne que si elle transmet un message avec un maximum de clarté et avec la plus grande dimension subjective possible (poésie, plaisir, imagination, humour).»

Ils évitent de développer un style propre et utilisent donc des symboles et des signes d'acception générale comme le soleil, la lune, les étoiles, le feu d'artifice. Pour obtenir la clarté voulue, ils recourent à la photo, au montage, aux cartes postales, aux collages, insignes, graffiti et écritures parfois enfantines, seuls ou combinés. Leurs affiches naissent du dialogue constant et de la collaboration de toute l'équipe, toujours dans la même intention: être compris, distraire et provoquer l'action. Le résultat intègre parfaitement le mot et l'écriture, parfois avec des jeux de mots, des ambiguïtés visuelles ou verbales, mais jamais aux dépens de la clarté du message. Peu importe qui se charge de quelle part du travail, pourvu que le résultat atteigne les objectifs fixés.

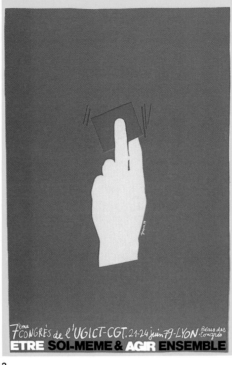

1

2

3

1 Political poster "Go there on my behalf"
2 Trade-Union poster, 7th congress of the UGICT-CGT, Lyon
3 Poster "Solidarity"
4 Political poster "To live, Vincennes"

1 Plakat der Ausstellung Grapus in Quimper
2 Gewerkschaftsplakat, 7. Kongress von UGICT-CGT, Lyon
3 Plakat «Solidarität»
4 Plakat «Die Universität von Vincennes muss leben»

1 Affiche politique «Allez-y de ma part»
2 Affiche syndicale, 7ème congrès de l'UGICT-CGT, Lyon
3 Affiche «Solidarité»
4 Affiche politique «Exister Vincennes»

4

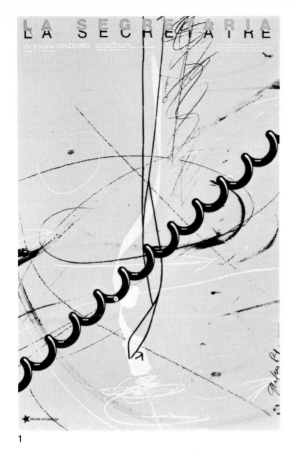

1

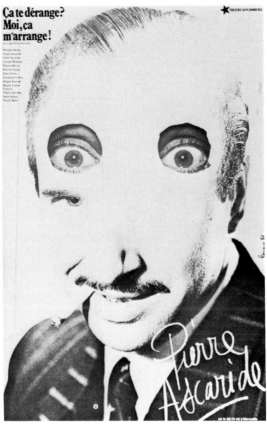

2

3

4

5

6

7

8

1

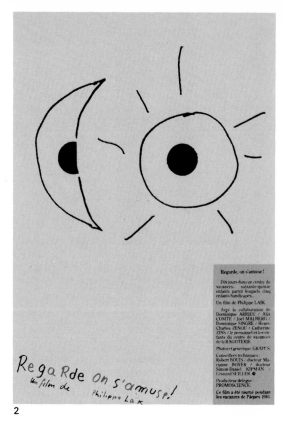

2

3

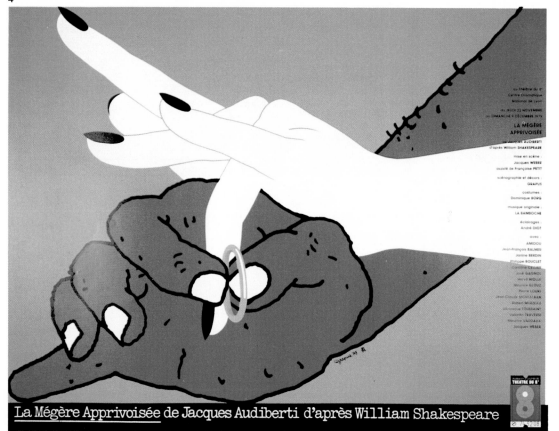

4

1 Theatre poster ''Les Cenci''
2 Poster ''Look, we enjoy ourselves''
3 Theatre poster ''The night just before the forest''
4 Theatre poster ''The Taming of the Shrew''

1 Theaterplakat «Les Cenci»
2 Filmplakat «Guck mal, uns macht's Spass!»
3 Theaterplakat «Die Nacht kurz vor dem Wald»
4 Theaterplakat «Der Widerspenstigen Zähmung»

1 Affiche théâtrale «Les Cenci»
2 Affiche de cinéma «Regarde, on s'amuse!»
3 Affiche théâtrale «La nuit juste avant les forêts»
4 Affiche théâtrale «La mégère apprivoisée»

1

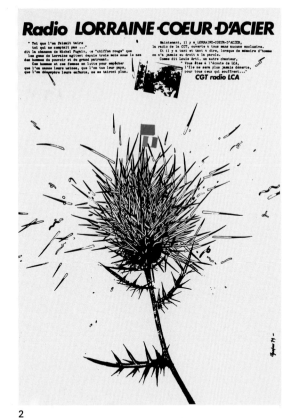

2

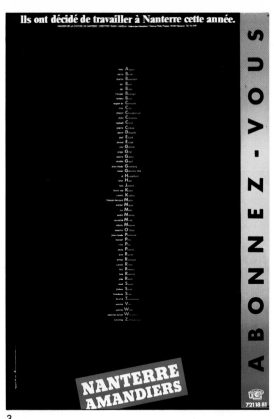

3

4

1 Poster "Autumn Festival at Montfermeil"
2 Radio poster "Lothringen, Heart of Steel"
3 Poster "Subscribe", House of Culture, Nanterre
4 Poster "Circus"

1 Plakat «Herbstfestival in Montfermeil»
2 Radioplakat «Lothringen, Herz aus Stahl»
3 Plakat «Abonnieren Sie!», Kulturhaus Nanterre
4 Plakat «Zirkus»

1 Affiche «Festival d'Automne à Montfermeil»
2 Radio Lorraine «Cœur d'acier»
3 Affiche «Abonnez-vous», Maison de la Culture, Nanterre
4 Affiche «Cirque»

Rudolph de Harak

*To Bill
with best wishes
Rudolph de Harak
1983*

Designer for more than 30 years, president of Rudolph de Harak & Associates, Inc., specializing in graphics, environmental and exhibition design. His work has been exhibited at the Museums of New York, Paris, Vienna, Amsterdam and Hamburg.

He has been a teacher of design and visual communications since 1952, he is also visiting professor at Yale University and professor of design at the Cooper Union School of Art and Architecture. He has taught and lectured at the Institutes, Colleges and Universities of Pittsburgh, Minneapolis, New York, Missouri, Virginia, Washington D.C., Ohio, Cincinnati.

He is a member of the American Institute of Graphic Arts, the AGI and the Advisory Committee to the United States Department of Transportation for the development of symbols for use in transportation related facilities.

Articles and examples of his work:
Graphis, Gebrauchsgraphik, Print, Linea Grafica and Progressive Architecture, and in books such as: Arts of the United States, Basic Typography, Internationale Ausstellungsgestaltung, Masters of Modern Art, Signet, Symbol, Signal, Who's Who in Graphic Art, Architectural Signing and Graphics, Trademarks and Symbols of the World, 12 United States Designers.

Awards from:
The American Institute of Architects, the American Institute of Graphic Arts, 1st Biennale Warsaw, 4th Biennale Arts Graphiques Brno, the New York Art Directors' Club, and the New York Type Directors' Club.

In 1981 he was the recipient of a grant from the National Endowment for the Arts for research on The History of Design.

Seit 30 Jahren als Designer tätig, Präsident der Rudolph de Harak & Associates, Inc., spezialisiert auf Grafik, Umwelt- und Ausstellungs-Design.
Seine Arbeiten wurden in folgenden Museen ausgestellt: New York, Paris, Warschau, Wien, Amsterdam und Hamburg.

Er unterrichtet Grafik-Design und Visuelle Kommunikation seit 1952, ist Gastdozent der Yale University und Professor an der Design-Fakultät der Cooper Union School of Art and Architecture.
Er unterrichtete an folgenden Colleges und Universitäten: Pittsburgh, Minneapolis, New York, Missouri, Virginia, Washington DC, Ohio, Cincinnati.

Er ist Mitglied des American Institute of Graphic Arts, der Alliance Graphique Internationale und des Beirats des «United States Department of Transportation» zur Schaffung von Symbolen für das Transportwesen.

Veröffentlichungen:
Graphis, Gebrauchsgraphik, Print, Linea Grafica, Progressive Architecture und in folgenden Büchern: Arts of the United States, Basic Typography, Internationale Ausstellungsgestaltung, Masters of Modern Art, Signet, Symbol, Signal, Who's Who in Graphic Art, Architectural Signing and Graphics, Trademarks and Symbols of the World, 12 United States Designers.

Anerkennungen:
American Institute of Architects, American Institute of Graphic Arts, 1st Biennale Warschau, 4. Biennale Brno, New York Art Directors' Club, New York Type Directors' Club.

1981 Forschungsstipendium für The History of Design.

Graphiste depuis plus de 30 années, président de la Rudolph de Harak & Associates, Inc., il est spécialisé dans le graphisme et la conception formelle de l'environnement et de l'exposition. Ses travaux ont été exposés aux musées de New York, Paris, Vienne, Amsterdam et Hambourg.

Depuis 1952, il enseigne aussi l'esthétique industrielle et la communication visuelle, et il est chargé de cours à la Yale University et professeur de design à la Cooper Union School of Art and Architecture. Il a enseigné aussi aux instituts, «colleges» et universités de Pittsburgh, Minneapolis, New York, Missouri, Virginia, Washington D.C., Ohio, Cincinnati.

Il est membre du «American Institute of Graphic Arts», de l'AGI et du Comité consultatif du «United States Department of Transportation» pour la création de symboles destinés aux différents moyens de transport.

Publications:
Graphis, Gebrauchsgraphik, Print, Linea Grafica, Progressive Architecture, ainsi que dans les livres suivants: Arts of the United States, Basic Typography, Internationale Ausstellungsgestaltung, Masters of Modern Art, Signet, Symbol, Signal, Who's Who in Graphic Art, Architectural Signing and Graphics, Trademarks and Symbols of the World, 12 United States Designers.

Prix reçus:
American Institute of Architects, American Institute of Graphic Arts, Ire Biennale de Varsovie, 4e Biennale des arts graphiques à Brno, New York Art Directors' Club et le New York Type Directors' Club.

En 1981, il a obtenu une bourse du «National Endowment for the Arts» pour une étude sur l'histoire du design.

Rudolph de Harak is a problem solver. This can be said of all designers in varying degrees but some of his achievements are perfect examples of this most essential design function. I think particularly of his two clock designs. His clock dial I consider the definitive solution where simplicity and clarity form a perfect equation to show the figures in a combination of twice three vertical and twice three horizontal parallel lines.

It is aesthetically highly satisfactory through its simple symmetry and perceptually optimal configuration; three lines symbolizing three numerals can be best taken in and easily differentiated at one glance. Until I saw this solution I always thought the italian clock dial best, which consists of twelve radial lines with one-twelfth increments in width for numerals 1 to 12. Although this solution is extremely simple and beautifully symbolic of the running out of time as in a hourglass, it is less easy to understand quickly than the one by Rudolph de Harak.

The other clock design, when a different brief in a different context requires a different solution, is

Rudolph de Harak ist ein Problemlöser. Das kann in unterschiedlichen Graden von allen Designern gesagt werden. Einige seiner Arbeitsergebnisse sind jedoch perfekte Beispiele dieser wichtigen Design-Funktion. Ich denke dabei besonders an seine beiden Uhrenentwürfe. Sein Zifferblatt sehe ich als die definitive Lösung in bezug auf Einfachheit und Klarheit an, wo die Zahlen in einer Kombination von zweimal je drei senkrechten und drei waagrechten parallelen Linien erscheinen. Diese Lösung ist ästhetisch hervorragend in ihrer einfachen Symmetrie und ebenso erfolgreich in ihrer Struktur, was die Wahrnehmung betrifft. Mit einem Blick können die drei Linien als drei Zahlen verstanden werden. Bevor ich diese Lösung sah, hielt ich immer die italienische Uhr für die beste, die 12 radial angeordnete Linien als Zahlen hat, die von 1 bis 12 je um ein Zwölftel stärker werden. Obwohl diese Version besonders einfach ist und auch sehr symbolisch in ihrem Hinweis auf die zu Ende gehende Zeit, wie eine Stundenuhr, wird sie nicht so leicht verstanden und wahrgenommen wie die Uhr von Rudolph de Harak.

Rudolph de Harak sait découvrir des solutions aux problèmes. A des degrés variés, on peut l'affirmer de tous les dessinateurs, mais certains de ses travaux sont des exemples parfaits de cette importante fonction de l'art graphique. Je pense en particulier à ses deux projets d'horloge. Ses cadrans me semblent la solution définitive en matière de clarté et de simplicité: les chiffres apparaissent dans une combinaison de deux fois trois parallèles verticales et trois horizontales. La solution est excellente du point de vue esthétique dans sa simple symétrie, et tout aussi réussie dans la perception de sa structure. D'un coup d'œil, les trois lignes sont comprises comme trois chiffres. Avant de voir celle-ci, j'ai toujours estimé l'horloge italienne la meilleure, avec ses 12 lignes radiales qui épaississent chaque fois d'un douzième entre 1 et 12. Malgré la simplicité de cette version et sa valeur symbolique par rapport au temps tirant à sa fin, elle n'est pas aussi facile à comprendre et à percevoir que le modèle de Rudolph de Harak.

Sa deuxième horloge, affectée d'une autre mission et située dans un autre environnement, est archi-

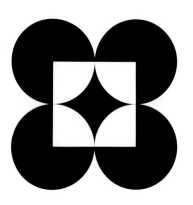

Trademarks: Kurt Versen Lighting Company, United Nations Plaza Hotel, Alan Guttmacher Institute (for family planning) and McGraw Hill Paperbacks

Warenzeichen: Kurt Versen (Beleuchtungsfirma), United Nations Plaza Hotel, Alan Guttmacher Institute (für Familienplanung) und McGraw-Hill Paperbacks

Marques de fabrique: Kurt Versen (entreprise d'éclairage), United Nations Plaza Hotel, Alan Guttmacher Institute (pour recherche et éducation publique), McGraw-Hill Paperbacks

his architectural clock which forms a three floor facade on a 32-floor building in downtown New York. For that reason the clock had to have a special and unique character of its own with the aim of making the building an environmental asset. The clock face consists of seventy-two square modules each 1.25 metres. The first horizontal row of twelve represents the hours and the five times twelve modules below indicate the minutes and seconds. The exact time is shown by the relevant squares lighting up so that there is a constant light-kinetic effect — especially dramatic at night. The whole building inside and out is a visual delight full of the unexpected, whether telephone kiosks in human shape, bright built-in chairs bent in steelplate, or a neon-surrounded tunnel which must be gone through to reach the elevators. The floor numerals, made up of light bulbs standing off the walls on stalks of different lengths, are clearly legible from a distance but dissolve into random stars as you approach them.

Seine zweite Uhr, bei der eine andere Aufgabenstellung und Umgebung zutrifft, ist die architektonische Uhr, in downtown New York, die sich an einem 32stöckigen Gebäude über drei Stockwerke erstreckt. In diesem Fall wurde das Gebäude als Mittel benutzt, der Uhr einen besonderen Charakter zu verleihen. Das Zifferblatt setzt sich aus 72 quadratischen Modulen von je 1,25 Meter zusammen. Die erste horizontale Modullinie repräsentiert die Stunden, während die fünf darunterliegenden Modulreihen die Minuten und Sekunden darstellen. Durch Aufleuchten der jeweiligen Quadrate wird die Zeit angezeigt. Dadurch wird ein licht-kinetischer Effekt erzielt, der nachts besonders dramatisch wirkt. Das ganze Gebäude ist sowohl innen wie aussen ein visuelles Vergnügen, voller Überraschungen, ob es sich um Telefonzellen in Gestalt von Menschen, bunte eingebaute Sitzgelegenheiten oder einen mit Neonlichtern ausgestatteten Tunnel handelt, durch den man die Aufzüge erreicht. Die Stockwerkskennzeichnungsnummern bestehen aus Glühbirnen, die auf unterschiedlich langen Sockeln in ihrer Fassung von der Wand abstehen. Sie sind daher von weitem klar zu erkennen und lösen sich in Zufallssternmuster auf, je näher man an sie herankommt.

tectonique. Elle s'étend sur trois des 16 étages d'un immeuble peu attrayant dans les bas quartiers de New York. Le bâtiment, dans ce cas, a servi à donner à l'horloge un caractère particulier. Le cadran se compose de 72 modules carrés de 1,25 m chacun. La première rangée horizontale de modules représente les heures et les cinq autres, audessous, les minutes. Le temps est indiqué par l'illumination des carrés correspondants. L'effet luminocinétique est particulièrement dramatique la nuit. Tout l'édifice est un plaisir pour les yeux, à l'intérieur comme au-dehors, plein de surprises, avec des cabines téléphoniques en forme d'êtres humains, des sièges incorporés de toutes les couleurs ou un tunnel éclairé au néon et menant aux ascenseurs. Les numéros d'identification des étages consistent en ampoules électriques que des socles de hauteur différente éloignent plus ou moins du mur. Ils se reconnaissent donc facilement de loin, mais se dissolvent en étoiles aléatoires à votre approche.

Brilliant solution for a clock dial; maximum clarity is achieved by maximum simplicity

Brillante Lösung des Zifferblatts einer Uhr; maximale Klarheit wurde durch grösste Einfachheit erreicht

Brillante solution pour le cadran d'une horloge; un maximum de clarté est réalisé grâce à un maximum de simplicité

1

2

3

1
A clock becomes an architectural feature. 127 John Street is a large building in the financial district of New York. The designer's brief asked for environmental improvements inside and outside the building, to give it character and distinction. The clock consists of 72 square modules, three floors high. The top row shows the hours, the other five rows the minutes and seconds — a complete integration of time and space.
2
The address and the logotye are sometimes shown on canvas, sometimes formed by small chromium spheres
3
The entrance to the building at groundfloor level is through a tunnel illuminated in neon light

1
Eine Uhr wird zur architektonischen Besonderheit. 127 John Street ist ein grosses Gebäude in New York. Die Design-Aufgabe war eine innere und äussere Verbesserung des Gebäudes. Das Gebäude sollte einen persönlichen Charakter erhalten. Die Uhr besteht aus 72 quadratischen Modulen, die sich über drei Stockwerke erstrecken. Die oberste Reihe gibt die Stunden an, die anderen fünf Reihen die Minuten und Sekunden, eine völlige Integration von Zeit und Raum.
2
Die Adresse und die Logotype werden manchmal auf Leinen gezeigt und manchmal durch kleine Glühbirnen dargestellt
3
Der Eingang des Gebäudes auf Strassenebene führt durch einen hellbeleuchteten Korridor

1
Une horloge devient une œuvre architecturale. A New York, à la John Street No. 127, se trouve un grand immeuble auquel le graphiste devait conférer un caractère distinctif et distingué en améliorant l'environnement intérieur et extérieur du bâtiment. L'horloge se compose de 72 modules carrés d'une hauteur de trois étages. La rangée supérieure indique les heures, les autres cinq rangs les minutes et les secondes. Une intégration parfaite du temps et de l'espace a été réalisée.
2
L'adresse et le logotype apparaissent parfois sur une toile de fond, parfois sous forme de petites lampes
3
L'entrée de l'immeuble au rez-de-chaussée mène à travers un corridor fortement éclairé

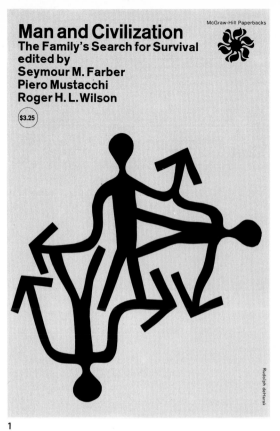

Man and Civilization
The Family's Search for Survival
edited by
Seymour M. Farber
Piero Mustacchi
Roger H. L. Wilson

McGraw-Hill Paperbacks

$3.25

Rudolph deHarak

1

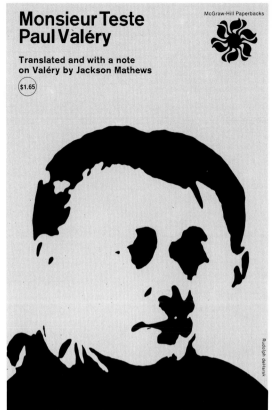

Monsieur Teste
Paul Valéry

McGraw-Hill Paperbacks

Translated and with a note
on Valéry by Jackson Mathews

$1.65

Rudolph deHarak

2

Personality
and Psychotherapy
An Analysis in Terms of
Learning, Thinking, and Culture

John Dollard
Neal E. Miller

McGRAW-HILL PAPERBACKS

$3.25

3

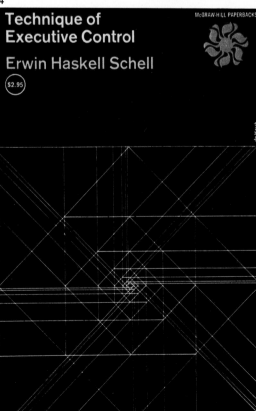

Technique of
Executive Control
Erwin Haskell Schell

McGRAW-HILL PAPERBACKS

$2.95

de Harak

4

Four bookcovers for paperbacks
Vier Buchhüllen für Taschenbücher
Quatre couvertures pour livres de poche

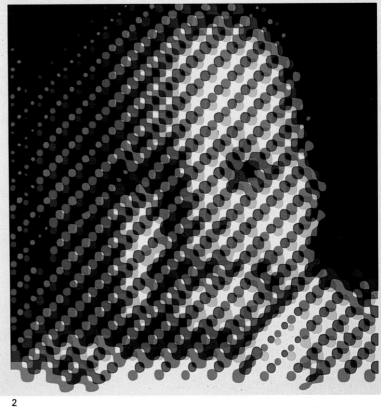

1 A cover for the Italian magazine "Linea Grafica"
2 Cover for "Perspectives", a family planning magazine

1 Titelseite des Magazins «Linea Grafica»
2 Titelseite für das Familienplanungsmagazin «Perspectives»

1 Couverture pour le magazine italien «Linea Grafica»
2 Couverture pour «Perspectives», revue sur le planning familial

1

2

1
The poster for the "Rufus Porter" exhibition at the Hudson River Museum. Collaborator: Frank Benedict
2
Shopping bags for the Metropolitan Museum of Art's Book store. Collaborator: Janice Bergen

1
Plakat für die Ausstellung «Rufus Porter» im Hudson River Museum. Mitarbeiter: Frank Benedict
2
Einkaufstaschen für die Buchhandlung des Metropolitan Museum of Art. Mitarbeiter: Janice Bergen

1
Affiche pour l'exposition «Rufus Porter» au Hudson River Museum. Collaborateur: Frank Benedict
2
Sacs d'achat pour la librairie du Metropolitan Museum of Art. Collaborateur: Janice Bergen

1

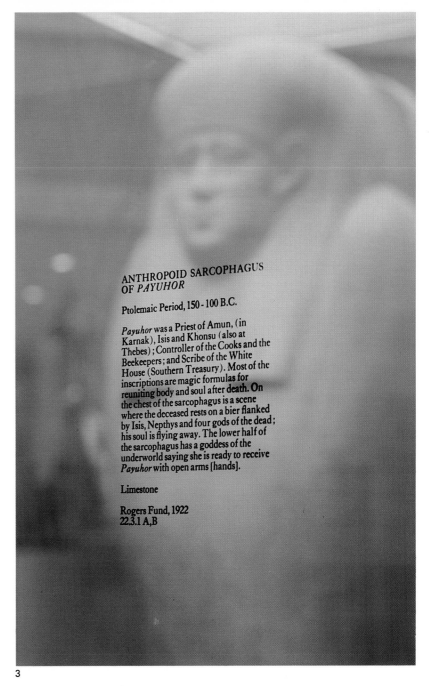

ANTHROPOID SARCOPHAGUS
OF *PAYUHOR*

Ptolemaic Period, 150 - 100 B.C.

Payuhor was a Priest of Amun, (in
Karnak), Isis and Khonsu (also at
Thebes); Controller of the Cooks and the
Beekeepers; and Scribe of the White
House (Southern Treasury). Most of the
inscriptions are magic formulas for
reuniting body and soul after death. On
the chest of the sarcophagus is a scene
where the deceased rests on a bier flanked
by Isis, Nepthys and four gods of the dead;
his soul is flying away. The lower half of
the sarcophagus has a goddess of the
underworld saying she is ready to receive
Payuhor with open arms [hands].

Limestone

Rogers Fund, 1922
22.3.1 A,B

2

3

1
"A Guide to the Metropolitan Museum of Art", an introductory
display to the Egyptian Section
2
This story can also be bought as an accordion folded book
3
Captions for displays are legibly yet discreetly printed on glass

1
«A Guide to the Metropolitan Museum of Art», ein Einführungs-
display zur ägyptischen Abteilung
2
Diese Chronologie kann auch als Leporello erstanden
werden
3
Lesbare, auf Glas gedruckte Bildunterschriften

1
«A Guide to the Metropolitan Museum of Art», display d'introduction à la section égyptienne
2
Cette chronologie existe aussi sous forme de plie en zig zag
3
Les légendes restent bien lisibles, malgré l'impression discrète
sur verre

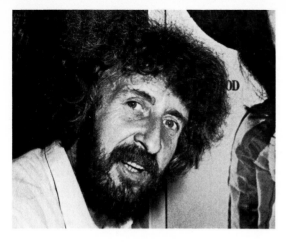

Günther Kieser

1930	Born in Kronberg, Germany
1946–49	Studied at Werkkunst-Schule, Offenbach/Main
1951	Works freelance: posters for radio and TV of Hessen broadcasting; posters for concerts, tours, groups, festivals, films, theatre and opera, exhibitions and museums; design of record-covers; design for exhibitions, stage decor and film sets
1981	Professor for Graphic Design, Gesamthochschule Wuppertal

Publications: Graphis, Novum, etc.
One-man shows: New York, Montreux, Bonn, Essen
Work in museums of New York, Zürich, Berlin, Essen
Member of the Alliance Graphique Internationale, the Bund Deutscher Graphiker and the Deutscher Werkbund

1930	Geboren in Kronberg, Deutschland
1946–49	Studium an der Werkkunst-Schule, Offenbach/Main
1951	Freischaffender Künstler: Plakate für Radio und Fernsehen des Hessischen Rundfunks; Plakate für Konzerte, Tourneen, Gruppen, Festivals, Filme, Theater und Oper, Ausstellungen und Museen; Entwürfe für Schallplattenhüllen; Ausstellungsgestaltungen, Bühnenbilder und Filmdekor
1981	Professor für Grafik-Design an der Gesamthochschule Wuppertal

Veröffentlichungen: Graphis, Novum usw.
Einzelausstellungen: New York, Montreux, Bonn, Essen
Arbeiten in folgenden Sammlungen: New York, Zürich, Berlin, Essen
Mitglied der Alliance Graphique Internationale, des Bundes Deutscher Graphiker und des Deutschen Werkbundes

1930	Né à Kronberg, Allemagne
1946–49	Etudes à la Werkkunst-Schule, Offenbach/Main
1951	Travaille comme graphiste indépendant: affiches pour la Radio et la Télévision du Pays de Hesse; affiches pour des concerts, tournées, groupes divers et festivals, films, théâtre et opéra, expositions et musées; conception de pochettes de disques; conception formelle d'expositions, de décors scéniques et cinématographiques
1981	Professeur d'art graphique à la Gesamthochschule Wuppertal

Publications: Graphis, Novum, etc.
Expositions individuelles: New York, Montreux, Bonn, Essen
Œuvres dans les musées de New York, Zurich, Berlin, Essen
Membre de l'Alliance Graphique Internationale, du Bund Deutscher Graphiker et du Deutscher Werkbund

He is a loner, who experiences, loves and enjoys the world as he finds it and most of the time music is a very important part of this world. Photography is an important tool towards achieving the effects he is trying to convey. Montage, super-imposition, reflections all are used, separately and together to achieve his high aims. In some of his photographic record covers, where things and people can be discovered in the reflections of the glass of a shop window, without however, obscuring what is displayed inside, he creates a fourth dimension. He follows Alice into a — for him — penetrable looking glass world and he makes us, the onlookers, experience this new magic with him. Sometimes super-realist and sometimes surrealist, he takes known people and objects and transforms them into a dreamworld, where logic has gone and everything

Er ist ein Einzelgänger, der die Welt auf seine Weise geniesst, liebt und darin Erfahrungen macht. Meistens spielt Musik dabei eine bedeutende Rolle. Die Fotografie ist für ihn ein wichtiges Werkzeug, um die Effekte zur Übermittlung seiner Botschaften zu erreichen. Er benutzt Montage, Superimpositionen und Reflexionen entweder einzeln oder gemischt, um seine hohen Ziele zu erreichen. Auf einigen Schallplattenhüllen, bei denen Gegenstände und Menschen in den Spiegelungen von Schaufenstern erscheinen, ohne jedoch die Auslagen im Schaufenster zu verdecken, kreiert er eine vierte Dimension. Er verfolgt Alice in eine – für ihn – begehbare Welt hinterm Spiegel und lässt uns, die Betrachter, an dem Zauber dieser neuen Erfahrung teilnehmen. Er wählt manchmal, teils als Superrealist oder auch als Surrealist, wohlbe-

C'est un solitaire, qui goûte le monde à sa manière, l'aime et y fait ses expériences. Souvent la musique joue un rôle déterminant dans cet univers. La photographie est pour lui un instrument important pour obtenir les effets traduisant ses messages. Il recourt au montage, aux superimpositions et aux réflexions, ou encore au tout ensemble, pour atteindre ses objectifs ambitieux. Sur certaines pochettes de disque où objets et personnes apparaissent dans le miroitement de vitrines, sans dissimuler pourtant l'étalage, il crée une quatrième dimension. Il suit Alice dans un monde où il a accès, derrière le miroir, et fait participer les spectateurs à la magie de cette expérience nouvelle. En artiste à la fois hyperréaliste et surréaliste, il choisit parfois des personnages ou des objets bien connus et les transpose dans un monde onirique où la logique

is possible — so that even the businessman can rediscover his sense of wonder which he lost as a small child a long time ago.

This fact made him work all his life in the world of make-believe, music, jazz, film and theatre and radio, where reality is always at least once removed.

He is a passionate hand-glider and is easy to understand that there — suspended in mid-air — he feels most at home and can find his true self.

kannte Leute oder Gegenstände und überträgt sie in eine Traumwelt, wo keine Logik mehr existiert und alles möglich ist. So kann sogar ein Geschäfts-mann seine Fähigkeit zu staunen wieder entdek-ken, die er vor langer Zeit als kleines Kind verloren hatte.

Das ist auch der Grund für Günther Kiesers lebens-langes Arbeiten auf dem Gebiet, wo die Wirklich-keit ein wenig in die Ferne rückt, in der Musik, dem Jazz, Film, Theater und Rundfunk.

Er ist ein passionierter Deltasegler, und man kann sehr gut verstehen, wie er sich dort oben im schwebenden Zustand zwischen Himmel und Erde zu Hause fühlt und sein wahres Selbst findet.

disparaît et où tout est possible. Un homme d'af-faires peut ainsi redécouvrir sa faculté de s'éton-ner, qu'il croyait perdue depuis l'enfance.

C'est la raison pour laquelle Günther Kieser a tra-vaillé sa vie durant dans des domaines où la réalité s'estompe un peu: musique, jazz, cinéma, théâtre et radio.

C'est un passionné du planeur Delta et l'on com-prend très bien qu'il se sente à l'aise planant entre ciel et terre en état d'apesanteur, et retrouvant là son véritable moi.

1 Theatre poster "Dr. Faust"
2 Poster "The Wrong Protective Clothing"

1 Theaterplakat «Dr. Faust»
2 Plakat «Falsche Schutzkleidung»

1 Affiche de théâtre «Dr Faust»
2 Affiche «Vêtements de protection inappropriés»

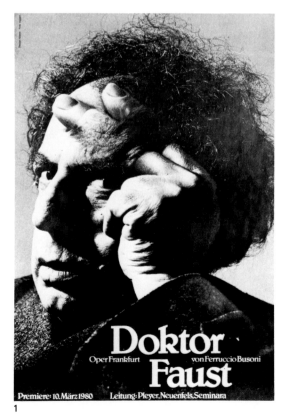

1

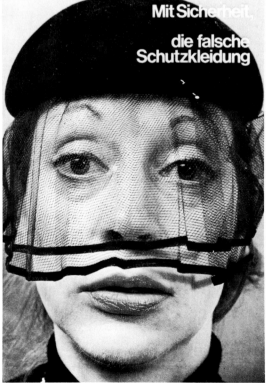

2

1

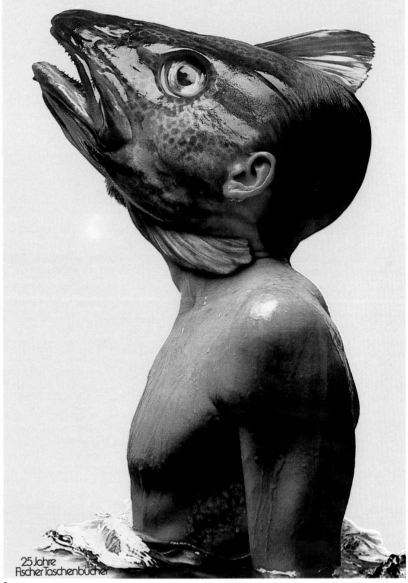

2

1 Poster for the BMW museum
2 Poster for a publisher
3–6 Record covers

1 Plakat für das BMW-Museum
2 Plakat für einen Verleger
3–6 Schallplattenhüllen

1 Affiche pour le Musée BMW
2 Affiche pour un éditeur
3–6 Pochettes de disques

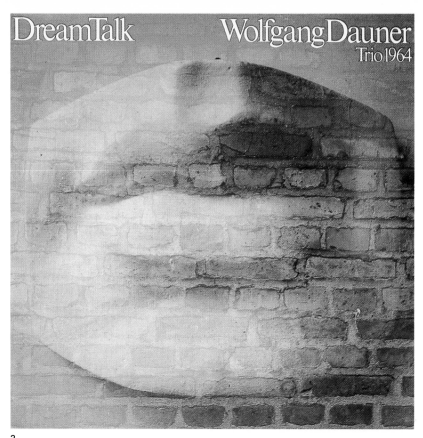

DreamTalk WolfgangDauner
Trio 1964

3

AttilaZoller&JimmyRaney JIM&I
Live In Frankfurt

4

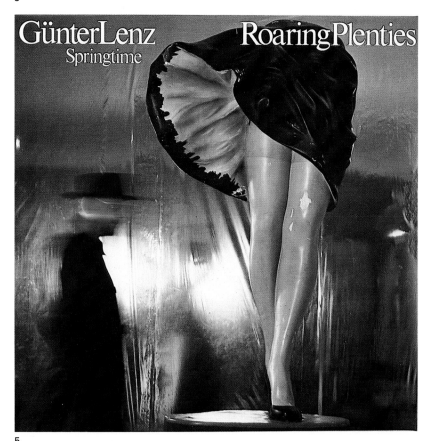

GünterLenz RoaringPlenties
Springtime

5

Washboard Doc, Lucky&Flash
SpecialGuest
LouisianaRed
EarlyMorning
Blues

6

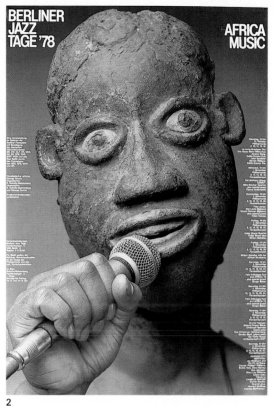

1

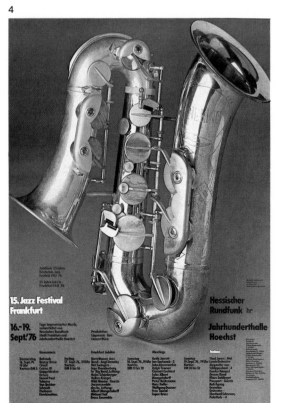

2

3

4

5

6

7

1

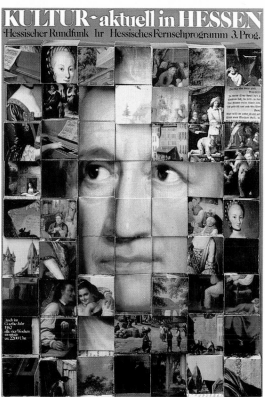

2

3

4

1–4 Posters for the "Hessischer Rundfunk"
1–4 Plakate für den Hessischen Rundfunk
1–4 Affiches pour «Hessischer Rundfunk»

1

2

1 Poster for Braun
2 Poster for BASF

1 Plakat für die Firma Braun
2 Plakat für BASF

1 Affiche pour la Maison Braun
2 Affiche pour BASF

Morteza Momayez

1936	Born in Iran	1936	Geboren in Iran	1936	Né en Iran
1952	Illustrator for journals, magazines and books	1952	Illustrator für Journale, Magazine und Bücher	1952	Illustration de journaux, magazines et livres
1963–64	Worked in advertising agencies	1963–64	Arbeit in Werbeagenturen	1963–64	Collaboration à des agences de publicité
1964	B.A. Faculty of Fine Arts, Tehran University	1964	B.A. Faculty of Fine Arts, Universität von Teheran	1964	B. A. Faculty of Fine Arts, Université de Téhéran
1961–78	Art director to various magazines, Tehran	1961–78	Art Director mehrerer Magazine, Teheran	1961–78	Direction artistique de plusieurs magazines, Téhéran
1968	Postgraduate studies in Interior Architecture, Paris	1968	Nachdiplomstudien in Innenarchitektur, Paris	1968	Etudes complémentaires en architecture d'intérieur, Paris
1969	Own Studio	1969	Eigenes Studio	1969	Fondation de son propre atelier
1969–79	Art director and costume designer for theatre and film	1969–79	Art Director und Kostüm-Designer für Theater und Film	1969–79	Directeur artistique et créateur de costumes de théâtre et de cinéma
1969	Professor of Graphic Design, Tehran University	1969	Professor für Grafik-Design, Universität von Teheran	1969	Professeur de graphic design, Université de Téhéran
1971–73	Director of three animated films, Tehran	1971–73	Direktor von drei Zeichentrickfilmen, Teheran	1971–73	Direction de trois dessins animés, Téhéran
1975–77	Professor of Decorative Arts College	1975–77	Professor für Kunstgewerbe	1975–77	Professeur des arts décoratifs
1978	Professor of Farabi University	1978	Professor an der Farabi-Universität	1978	Professeur à la Farabi University
1973	Head of Plastic Arts Section, UNESCO Commission, Iran	1973	Leiter der Abteilung Skulpturkunst der UNESCO-Kommission, Iran	1973	Direction de la Section des arts plastiques de la commission de l'UNESCO, Iran
1975	Member of International Advertising Association, USA	1975	Mitglied der International Advertising Association, USA	1975	Membre de l'International Advertising Association, USA
1977	Member of AGI	1977	Mitglied der AGI	1977	Membre de l'AGI

Publications:
Graphic Art in Iran, Drawing and Painting, What is design?, Lay-out Design, Dictionary of International Plastic Arts, Magazine Lay-out Design, Slogans and Titles, Visual Design in the Persian Alphabet

Exhibitions:
Art Biennale Tehran, Poster Biennale Warsaw, Film Posters Cannes, Film Posters Chicago, Design Biennale Brno, Galleries and Museums in Tehran, Posters Annecy Film, Posters Australia Film, Six one-man shows in Tehran

Veröffentlichungen:
Grafische Kunst in Iran, Zeichnen und Malerei, Was ist Design?, Lay-out-Design, Lexikon der «International Plastic Arts», Magazin-Lay-out-Design, Slogans und Titel, Visuelles Design im persischen Alphabet

Ausstellungen:
Kunst-Biennale Teheran, Plakat-Biennale Warschau, Filmplakate Cannes, Filmplakate Chicago, Design-Biennale Brno, Galerien und Museen in Teheran, Filmplakate Annecy, Filmplakate Australien, sechs One-man-Ausstellungen in Teheran

Publications:
L'art graphique en Iran, Dessin et peinture, Qu'est-ce que le design?, Lay-out Design, Dictionnaire des «International Plastic Arts», Magazine Lay-out Design, Slogans et titres, Design visuel dans l'alphabet persan

Expositions:
Biennale d'art de Téhéran, Biennale de l'affiche de Varsovie, Affiches cinématographiqes de Cannes, Affiches cinématographiques de Chicago, Biennale du design de Brno, galeries et musées de Téhéran, Affiches cinématographiques d'Annecy, Affiches du film australien, six expositions individuelles à Téhéran

Morteza Momayez is a graphic designer in Iran. He is of astonishing versatility. Seeing that communications with Iran are at the moment non-existent, it was very fortunate that so much of his excellent work could be obtained. Looking at his posters, trademarks and magazine lay-outs, he might be living and working in any country in Europe or North America. The only give-away is the arabic lettering. He is obviously fully aware of what is going on in graphic design anywhere in the world.

His posters are full of ideas showing an excellent sense of colour and a sensitive approach to type and lay-out. All show a consistent freshness, vitality and originality. His work for magazines is very much of the '80's and each double-spread presents a new surprise. The contrast between the Persian lettering and the heavy black of the photographs, reduced to line treatment are beautiful examples of the interplay of lines, solids, grey text within the white space. One looks at them with the same excitement as was experienced when the first issues of Twen magazine appeared in the early '60's only they belong to this decade. His trademarks are extraordinary examples of integrating the intricacies of Persian ornamentation and the latest graphics of the West. This rare and happy — not easy to achieve — mixture make them unique. Dan Reisinger has coped with similar two-language problems equally successfully. In both cases one has to remember that Persian and Hebrew one read from right to left and English from left to right, which makes the challenge of a good solution all the greater.

Morteza Momayez ist Grafik-Designer in Iran. Seine Arbeiten zeigen eine ganz erstaunliche Vielseitigkeit. Es war ein Glück, dass trotz der fast nicht existierenden Kommunikation mit Iran im Moment, eine so grosse Auswahl seiner exzellenten Arbeiten erhältlich war. Bei der Durchsicht seiner Plakate, Warenzeichen und Magazinlayouts könnte man annehmen, dass er in jeglichem europäischen Land oder sogar Nordamerika zu Hause sein könnte. Der einzige Hinweis auf sein Land ist die arabische Schrift. Er scheint über das, was im Grafik-Design in anderen Ländern passiert, genau informiert zu sein.

Seine Plakate zeigen eine Vielfalt von Ideen und einen ganz ausgezeichneten Farbsinn wie einen sehr feinfühligen Umgang mit Schrift und Layout. Er besitzt eine beständige Frische, Vitalität und Originalität. Seine Arbeiten für Magazine sind sehr im Stil der 80er Jahre, und jede Doppelseite ist eine neue Überraschung. Der Kontrast zwischen dem arabischen Text und dem tiefen Schwarz seiner Fotografien, hartkopiert, ist ein schönes Beispiel eines Zwischenspiels von Linien, dunklen Flächen und Grautönen innerhalb der weissen Fläche. Man betrachtet sie mit der gleichen Begeisterung wie seinerzeit die ersten Ausgaben des «Twen»-Magazins in den frühen 60er Jahren, nur sind diese Arbeiten hier aus unserer jetzigen Dekade. Seine Warenzeichen sind erstaunliche Beispiele von einer gelungenen Integrierung der sehr reichen, komplizierten arabischen Ornamente und den neusten grafischen Bewegungen des Westens. Diese rare und sehr erfolgreiche Mischung, die nicht leicht zu erreichen ist, macht sie besonders einmalig. Dan Reisinger hatte ähnliche Aufgaben in seinen zweisprachigen Problemen. In beiden Fällen sollte man sich daran erinnern, dass im Arabischen und im Hebräischen von rechts nach links gelesen wird, wogegen im Englischen von links nach rechts, was den Ansporn zu einer guten Lösung noch verstärkt.

Morteza Momayez travaille comme graphiste en Iran. Ses œuvres offrent une variété inouïe. Malgré l'absence presque complète de communication avec l'Iran, en ce moment, c'est un bonheur qu'un tel choix de ses excellents travaux soit disponible. Devant ses affiches, marques de produits et projets de conception formelle de magazines, on pourrait le croire chez lui dans n'importe quel pays d'Europe ou d'Amérique du Nord. Le seul indice de sa nationalité réside dans l'écriture arabe. Il semble parfaitement au courant de ce que les arts graphiques produisent sous d'autres cieux.

Ses affiches débordent d'idées et trahissent un extraordinaire sens de la couleur, comme une grande finesse dans l'utilisation de l'écriture et de la disposition. Il possède une solide vitalité et une fraîche originalité. Ses travaux pour des magazines s'inscrivent tout à fait dans la ligne des années 80, et chaque double page est une surprise nouvelle. Le contraste entre le texte persan et le noir intense de ses photos fournit de beaux exemples d'imbrications de lignes, surfaces foncées et grisés à l'intérieur d'un espace blanc. Ils suscitent la même admiration que les premiers numéros du magazine Twen, au début des années 60, sauf que ces travaux-ci appartiennent à notre décennie. Son style se caractérise par une intégration très heureuse des ornements persans, riches et compliqués, et des dernières tendances graphiques occidentales. Ce mélange rare, aussi réussi que difficile à atteindre, fait son originalité toute particulière. Dan Reisinger a eu des problèmes comparables, dans son monde bilingue. Dans les deux cas, il faut se rappeler que le persan tout comme l'hébreu se lisent de droite à gauche, contrairement à l'anglais, ce qui renforce encore l'incitation à une bonne solution.

1

2

3

4

1 Reza Abassi Arts and Cultural Center
2 Gazal — an Iranian film
3 Asian Cultural Documentation Center, Tehran
4 Iranian Musicians Society

1 Reza Abassi Arts and Cultural Center
2 Gazal – ein iranischer Film
3 Asian Cultural Documentation Center, Teheran
4 Iranian Musicians Society

1 Reza Abassi Arts, Centre de l'Art et de la Culture
2 Gazal, film iranien de 1974
3 Centre asiatique de documentation culturelle, Téhéran
4 Société musicale iranienne

"I live through my eyes. I speak the language of image, because it is a free language that cannot be controlled and confined within the obtrusive and prejudiced boundaries of literature and politics. The beauties of the language of image are not hidden under the rules of grammar. All feel these beauties very easily, enjoy them and perceive the multiplicity of national culture without any mediator or any translator. The language of image in graphic art is more beautiful, more accurate and more technical than in any other visual art, because graphic art is a comprehensive art that can easily utilize everything and take advantage of them. Graphic art is the precise mirror of time. It thinks about the entire details of life and all the moments of life are reflected in graphic works. A graphic designer or a graphic artist is closest and most familiar with the atmosphere and the content of society. His works have access to the privacy of each individual. If you cast a glance on your surroundings at any moment and in any place, you would find a graphic work next to you. Graphic art is the sign of human being. It is his signature; it is his name. Graphic art is signal. I strive that each work be a signal of me. A signal is the plainest and fastest indicator to develop relations amongst peoples. It gives direct and explicit hint, however you receive it, according to your wishes and spirit. You receive it as you like it and that is the best relationship. Signal is the purest medium of relating. For instance, a smile is a happy signal for everybody and the image of a smile in the human imagination has beautiful and memorable association.»

Morteza Momayez schreibt über sich selbst: Ich lebe hauptsächlich durch meine Augen. Ich drücke mich durch Bilder aus, denn diese Sprache ist für mich frei von hindernden und voreingenommenen Kontrollen der Literatur und der Politik. Der Reiz der Sprache in Bildern versteckt sich nicht hinter Grammatikregeln. Jeder empfindet diese Reize sehr leicht, geniesst sie und kann nationale Kultureigenarten ohne einen Vermittler oder Übersetzer aufnehmen. Die bildliche Sprache ist im Grafik-Design schöner und akkurater und auch technischer als in jedem anderen visuellen Kunstbereich. Grafik-Design ist eine verständliche Kunst, sie kann von allem Gebrauch machen und daraus einen grossen Vorteil ziehen. Die grafische Kunst ist ein Spiegelbild ihrer Zeit. Sie macht sich Gedanken über jegliche Einzelheiten unseres Lebens, und alle Lebensmomente sind in grafischen Arbeiten wiedergegeben. Ein Grafik-Designer oder ein grafischer Künstler ist besonders nahe und vertraut mit der Atmosphäre und dem Inhalt einer Gesellschaft. Seine Arbeiten zeigen Zugang zu dem Eigenleben eines jeden Individuums. Zu welcher Zeit auch immer und an welchem Platz auch immer wir unserer Umwelt Aufmerksamkeit schenken, werden wir immer grafische Arbeiten um uns herum entdecken. Grafische Kunst weist auf ein menschliches Wesen hin, sie trägt seine Unterschrift und seinen Namen. Grafische Kunst ist ein Signal. Ich versuche es zu erreichen, dass jede einzelne Arbeit ein Signal von mir darstellt. Ein Signal ist das einfachste und schnellste Mittel, Beziehungen zwischen Menschen herzustellen. Es gibt einen direkten und eindeutigen Hinweis, jedoch nehmen wir dieses Signal unseren Wünschen und unserer momentanen Verfassung entsprechend auf. Man nimmt es so auf, wie es einem gefällt, und das ist die beste Beziehung. Das Signal ist das klarste Mittel für eine Beziehung. Zum Beispiel ein Lächeln ist ein glückliches Signal für jeden, und das Bild eines Lächelns ruft im Bereich der menschlichen Vorstellungskraft schöne und erinnerungswürdige Assoziationen herbei.

Morteza Momayez se décrit ainsi: «Je vis principalement par les yeux. Je m'exprime par des images, car ce langage est pour moi libéré des contrôles et des obstacles de la littérature et de la politique. L'attrait de la langue imagée ne se dissimule pas derrière des règles grammaticales. Chacun l'éprouve très facilement, la goûte et peut saisir les particularités culturelles d'une nation sans l'entremise d'un traducteur. Dans l'art graphique, le langage est plus beau, plus soigneux et aussi plus technique que dans n'importe quel art visuel. C'est un art compréhensible, qui peut tirer parti et même profit de tout. Il reflète son époque. Il se livre à une réflexion sur tous les détails de notre vie et tous ses instants. Un dessinateur en art graphique est particulièrement proche et familier de l'atmosphère et du contenu d'une société. Ses travaux montrent l'accès à la vie propre de tout individu. A quelque moment et en quelque lieu que nous observions notre environnement, nous découvrirons toujours des œuvres graphiques autour de nous. L'art graphique trahit l'humain, porte sa signature et son nom. C'est un signal. Je tâche d'obtenir que chacun de mes travaux émette un signal de moi-même. Un signal représente le moyen le plus simple et le plus rapide d'établir des relations entre les hommes. Il donne une indication directe et sans équivoque, mais nous l'accueillons selon nos désirs et notre humeur du moment. Nous l'accueillons comme il nous plaît, et c'est la meilleure relation. Le signal est le moyen le plus clair pour établir une relation. Un sourire, par exemple, est un signal heureux pour tous et l'image d'un sourire appelle de belles et mémorables associations dans le domaine de l'imagination humaine.»

1	2	3	4
	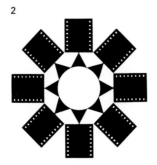		

1 Azad Theatre Group
2 Iranian Film Directors Ass.
3 Iranian Expert Accountant Society
4 Farabi Film Center

1 Azad Theatre Group
2 Iranian Film Directors Ass.
3 Iranian Expert Accountant Society
4 Farabi Film Center

1 Groupe théâtral Azad
2 Association iranienne des directeurs de films
3 Iranian Expert Accountant Society
4 Farabi Film Center

نمی‌توان او را دید و زنده ماند

«شب»

اولین عشق

بختک

نبرد تن به تن آقای فراست

1–5 Illustration for a monthly magazin
1–5 Illustration für eine Monatszeitschrift
1–5 Illustration pour une revue mensuelle

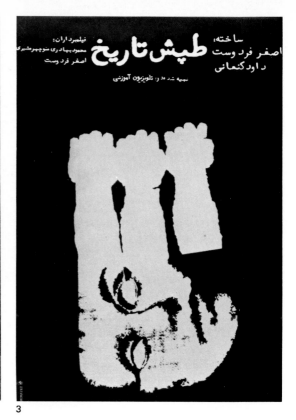

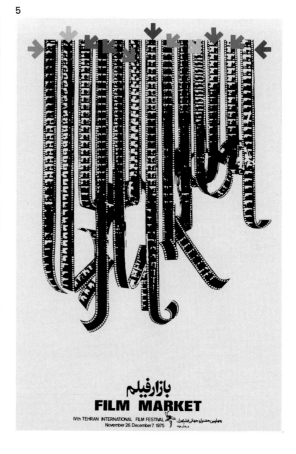

1 Poster "The Cinema of Michelangelo Antonioni"
2 Poster "Iranian Film"
3 Iranian film poster
4 Poster "The Films of Andrej Wajda"
5 Poster "Film Bazaar", Tehran International Film Festival

1 Plakat «Das Kino von Michelangelo Antonioni»
2 Plakat «Iranischer Film»
3 Iranisches Filmplakat
4 Plakat «Die Filme von Andrej Wajda»
5 Plakat «Film Bazaar», Teheran International Film Festival

1 Affiche «Les films de Michelangelo Antonioni»
2 Affiche «Le film iranien»
3 Affiche pour un film iranien
4 Affiche «Les films d'Andrej Wajda»
5 Affiche «Film Bazaar», Festival international du film iranien

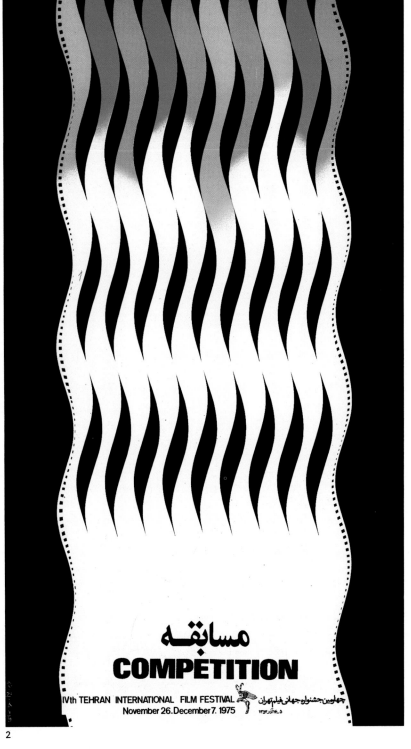

1 Poster "Farabi Film Center"
2 Poster "Competition", Tehran International Film Festival

1 Plakat «Farabi Film Center»
2 Plakat «Competition», Teheran International Film Festival

1 Affiche pour le «Farabi Film Center»
2 Affiche «Concours», Festival international du film iranien

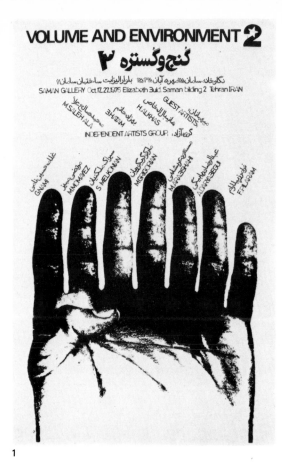

1

2

3

4

5

1 Poster for an art exhibition
2 Poster ''First Asian Graphic Design Biennale''
3 Poster ''Iranian Theatre''
4 Poster ''Iranian Concert''
5 Poster ''100th Anniversary of Ali Akbar Deh Khoda''

1 Plakat für eine Kunstausstellung
2 Plakat «Erste asiatische Grafik-Design-Biennale»
3 Plakat «Iranisches Theater»
4 Plakat «Iranisches Konzert»
5 Plakat «100. Geburtstag von Ali Akbar Deh Khoda»

1 Affiche pour une exposition d'art
2 Affiche «Première biennale asiatique d'art graphique»
3 Affiche «Le théâtre iranien»
4 Affiche «Concert iranien»
5 Affiche «Le centenaire d'Ali Akbar Deh Khoda»

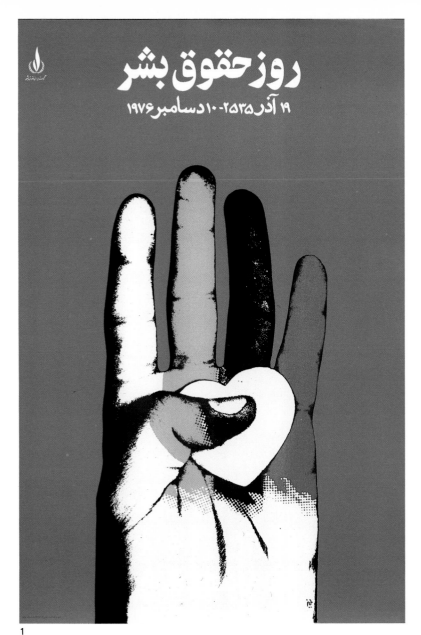

1

2

1 Poster "Human Rights"
2 Poster "Air Pollution"

1 Plakat «Menschenrechte»
2 Plakat «Luftverunreinigung»

1 Affiche «Les droits de l'homme»
2 Affiche «La pollution de l'air»

Bruno Monguzzi

1941	Born in Tessin, Switzerland
1956–61	Studies graphic design in Geneva, typography, photography and Gestalt psychology in London
1961–63	Works with Studio Boggeri, Milan
1963–64	Lecturer at Cini Foundation, Venice
1965–67	Exhibit and graphic design in USA and Canada (Expo '67)
1968–	Editorial, exhibit and graphic design in Milan
1971	Receives the Bodoni prize for having made a definite contribution to the improvement of Italian graphic design
1971–	Teaches the psychology of perception and typographic design at the Lugano School of Applied Arts
1979	Becomes member of the Alliance Graphique Internationale
1981	Attends the Aspen Design Conference as an IBM Fellow
1982	Visiting professor at the Cooper Union School for the Advancement of Art and Science, New York

1941	Geboren im Tessin, Schweiz
1956–61	Studien für Grafik-Designer in Genf, Typografie, Fotografie und Gestaltpsychologie in London
1961–63	Mitarbeiter im Studio Boggeri, Mailand
1963–64	Gastvorlesungen für die Cini-Foundation, Venedig
1965–67	Ausstellungs- und Grafik-Design in den USA und in Kanada (Expo '67)
1968–	Buch-, Grafik- und Ausstellungs-Design in Mailand
1971	Preisverleihung Bodoni-Preis für Beiträge zur Verbesserung des italienischen Grafik-Designs
1971–	Lehrtätigkeit in Wahrnehmungs-psychologie und Typografie an der Kunstgewerbeschule Lugano
1979	Mitglied der Alliance Graphique Internationale
1981	Teilnahme an der Aspen-Design-Konferenz als IBM Fellow
1982	Gastprofessor an der Cooper Union School for the Advancement of Art and Science, New York

1941	Né au Tessin, Suisse
1956–61	Etudes d'art graphique à Genève, de typographie, photographie et psychologie de la Forme à Londres
1961–63	Collaborateur du Studio Boggeri, Milan
1963–64	Chargé de cours à la Fondation Cini, Venise
1965–67	Graphisme et architecture d'expositions aux USA et au Canada (Expo '67)
1968–	Catalogues, affiches, graphisme et architecture d'expositions à Milan
1971	Reçoit le prix Bodoni pour son importante contribution à la promotion des arts graphiques en Italie
1971–	Enseigne la psychologie de la perception et la typographie à l'Ecole des Arts appliqués de Lugano
1979	Membre de l'Alliance Graphique Internationale
1981	Participe à la Conférence internationale de design à Aspen en tant que IBM Fellow
1982	Professeur invité à la Cooper Union School for the Advancement of Art and Science, New York

Bruno Monguzzi writes about himself: "I was born and spent my childhood in Tessin, the Italian part of Switzerland, some forty years ago. I was brought up in a rather Italian schizophrenic way, between Catholicism and Marxism, having a liberal Catholic mother and a strict socialist father. Then my family decided to move to the most Calvinist city, Geneva, where eventually I began to study graphic design, asking myself and my teachers endlessly and without much success all kinds of 'pourquoi?' that were later to become 'why?' having moved to London. It is here that I began to study perception and that I

Bruno Monguzzi schreibt über sich selbst: «Ich wurde vor etwa 40 Jahren im Tessin, der italienischen Schweiz, geboren und verbrachte dort meine Kindheit. Meine Erziehung war eine ziemlich italienische, hin- und hergerissen zwischen Katholizismus und Marxismus, bedingt durch meine liberal katholische Mutter und meinen streng sozialistischen Vater. Dann entschloss sich meine Familie, in die sehr calvinistische Stadt Genf zu ziehen, wo ich schliesslich Grafik-Design zu studieren begann. Ich stellte mir und meinen Lehrern endlos, und ohne viel Erfolg, die verschiedensten Arten von

Bruno Monguzzi dit de lui-même: «Je suis né il y a une quarantaine d'années au Tessin, la partie italienne de la Suisse, et c'est là que j'ai passé mon enfance. Mon éducation? Passablement italienne, ballottée entre le catholicisme et le marxisme, entre ma mère, catholique libérale, et mon père, socialiste strict. Ma famille s'est ensuite installée dans la très calviniste Genève, où j'ai entrepris des études d'arts graphiques. A mes professeurs comme à moi-même, je demandais sans trêve ni grand succès ‹pourquoi›, tous les ‹pourquoi› possibles, qui sont devenus des ‹why› lorsque je suis

decided graphic design could be a problem solving profession instead of a problem making one as I was inclined to believe up to that point. On the day I was twenty, I do not like birthdays, I jumped on a plane. I had just come across an issue of 'Neue Grafik' with an article about the Milanese Studio Boggeri and wanted to know this man. The elevator of 3 Piazza Duse was very tiny and very slow. On my way up to the sixth floor I felt uncomfortable. And for the next two years I was going to go through this same feeling. I had fallen in love with the man, his ideas, his office. And eventually, ten years later (Antonio would sometimes complain about Swiss designers being slow), in a less platonic way, with his daughter. In the meantime I had given lectures at the Cini Foundation in Venice and worked on different projects between Canada and the States. My efforts to make type read, to my great surprise and to my greater pleasure, were noticed in 1971 when I was assigned the Bodoni prize 'having made a definite contribution to the betterment of Italian graphic design'."
Bruno Monguzzi is a priori typographer, an artist in space, whether in the two dimensions of print and poster or in the three dimensions of exhibitions and architecture. His catalogues for "Majakovskij" and "Italian Furniture Design" at Cologne, as his book on "Studio Boggeri", are exciting kinetic events in space and time. The sequence of pages from front to back cover is like an animated film — a perfect balance of variety and continuity.

‹pourquoi›, die später ‹why› wurden, als ich nach London zog. Hier begann ich das Studium der Wahrnehmungslehre und begriff, dass Grafik-Design eine problemlösende Tätigkeit sein kann und nicht, wie ich bis dahin angenommen hatte, eine problemschaffende. An meinem zwanzigsten Geburtstag – ich mag keine Geburtstage – bestieg ich kurzentschlossen ein Flugzeug. Ich hatte gerade einen Artikel in einer Ausgabe von ‹Neue Grafik› über das Mailänder Studio Boggeri gelesen und wollte diesen Mann kennenlernen. Der Lift in der Piazza Duse 3 war winzig und sehr langsam. Auf meinem Weg nach oben bis zum 6. Stock fühlte ich mich etwas ungemütlich. Dieses Gefühl dauerte für die nächsten zwei darauffolgenden Jahre an. Ich war einfach verliebt in diesen Mann, in seine Ideen und sein Büro, und zehn Jahre später (Antonio beschwerte sich manchmal darüber, dass Schweizer Designer etwas langsam sind) verliebte ich mich in etwas weniger platonischer Weise in seine Tochter. Zwischendurch hatte ich an der Cini Foundation in Venedig unterrichtet und arbeitete an verschiedenen Projekten zwischen Kanada und den USA. Meine Bestrebungen, Typografie lesbar zu machen, wurden zu meinem grossen Erstaunen und zu meiner Freude 1971 mit dem Bodoni-Preis belohnt, ‹für seinen Beitrag zur Verbesserung des italienischen Grafik-Designs›.»
Bruno Monguzzi ist vorerst Typograf, ein Künstler im Raum, ob in der Zweidimensionalität des Drucks und der Plakate oder auf dem dreidimensio-

parti pour Londres. C'est ici que j'ai commencé à étudier la perception, comprenant que les arts graphiques pouvaient résoudre des problèmes de communications et non en créer, comme je l'avais cru jusque-là. Pour mon vingtième anniversaire – je n'aime pas les anniversaires –, j'ai sauté sur un avion. Dans un numéro de ‹Neue Grafik›, je venais de voir un article sur le Studio Boggeri de Milan, et je voulais connaître cet homme. L'ascenseur de Piazza Duse 3 était minuscule et très lent. Pendant ma longue montée vers le sixième étage, je me sentais peu à l'aise. Ce sentiment devait durer les deux années suivantes. J'étais simplement tombé amoureux de cet homme, de ses idées et de son bureau. Dix ans plus tard enfin (Antonio se plaignait parfois de la lenteur des dessinateurs suisses), je suis tombé amoureux de sa fille, un peu moins platoniquement cette fois. Entre-temps j'avais enseigné à la Cini Foundation de Venise et je travaillais à divers projets, entre le Canada et les Etats-Unis. A mon grand étonnement et ma plus grande joie, mes efforts pour rendre la typographie lisible ont été honorés, en 1971, du prix Bodoni, ‹ayant apporté une effective contribution pour une meilleure qualification du graphisme italien›.»
Bruno Monguzzi est d'abord un typographe, un artiste dans l'espace, soit dans les deux dimensions de l'impression et de l'affiche, soit dans les trois dimensions des expositions et de l'architecture. Ses catalogues pour «Majakovskij» et «Italienisches Möbeldesign» de Cologne, comme son livre sur le

Poster for the zone councils of the city of Milan to request voluntary help immediately after the Irpinia earthquake

Plakat für die Ortsämter der Stadt Mailand zur Aufforderung von freiwilliger Hilfe nach dem Irpinia-Erdbeben

Affiche pour les bureaux de district de la ville de Milan faisant appel à des volontaires après le tremblement de terre d'Irpinia

Within the constraints of the grid there takes place a wild and constantly surprising performance of typography, layout, colour and white space—all this with due respect being shown to content. It is like an amazing, well-rehearsed and disciplined circus, all controlled down to the minutest details by ring-master Bruno Monguzzi. As the two catalogues have 312 and 128 pages respectively, the illustrations of double-spreads shown within this book, can only have the frustrating merit of a film trailer. His exhibitions (always in collaboration with distinguished architects) show the ease with which he handles type in space, No doubt the architects call on him so frequently to collaborate with them because they know he can contribute something they themselves lack, which, however, is worth incorporating.

Type and typography become very important elements of architecture. This is also well demonstrated by his sign scheme for a hospital and often even by his posters. He proves through his work the maxim 'typography is the matrix of graphic design'.

nalen Gebiet der Ausstellungen und der Architektur. Seine Kataloge für «Majakovskij» und «Italienisches Möbeldesign» wie auch sein Buch «Studio Boggeri» stellen reizvolle kinetische Ereignisse in Raum und Zeit dar. Die Reihenfolge der Seiten von Anfang bis Ende ist gleich einem Film, ein perfektes Gleichgewicht zwischen Variation und Kontinuität. Innerhalb der durch den Raster gegebenen Einschränkungen spielt sich ein lebendiges Toben von Typografie und Layout, von Farbe und weissen Flächen ab, wobei aber gegenüber dem Inhalt der Darstellungen genügend Respekt bewahrt wird. Man bekommt den Eindruck eines disziplinierten Zirkus, in dem nach gründlicher Generalprobe alles bis zum kleinsten Detail vom Ringmeister Bruno Monguzzi kontrolliert wird. Da die beiden Kataloge jeweils 312 und 128 Seiten haben, können die wenigen hier gezeigten Seiten nur den frustrierenden Eindruck einer Filmvorschau haben. Seine Ausstellungen, jeweils in Zusammenarbeit mit namhaften Architekten, zeigen, wie sicher er im Umgang von Schrift im Raum ist. Es ist verständlich, dass ihn Architekten häufig um Zusammenarbeit bitten, denn sie wissen, dass er einen Beitrag leisten kann, zu dem sie selbst nicht in der Lage sind und dessen Einbeziehung sich lohnt.

Schrift und Typografie werden sehr wichtige Elemente der Architektur. Das beweist er erfolgreich in seinem Zeichensystem für ein Krankenhaus und oft sogar auf seinen Plakaten. Er unterstellt seine Arbeiten der Maxime «Typografie ist die Mutter des Grafik-Designs».

«Studio Boggeri», constituent de passionnants événements cinétiques dans le temps et dans l'espace. Du début à la fin, la suite des pages se déroule comme un film, un équilibre parfait entre variation et continuité. Dans les limites du cadre imposé se déchaînent typographie et disposition, couleur et surfaces blanches, dans un respect subtil du contenu. Il s'en dégage l'impression d'un cirque discipliné où, après une répétition générale minutieuse, tout, jusqu'au moindre détail, est contrôlé par le maître de manège Bruno Monguzzi. Par rapport aux 312 et 128 pages des deux catalogues, les quelques illustrations présentées ici ne peuvent éveiller que la sensation frustrante d'un échantillon. Ses expositions, toujours en collaboration avec des architectes de renom, montrent sa sûreté à manier l'information dans l'espace. Si des architectes recherchent aussi souvent sa participation, c'est qu'ils le savent capable de fournir une contribution qui n'est pas à leur portée, mais qui en vaut la peine.

La lettre et la typographie deviennent des éléments essentiels de l'architecture. Il le prouve à profusion dans son système de signes pour un hôpital, et souvent même dans ses affiches. Ses œuvres démontrent la vérité de la formule «la typographie est la mère des arts graphiques».

1
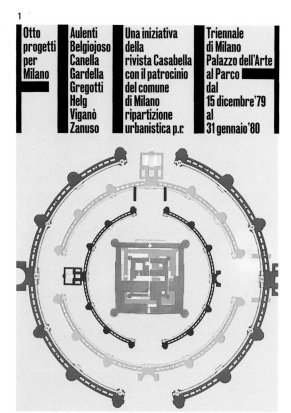

2
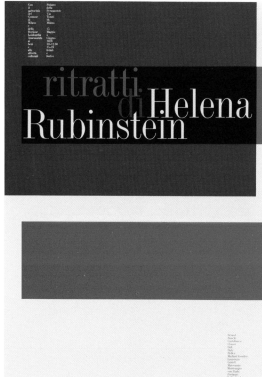

3

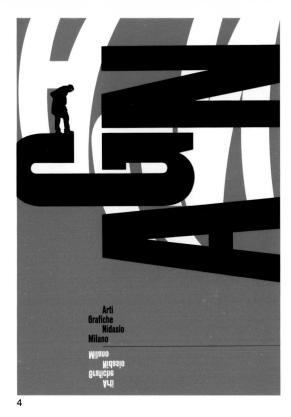

4

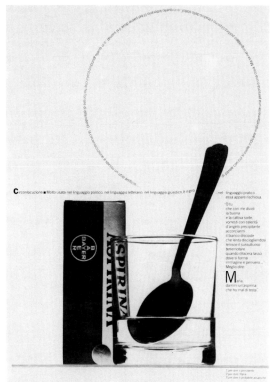

5

6

7

8

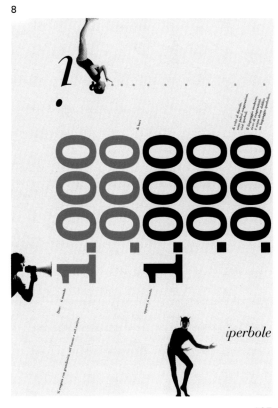

1 Poster for a town planning exhibition at the Milan Triennale (designed with Roberto Sambonet)
2 Poster for an exhibition of portraits by various artists of Helena Rubinstein
3 Poster for a travelling exhibition about three cultural protagonists of the Russian Revolution, Majakovskij, Mejerhol'd, Stanislavskij
4–8 Pages from a publication for ''Arti Grafiche Nidasio'' in Milan about communication terms

1 Plakat für eine Städteplanungsausstellung der Mailänder Triennale (Zusammenarbeit mit Roberto Sambonet)
2 Plakat einer Porträt-Ausstellung über Helena Rubinstein unter Teilnahme mehrerer Künstler
3 Plakat einer Wanderausstellung über Majakovskij, Mejerhol'd Stanislavskij, drei kulturelle Protagonisten der Russischen Revolution
4–8 Seiten aus einer Veröffentlichung für «Arti Grafiche Nidasio», Mailand, über verschiedene Ausdrücke der Kommunikation

1 Affiche pour une exposition sur l'urbanisme à la Triennale de Milan (en collaboration avec Roberto Sambonet)
2 Affiche pour une exposition de portraits de Helena Rubinstein par différents artistes
3 Affiche d'une exposition itinérante sur trois protagoistes culturels de la Révolution russe, Majakovskij, Mejerhol'd, Stanislavskij
4–8 Pages d'une publication pour «Arti Grafiche Nidasio» à Milan sur différentes formes de communication

This catalogue should be seen like a film sequence in space and time. The grid imposes a strong and rigid continuity, within which a surprising variety unfolds. The combination of the spirit of the twenties and that of the eighties shows a masterly sensitivity and empathy, which makes the book (128 pp.) an outstanding example of modern and period typographic style and lay-out. (Compare with pp. 154, 155, Weingart.)

Man sollte diesen Katalog als Filmablauf sehen. Der Raster zwingt zu starker, fast starrer Fortsetzung, aber trotz dieser Einengung gibt es Überraschungen und Vielseitigkeit. Der Zeitgeist der zwanziger und achtziger Jahre wird mit viel Einfühlungsvermögen vereint. Das Buch (128 Seiten) ist ein meisterhaftes Beispiel des heutigen und derzeitigen Stils und Layouts. (Vergleiche mit Seiten 154, 155, Weingart.)

Ce catalogue doit être vu comme une séquence filmique dans le temps et dans l'espace. La grille typographique impose une forte continuité à l'intérieur de laquelle se déploie une surprenante variété. La combinaison de l'esprit des années vingt avec celui des années quatre-vingts démontre une sensibilité magistrale et rend ce livre de 128 pages un éminant exemple de dessin typographique et de mise en pages où l'apport contemporain se fond avec celui de l'histoire.

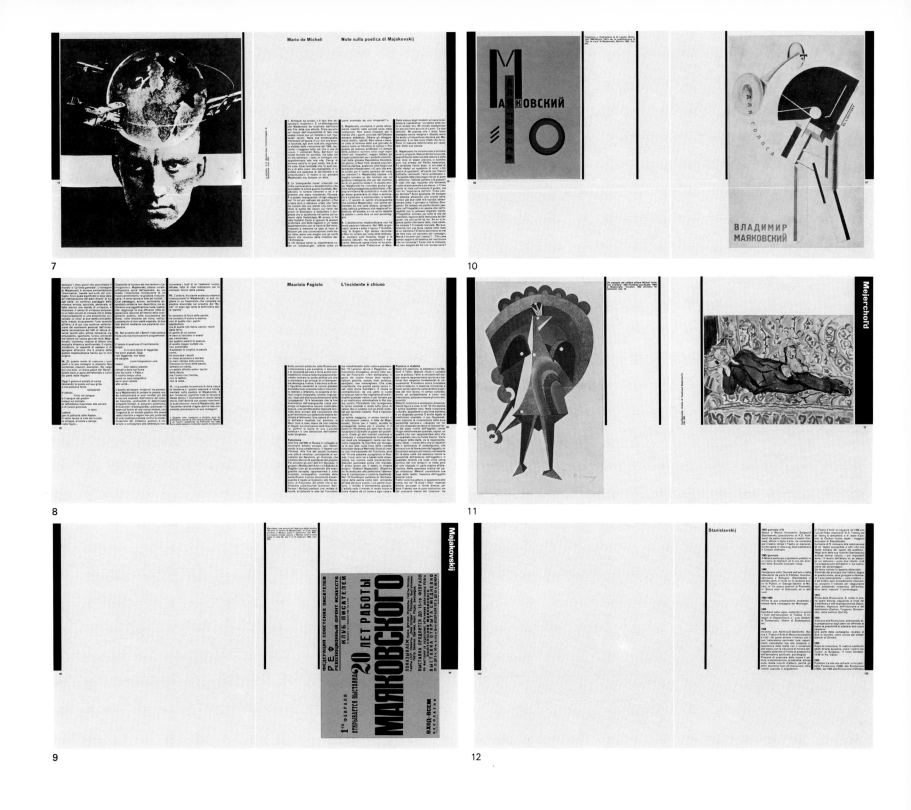

7

8

9

10

11

12

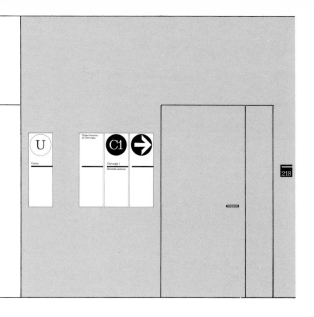

1

1
Hospital signage system for Regione Piemonte, Italy (in association with the architects Giancarlo Ortelli and Stefano Signoretti)
2
Exhibit design for a travelling exhibition on Caravaggio (in association with Roberto Sambonet and Giancarlo Ortelli)
3
Poster for the exhibition "Processo per il museo" (Trial for the
museum)

1
Zeichensystem für Krankenhaus Regione Piemonte, Italien (in
Zusammenarbeit mit den Architekten Giancarlo Ortelli und Ste-
fano Signoretti)
2
Design der Wanderausstellung über Caravaggio (in Zusammen-
arbeit mit Roberto Sambonet und Giancarlo Ortelli)
3
Ausstellungsplakat «Processo per il museo» (Prozess für das
Museum)

1
Système de signalisation pour hôpital, Regione Piemonte, Italie
(en collaboration avec les architectes Giancarlo Ortelli et Stefano Signoretti)
2
Conception formelle de l'exposition itinérante sur Caravaggio
(en collaboration avec Roberto Sambonet et Giancarlo Ortelli)
3
Affiche pour l'exposition «Processo per il museo» (Procès pour
le musée)

2

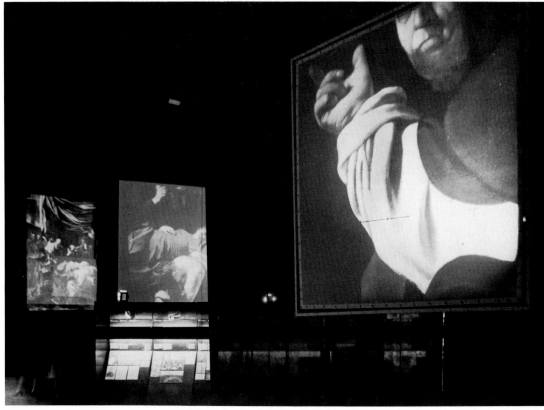

3

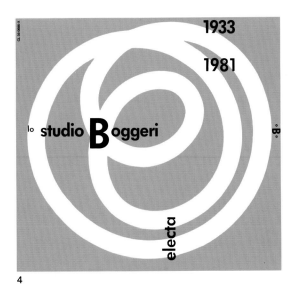

4

5

4, 5
Book editing and design for the Studio Boggeri, also exhibition
design for Studio Boggeri at the Milan Triennale (in association
with Giancarlo Ortelli)
6, 7
Poster and design for the exhibition "Raffaello" (in association
with Roberto Sambonet and Giancarlo Ortelli)

4, 5
Konzeption des Buches sowie Ausstellungsgestaltung «Studio
Boggeri» für die Mailänder Triennale (in Zusammenarbeit mit
Giancarlo Ortelli)
6, 7
Gestaltung für Plakat und Ausstellung «Raffaello» (Entwurf in
Zusammenarbeit mit Roberto Sambonet und Giancarlo Ortelli)

4, 5
Conception du livre ainsi que création du projet d'exposition
«Studio Boggeri» pour la Triennale de Milan (en collaboration
avec Giancarlo Ortelli)
6, 7
Affiche et conception de l'exposition «Raffaello» (en collaboration avec Roberto Sambonet et Giancarlo Ortelli)

6

7

Siegfried Odermatt is self-taught, he worked briefly with an industrial designer and 3 years with Hans Falk on freelance basis. 3 years in an advertising agency, since 1950 he has worked on his own.
Prizes and distinctions:
Typomundus 1965, 1970, Warsaw Biennale 1970, 1980.

After one year at the School of Applied Arts Zürich, *Rosmarie Tissi* was apprenticed for four years. Since 1968, collaboration with Siegfried Odermatt.
Prizes and distinctions:
3 times Swiss scholarship for applied arts, Typomundus 1965, 1970, Type Directors' Club of New York 1966, 4th International Calendar Competition, Germany 1972, several first prizes in symbol and poster competitions.

Both had exhibitions of their work in: New York 1966, Stuttgart 1967, Wuppertal 1968, Hof-Saale 1972. They also participated in group exhibitions in: Paris 1971, Milan 1974, Brussels 1975. Since 1974, they are members of the Alliance Graphique Internationale.

Odermatt & Tissi, a Swiss team of two, show in their work a new and fresh approach to and partly against the Swiss graphic perfection, which we have known for so long — maybe it is the dawning of a new Zeitgeist. To work as a team is also somewhat of a Helvetic innovation, although it is prevalent in the US, UK, Germany and France (see de Harak, Fletcher, Rambow, Lienemeyer and Grapus examples in this book).
On their creative philosophy they have the following to say: "We have deliberately kept our team small in order to keep a limited field of graphic design under close personal control. Graphic design is to both of us a vehicle of communication, and we generally limit ourselves to the media of

Siegfried Odermatt ist Autodidakt, arbeitete kurze Zeit mit einem Industriegrafiker und war während 3 Jahren freier Mitarbeiter von Hans Falk. Nach weiteren 3 Jahren in einer Werbeagentur machte er sich 1950 selbständig.
Auszeichnungen:
Typomundus 1965 und 1970 sowie an der Plakatbiennale Warschau 1970 und 1980.

Rosmarie Tissi machte nach einem Jahr Kunstgewerbeschule Zürich eine 4jährige Berufslehre. Seit 1968 Ateliergemeinschaft mit Siegfried Odermatt.
Auszeichnungen:
3mal Eidgenössisches Stipendium für angewandte Kunst, Typomundus 1965 und 1970, Type Directors' Club of New York 1966 sowie am 4. Internationalen Kalender-Wettbewerb Deutschland 1972, verschiedene erste Preise an Signet- und Plakat-Wettbewerben.

Beide hatten Einzelausstellungen in New York 1966, in Stuttgart 1967, in Wuppertal 1968, in Hof-Saale 1972. Sie nahmen an Gruppenausstellungen teil in Paris 1971, Mailand 1974 und Brüssel 1975. Seit 1974 sind sie Mitglieder der Alliance Graphique Internationale.

Odermatt & Tissi, ein Schweizer Team von zwei Designern, zeigen in ihren Arbeiten eine neue, frische Einstellung zu der und zum Teil auch gegen die Schweizer Grafik-Perfektion, die wir seit langem kennen. Vielleicht handelt es sich um den Beginn eines neuen Zeitgeistes. Die Teamarbeit ist auch etwas Neues in der Schweiz, obwohl sie in den USA, in England, Deutschland und Frankreich allgemein verbreitet ist (siehe Beispiele von de Harak, Fletcher, Rambow, Lienemeyer und Grapus in diesem Buch). Über ihre Philosophie zur Kreativität sagen sie folgendes: «Wir halten unser Team absichtlich klein, um ein begrenztes Gebiet des Grafik-Designs unter enger persönlicher Kontrolle zu halten. Für uns beide ist Grafik-Design ein Kommu-

Siegfried Odermatt est un autodidacte; il collabora brièvement avec un graphiste industriel et fut pendant 3 ans collaborateur libre de Hans Falk; après 3 années dans une agence de publicité, il s'établit à son propre compte à partir de 1950.
Prix et distinctions: Typomundus 1965, 1970, Biennale de Varsovie 1970, 1980.

Après une année à l'Ecole des arts et métiers de Zurich, *Rosmarie Tissi* fit un apprentissage de 4 ans. Depuis 1968, collaboration avec Siegfried Odermatt.
Prix et distinctions: 3 fois bourse fédérale des arts appliqués, Typomundus 1965, 1970, Type Directors' Club of New York 1966, 4e concours international du calendrier, Allemagne 1972, divers premiers prix à des concours de symboles et d'affiches.

Expositions individuelles des travaux des deux artistes à: New York 1966, Stuttgart 1967, Wuppertal 1968, Hof-Saale 1972. Participation à des expositions collectives à: Paris 1971, Milan 1974, Bruxelles 1975. Depuis 1974 ils sont membres de l'Alliance Graphique Internationale.

Les deux graphistes suisses Odermatt & Tissi montrent dans leurs travaux une attitude nouvelle et rafraîchissante sur (et en partie contre) la perfection graphique suisse que nous connaissons de longue date. Peut-être une nouvelle ère s'ouvre-t-elle. Le travail d'équipe est aussi une nouveauté en Suisse, bien que les Etats-Unis, l'Angleterre, l'Allemagne et la France le pratiquent fréquemment (voir les exemples de Harak, Fletcher, Rambow, Lienemeyer et Grapus dans cet ouvrage).
Sur leur philosophie de la créativité, voici ce qu'ils disent: «Nous en restons volontairement à une petite équipe, pour contrôler personnellement un domaine réduit des arts graphiques. Pour nous, le ‹graphic design› est un support de communication,

typography, photography and technical drawing. What we stress in our work is a conceptual idea which we try to develop in our design. Thus we use our media in the manner of elements, assembling them into an informative whole. Generally we arrive at the solutions of our design-problems by means of what could be called a dialectical process: we try to analyse the given content of the intended message into segments which can be translated into the various media we use and then form a synthesis accordingly.

Although we both work in the same manner, we often arrive at startlingly different solutions. Although our manner of work may seem rather intellectual, intuition inevitably plays a distinctive role. As we complement each other in this often argumentative process, many of our works cannot be fairly attributed to either of us, they are the product of the team. However, many years of collaboration have led us to rather intimate knowledge of our 'graphic brains'.

Generally speaking we tend to use simple, distinctive patterns of design and thus often arrive at signal-type solutions which can easily be remembered and individually recognized. Our main differences are congenial; while Rosmarie Tissi has a more playfull approach to graphic problems, Siegfried Odermatt prefers the disciplined mental probing. However, both our work has developed in the same direction and thus bears the marks of a common style.''

nikationsträger, und wir begrenzen uns im allgemeinen auf die Medien der Typografie, Fotografie und technischen Zeichnungen. Was wir in unserer Arbeit betonen, ist die konzeptionelle Idee, die wir zu entwickeln versuchen. Daher benutzen wir unsere Medien als Einzelelemente, um ein informatives Ganzes zu erreichen. Im allgemeinen erzielen wir unsere Problemlösungen durch Mittel, die man einen dialektischen Prozess nennen kann. Wir versuchen, den vorgegebenen Inhalt der beabsichtigten Aussage in Segmenten zu analysieren, die auf die verschiedenen Medien, die wir benutzen, übertragen werden können, und diese bilden dann entsprechend eine Synthesis.

Obwohl unsere Arbeitsweise die gleiche ist, erreichen wir oft völlig unterschiedliche Ergebnisse. Wenn auch unsere Arbeitsmethode ziemlich intellektuell erscheinen mag, spielt die Intuition doch eine starke Rolle. Da wir uns im Dialog der Auseinandersetzung ergänzen, können manche Arbeiten von uns eigentlich keinem von beiden persönlich zugeordnet werden. Sie sind das Ergebnis von Teamarbeit. Lange Jahre der Zusammenarbeit führten jedoch zu einer persönlichen Kenntnis der Denkweise des Partners.

Wir versuchen, einfache und charakteristische Darstellungen zu benutzen, und erreichen daher oft Signaltypen-ähnliche Lösungen, die leicht zu erkennen und zu behalten sind. Unsere Hauptunterschiede ergänzen sich jedoch erfolgreich. Während Rosmarie Tissi zu einer etwas spielerischen Art der Grafik-Problemlösung neigt, zieht Siegfried Odermatt eine disziplinierte, abstraktere Arbeitsweise vor. Die Arbeiten von uns beiden haben sich jedoch in die gleiche Richtung bewegt und besitzen heute einen uns gemeinsamen Stil.»

et nous nous bornons généralement aux médias de la typographie, de la photographie et du dessin technique. Ce que notre travail veut souligner, c'est l'idée conceptionnelle que nous tentons de développer. Nous exploitons donc nos médias comme des éléments isolés, pour obtenir un ensemble informatif. En général, nous atteignons nos solutions par des moyens que l'on pourrait qualifier de processus dialectique. Nous cherchons à analyser le contenu donné du message envisagé en segments pouvant se reporter sur les divers médias que nous utilisons et qui forment alors une synthèse correspondante.

Malgré la similitude de nos méthodes, nous aboutissons souvent à des résultats très différents. Dans son intellectualité apparente, notre travail laisse pourtant une large place à l'intuition. Comme nous nous complétons dans un dialogue contradictoire, certaines de nos œuvres ne peuvent vraiment être attribuées à l'un ou l'autre personnellement; elles sont le fruit du travail d'équipe. Cependant, de longues années de collaboration nous ont donné une connaissance personnelle de la pensée du partenaire. Voilà pourquoi nos avis divergent rarement sur la qualité de nos travaux individuels.

Nous essayons d'utiliser des motifs simples et caractéristiques, obtenant souvent des solutions du type signal, faciles à reconnaître et à mémoriser. Nos différences principales se complètent heureusement. Alors que Rosmarie Tissi tend vers une solution graphique plutôt enjouée, Siegfried Odermatt préfère un travail plus discipliné, abstrait. Mais nous évoluons dans la même direction et possédons désormais un style commun.»

1

2

3

1 Symbol for an industrial mill
2 Symbol for Kupferschmid Papers
3 Symbol for an architects' office

1 Signet für einen Mühlenbetrieb
2 Signet für Kupferschmid-Papiere
3 Signet für ein Architekturbüro

1 Emblème pour une minoterie
2 Emblème pour les papiers Kupferschmid
3 Emblème pour un bureau d'architecture

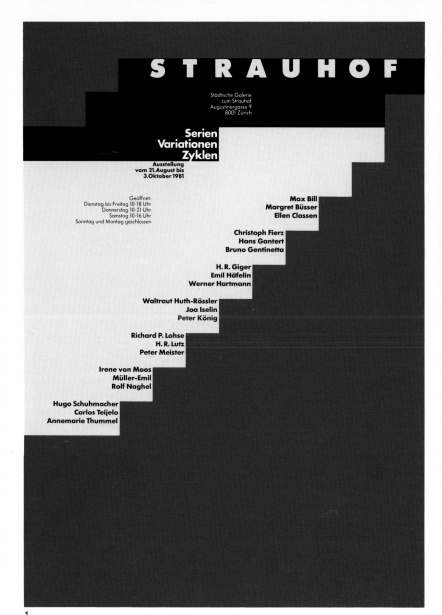

1
Poster for an exhibition "Series, variations, cycles"
2
Poster for exhibition "Design from the Netherlands" using
Dutch national colours to attract attention
3
Poster for Swissair

1
Plakat für die Ausstellung «Serien, Variationen, Zyklen»
2
Plakat für die Ausstellung «Design aus den Niederlanden», als
Blickfang wurden die Farben und die Einteilung der holländi-
schen Flagge verwendet
3
Plakat für Swissair

1
Affiche pour l'exposition «Séries, Variations, Cycles»
2
Affiche pour l'exposition «Design des Pays-Bas»; les couleurs et
l'aménagement du pavillon néerlandais ont servi d'impact visuel
3
Affiche pour Swissair

3

1

2

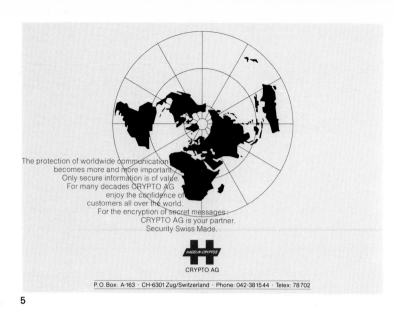

5

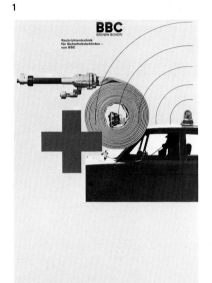

3

4

6

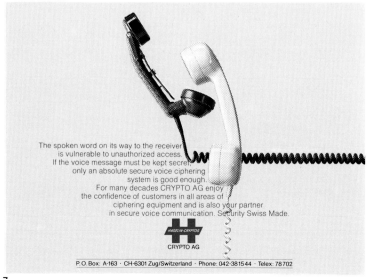

7

OFFSET
Seit 1948 wandelte sich unser Betrieb
von der Buchdruckerei zu einer leistungsfähigen Offsetdruckerei. Mit einer
Vierfarbendruckmaschine, drei Zweifarben-
druckmaschinen sowie drei Einfarbendruck-
maschinen drucken wir bis zum
maximalen Bogenformat von 72 × 102 cm.

Anton Schöb
Buchdruck – Offsetdruck
Foliendruck
Birchstrasse 102
8050 Zürich
Telefon 01-311 22 60

LICHTSATZ
Seit April 1981 produzieren wir unseren
Satz auf einer leistungsfähigen
Lichtsetzanlage:
Mit dem Texterfassungssystem
«Grafitex CDS-410» setzen wir in den Graden
4 bis 96 Punkt in Halbpunktabstufungen
auf maximal 287 mm Breite. Der mit dem
Texterfassungssystem on-line verbundene Kathoden-
strahlbelichter «Compugraphic cg 8600» belichtet
die gesetzten Texte dank neuartigem
Digitalisierungsverfahren in tadelloser Qualität.
Verlangen Sie Schriftmuster.

Anton Schöb
Buchdruck – Offsetdruck
Foliendruck
Birchstrasse 102
8050 Zürich
Telefon 01-311 22 60

8

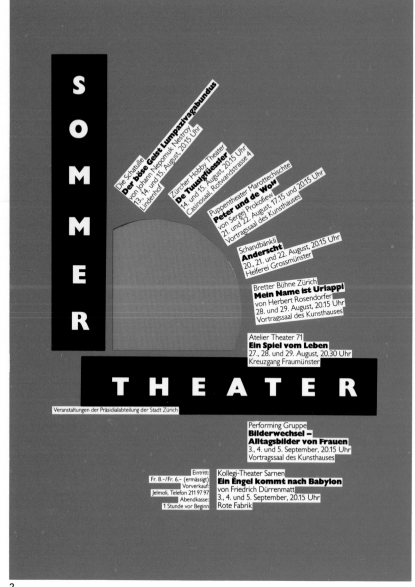

Poster for the Zürich summer theatre advertising 8 different
plays by amateur companies
Poster for the concert season in the Zürich theatre 11

Plakat für das Zürcher Sommertheater mit 8 verschiedenen
Laientheater-Vorführungen
Plakat für das Generalprogramm der Konzerte im Theater 11

Affiche sur le Théâtre d'été de Zurich avec 8 représentations
d'amateurs différentes
Affiche pour le programme général des concerts au Théâtre 11

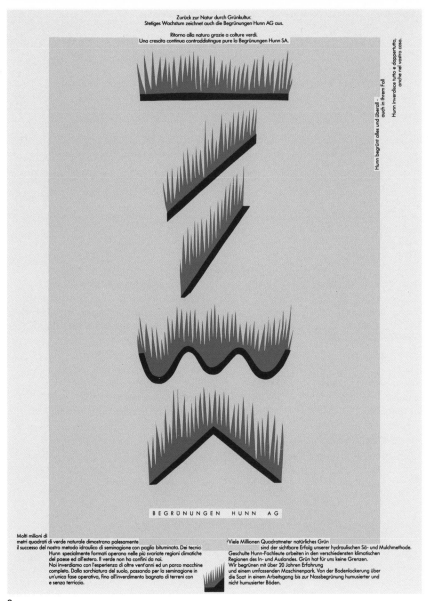

3

4

5

6

3
Poster for Hunn AG, a firm specialising in grass planting motor-way banks, ski runs, etc. Symbolic demonstration that all topo-graphical situations can be covered in grass
4
Symbol for Mettler & Co. AG, weavers, printers and exporters. The striped ''M'' seems like a piece of woven fabric
5
Symbol for Teamtex, a subsidiary of Mettler & Co. AG. This ''T'' should match the Mettler ''M'' without appearing to be too similar at first sight
6
Symbol for the indoor baths, Geroldswil, in the municipal, heraldic colours. It symbolises water under a roof

3
Plakat für Begrünungen Hunn AG; diese Firma begrünt Auto-bahnböschungen, Skipisten usw. Die symbolischen Darstellungen sollen zeigen, dass jede topografische Lage begrünbar ist
4
Signet für Mettler + Co. AG, Weberei, Druck, Export, St. Gallen. Das schraffierte «M» wirkt wie ein Stück gewebten Stoffes
5
Signet für Teamtex, eine Tochterfirma von Mettler + Co. AG. Das Signet musste dem Mettler-«M» angeglichen werden, ohne auf den ersten Blick ähnlich zu sein
6
Signet für das Hallenbad Geroldswil, in den Wappenfarben der Gemeinde. Das Zeichen symbolisiert Wasser unter Dach

3
Affiche pour la Société Hunn SA, spécialisée dans la plantation des bas-côtés d'autoroutes, pistes de ski, etc. Les représentations symboliques indiquent que toute topographie permet la création de zones de verdure.
4
Emblème pour la Société Mettler + Co. SA, Tisseranderie, Impression, Exportation, St-Gall. Le «M» hachuré fait l'effet d'une pièce d'étoffe tissée
5
Emblème pour Teamtex, une société affiliée de Mettler + Co. SA. Il fallait assimiler cet emblème au «M» de Mettler sans qu'il paraisse analogue du premier coup d'œil
6
Emblème pour la piscine couverte à Geroldswil, dans les couleurs d'armoiries de la commune. Cet emblème symbolise l'eau sous le toit

Rambow Lienemeyer van de Sand

Günter Rambow

1938	Born in Neustrelitz (Mecklenburg)
1954–58	Training as stained glass painter at the Staatliche Glasfachschule in Hadamar
1958–64	Studied at the Hochschule für bildende Künste in Kassel
1960	Founding of Studio Rambow+Lienemeyer in Kassel
1964	Studio in Stuttgart
1967	Studio in Frankfurt/Main
1967	Founding of Kohlkunstverlag
1974	Professor at the Gesamthochschule Kassel (Graphic design and photography)
1974	Member of AGI
1977	Member of DWB

Gerhard Lienemeyer

1936	Born in Bielefeld
1953–57	Apprenticed as graphic designer in industry
1959–64	Studied at the Hochschule für bildende Künste in Kassel
1960	Founding of Studio Rambow+Lienemeyer in Kassel
1964	Studio in Stuttgart
1967	Studio in Frankfurt/Main
1967	Founding of Kohlkunstverlag (publishers)
1974	Member of AGI
1977	Member of DWB

Michael van de Sand

1945	Born in Krefeld
1963–68	Studied at the Fachhochschule Niederrhein in Krefeld (graphic design and photography)
1969	Worked in Studio Rambow+Lienemeyer
1973	Partner in Studio Rambow, Lienemeyer, van de Sand
1977	Member of DWB

Günter Rambow

1938	Geboren in Neustrelitz (Mecklenburg)
1954–58	Ausbildung zum Glasmaler an der Staatlichen Glasfachschule in Hadamar
1958–64	Studium an der Hochschule für bildende Künste in Kassel
1960	Gründung Atelier Rambow+Lienemeyer in Kassel
1964	Atelier in Stuttgart
1967	Atelier in Frankfurt/Main
1967	Gründung des Kohlkunstverlages
1974	Professor an der Gesamthochschule Kassel (Grafik-Design und Fotografie)
1974	Mitglied der AGI
1977	Mitglied DWB

Gerhard Lienemeyer

1936	Geboren in Bielefeld
1953–57	Lehre als grafischer Zeichner in einem Industriebetrieb
1959–64	Studium an der Hochschule für bildende Künste in Kassel
1960	Gründung Atelier Rambow+Lienemeyer in Kassel
1964	Atelier in Stuttgart
1967	Atelier in Frankfurt/Main
1967	Gründung des Kohlkunstverlages
1974	Mitglied der AGI
1977	Mitglied DWB

Michael van de Sand

1945	Geboren in Krefeld
1963–68	Studium an der Fachhochschule Niederrhein in Krefeld (Grafik-Design und Fotografie)
1969	Im Atelier Rambow+Lienemeyer in Frankfurt/Main
1973	Partner im Atelier Rambow, Lienemeyer, van de Sand
1977	Mitglied DWB

Günter Rambow

1938	Né à Neustrelitz (Mecklenbourg)
1954–58	Formation en peinture sur verre à la Staatliche Glasfachschule à Hadamar
1958–64	Etudes à la Hochschule für bildende Künste à Kassel
1960	Fondation de l'atelier Rambow+Lienemeyer à Kassel
1964	Studio à Stuttgart
1967	Studio à Francfort/Main
1967	Fondation des Editions Kohlkunstverlag
1974	Professeur à la Gesamthochschule Kassel (arts graphiques et photographie)
1974	Membre de l'AGI
1977	Membre du DWB

Gerhard Lienemeyer

1936	Né à Bielefeld
1953–57	Apprentissage de dessinateur graphique dans une entreprise industrielle
1959–64	Etudes à la Hochschule für bildende Künste à Kassel
1960	Fondation de l'atelier Rambow+Lienemeyer à Kassel
1964	Fondation de l'atelier à Stuttgart
1967	Atelier à Francfort/Main
1967	Fondation des Editions Kohlkunstverlag
1974	Membre de l'AGI
1977	Membre du DWB

Michael van de Sand

1945	Né à Krefeld
1963–68	Etudes à la Fachhochschule Niederrhein à Krefeld (arts graphiques et photographie)
1969	Collaborateur dans l'atelier Rambow+Lienemeyer à Francfort/Main
1973	Partenaire de l'atelier Rambow, Lienemeyer, van de Sand
1977	Membre du DWB

Rambow Lienemeyer van de Sand formed a graphic design co-operative in Germany at about the same time and with similar motivation as Grapus to use the poster as a medium of social comment to make reality, once removed through photography, into an all the more impressive and convincing communication. Their many posters for plays, films and museums have made an enormous impact. Like Grapus they won prizes at the Poster Biennales at Warsaw and Brno as well as in many other countries. These photographers, designers, typographers all met at the Kassel Academy where they all were students of the very talented Hans Hillmann. Since then they have become teachers themselves and as such have been responsible for a whole new wave of joung German designers and typographers who find the camera a more appropriate tool than pencil, brush and colour.

They are worthy successors of John Heartfield when they use photomontage although of course their use of photography is entirely of today. Their motivation, however, is every bit as political, socially conscious and critical as that of the pioneer of this technique in the '20s. They show the empathy and surrealist imagination of Magritte and Hans Hillmann and they obtain lyrical and even painterly effects with photography; they seem to paint with a camera. Only unlike Magritte's international ambiguities their visual illusions always make a precise and unmistakable statement. They

Rambow Lienemeyer van de Sand schlossen sich etwa zur gleichen Zeit wie Grapus zu einer Design-Kooperative zusammen. Sie haben eine ähnliche Motivation, nämlich Plakate als Medium für sozialkritische Aussagen zu benützen. Durch geschickte Anwendung der Fotografie als Mittel der leichten Verfremdung erreichen sie eine besonders eindrucksvolle und erfolgreiche Kommunikation. Ihre vielen Plakate für Theater, Filme und Museen haben einen starken Eindruck hinterlassen. Ähnlich wie Grapus bekamen sie Preise auf der Warschauer Poster-Biennale, in Brno und in vielen anderen Ländern. Diese Fotografen, Designer und Typografen trafen sich alle an der Kasseler Akademie, als Studenten des hochbegabten Hans Hillmann. Inzwischen unterrichten sie selbst und sind für die Formierung einer neuen Welle von jungen deutschen Designern und Typografen verantwortlich, die die Kamera als ein passenderes Werkzeug ansehen, im Vergleich zu Bleistift, Pinsel und Farbe.

Sie sind würdige Nachfolger von John Heartfield im Gebrauch ihrer Fotomontagen, doch ihre Fotografie besitzt die Ausdrucksmittel unserer heutigen Zeit. Ihre Motivation ist aber genauso politisch, sozial bewusst und kritisch wie die Technik des Pioniers der 20er Jahre. Ihre Arbeiten besitzen das Einfühlungsvermögen und die surrealistische Fantasie von Magritte und Hans Hillmann. Ihre Fotografie erreicht lyrische Effekte und grenzt oft an

Rambow Lienemeyer van de Sand ont fondé à peu près à la même époque un atelier de caractère coopératif et ayant un but commun: utiliser l'affiche comme support de messages pour la critique sociale. En employant habilement la photographie comme moyen d'aliénation légère de la réalité, ils obtiennent une communication particulièrement expressive et efficace. Leurs nombreuses affiches de théâtre, cinéma et musées ont laissé une forte empreinte. Comme l'atelier Grapus, ils ont remporté des prix à la Biennale de l'affiche de Varsovie, à Brno et dans bien d'autres pays. Ces photographes, graphistes et typographes sont tous passés par l'Académie de Cassel, dans la classe du talentueux Hans Hillmann. Entre-temps, ils enseignent eux-mêmes et ont assuré la formation d'une nouvelle génération de graphistes et typographes allemands qui considèrent la caméra comme un outil plus approprié que le crayon, le pinceau ou la couleur.

Leurs montages photographiques en font les dignes successeurs de John Heartfield, mais leur photographie possède les moyens d'expression de notre époque. Leur motivation est aussi politique, sociale, consciente et critique que celle du pionnier de la technique, dans les années 20. Leurs œuvres possèdent l'intuition et l'imagination surréaliste de Magritte et de Hans Hillmann. Leur caméra obtient des effets lyriques et égale souvent le pinceau. Ils peignent sur pellicule, mais contrairement à l'ambi-

1 Poster for Städelmuseum, Frankfurt
2 Poster for Cologne art fair

1 Plakat für das Städelmuseum in Frankfurt
2 Plakat für den Kölner Kunstmarkt

1 Affiche pour le Städelmuseum à Francfort
2 Affiche pour la Foire d'art de Cologne

1   2

are part of a new German poster wave of photo-graphists, a group which includes such distin-guished designers as Holger Mathies, Frieder Grindler, Ingo Pape and Inge Werth.
Their posters endow the classic plays with a new and topical meaning, suggesting an urgent and often provocative message for today's public. The typography, or rather the text, forms always an integral part of their posters, arresting the passer-by in the street, catching his attention and dramati-cally conveying the message. They bear out Savig-nac's comment 'a poster should be a small scandal in the street'.

Malerei. Sie malen mit ihrer Kamera, jedoch anders als bei Magrittes absichtlichen Zweideutigkeiten, und machen mit ihren visuellen Illusionen immer eine präzise und unmissverständliche Aussage. Sie gehören zu einer neuen deutschen Bewegung von Foto-Grafikern, zu einer Gruppe von namhaften De-signern, zu denen auch Holger Mathies, Frieder Grindler, Ingo Pape und Inge Werth gehören.
Ihre Plakate verleihen den klassischen Stücken eine neue aktuelle Bedeutung mit einer dringenden und oft provokativen Aussage an das heutige Pu-blikum. Die Typografie oder vielmehr der Text ist immer ein integrierter Teil ihrer Plakate, der den Vorübergehenden auf der Strasse zum Anhalten bewegt, seine Aufmerksamkeit weckt und die Bot-schaft in dramatischer Weise übermittelt. Sie hal-ten sich an Savignacs Forderung, «ein Plakat muss immer ein kleiner Skandal auf der Strasse sein».

guïté voulue de Magritte, leurs illusions visuelles li-vrent toujours un message précis et catégorique.
Ils appartiennent à un nouveau mouvement alle-mand de photo-graphistes aux noms célèbres, parmi lesquels figurent Holger Mathies, Frieder Grindler, Ingo Pape et Inge Werth.
Leurs affiches confèrent aux pièces classiques une nouvelle actualité, avec un message pressant et souvent provocant au public moderne. La typogra-phie ou plutôt le texte fait toujours partie de leurs affiches, qui obligent le passant à s'arrêter, éveil-lent son attention et diffusent dramatiquement le message. Ils appliquent l'impératif de Savignac, pour qui «une affiche doit toujours être un petit scandale dans la rue».

1–9
Posters for S. Fischer publishers, Frankfurt

1–9
Plakate für den Verlag S. Fischer in Frankfurt

1–9
Affiches pour les Editions S. Fischer, Francfort

1

2

3

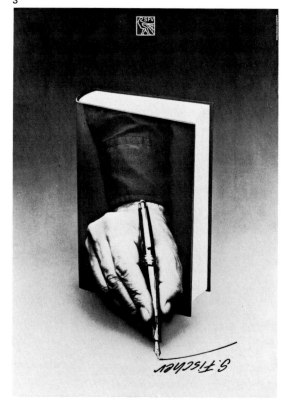

4

5

6

7

8

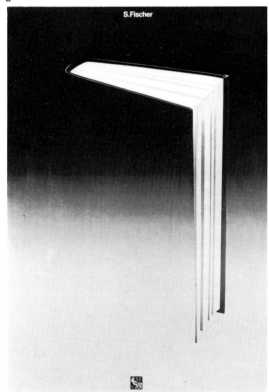

9

121

1

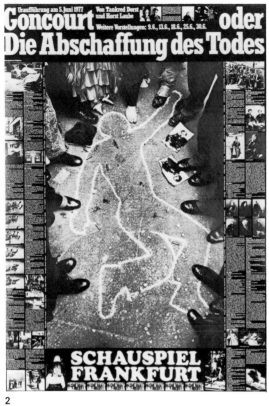

2

3

4

5

6

7

8

1
Poster for "Egoist" magazine
2–8
Posters for the Frankfurt playhouse

1
Plakat für die Zeitschrift «Egoist»
2–8
Theaterplakate für das Schauspiel Frankfurt

1
Affiche pour le magazine «Egoist»
2–8
Affiches théâtrales pour le spectacle de Francfort

1

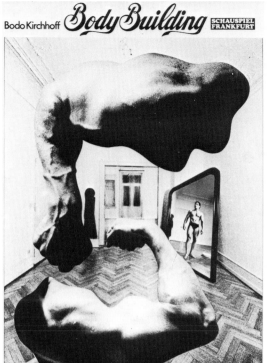

2

3

4

5

1, 2, 4, 5
Posters for the Frankfurt playhouse
3
Poster for the "am Turm" theatre, Frankfurt

1, 2, 4, 5
Theaterplakate für das Schauspiel Frankfurt
3
Plakat für das Theater am Turm in Frankfurt

1, 2, 4, 5
Affiches théâtrales pour le spectacle de Francfort
3
Affiche pour le théâtre à la tour

1

2

1, 2
Posters for René Block publishers, Berlin

1, 2
Plakate für die Edition René Block in Berlin

1, 2
Affiches pour les Editions René Block, Berlin

Dan Reisinger

1934	Born in Kanjiza, Yugoslavia	1934	Geboren in Kanjiza, Jugoslawien	1934	Né à Kanjiza, Yougoslavie
1949	Emigrated to Israel; worked as house-painter	1949	Emigriert nach Israel, begann als Häuseranstreicher	1949	Immigration en Israël, travail comme peintre en bâtiment
1951–54	Studied at Bezalel Academy of Art, Jerusalem (awarded Hermann Struck prize)	1951–54	Studium an der Bezalel Academy of Art, Jerusalem (Hermann-Struck-Preis)	1951–54	Etudes à la Bezalel Academy of Art, Jérusalem (prix Hermann Struck)
1954–57	Military service, publications designer, Israel Air Force	1954–57	Militärdienst, Design-Veröffentlichungen, israelische Luftwaffe	1954–57	Service militaire, publications sur le design, Armée de l'air israélienne
1957–58	Worked in Brussels, 1st prize in "Expo 58" poster competition	1957–58	Tätigkeit in Brüssel, 1. Preis für den «Expo 58»-Plakatwettbewerb	1957–58	Activité à Bruxelles, 1er prix du concours d'affiches de l'«Expo 58»
1958–60	Studied and worked in London, designed posters for BBC and General Post Office	1958–60	Studium und Praxis in London, Plakatentwürfe für BBC und die Hauptpost	1958–60	Etudes et travail pratique à Londres, projets d'affiches pour BBC et l'Office central des postes
1960–	Lives and works in Israel; married, 3 sons; member of Alliance Graphique Internationale; member of Art Directors' Club, New York; consultant to "Beautiful Israel Society"; design consultant to the "Bank of Israel"; former consultant to "Bezalel Academy of Art"	1960–	In Israel ansässig, verheiratet, 3 Söhne, Mitglied der Alliance Graphique Internationale, Mitglied des Art Director's Club, New York, Berater der «Beautiful Israel Society», Design Consultant der «Bank of Israel» und früherer Berater der «Bezalel Academy of Art»	1960–	Etablit en Israël, marié, 3 fils, membre de l'Alliance Graphique Internationale, membre du Art Directors' Club, New York, consultant de la «Beautiful Israel Society», Design Consultant de la «Bank of Israel» et ancien consultant de la «Bezalel Academy of Art»

Distinctions:
Recipient of Nordau Prize and Herzl Prize for his contribution to graphic art and design in Israel

Exhibitions:
One-man exhibition, Israel Museum Jerusalem, one-man exhibition at Helena Rubinstein Museum, Tel Aviv

His posters are included in many international collections and museums: Warsaw, Tokyo, New York

Anerkennungen:
Nordau-Preis, Herzl-Preis für seinen Beitrag im Bereich des Graphic Art and Design in Israel

Ausstellungen:
Einzelausstellung Israel Museum, Jerusalem, Einzelausstellung Helena-Rubinstein-Museum, Tel Aviv

Seine Plakate sind in verschiedenen internationalen Sammlungen und Museen vertreten: Warschau, Tokio, New York

Distinctions spéciales:
Prix Nordau, prix Herzl pour sa contribution à l'art et à la conception graphique en Israël

Expositions:
Exposition individuelle à Jérusalem, exposition individuelle Helena Rubinstein Museum, Tel Aviv

Ses affiches sont représentées dans diverses collections publiques et des musées internationaux: Belgrade, Varsovie, Tokyo, New York

On Dan Reisinger, comments Dr. Gaon, the curator of the Israel Museum Design pavilion: "Dan Reisinger's career, with its agressive, creative energy, parallels the development of Israel. As a growing nation, it created an atmosphere in which a bright and talented young man could apply his ideas with success — Dan Reisinger did it.

Dr. Gaon, der Kurator des Design-Pavillons im Israel-Museum, sagt über Dan Reisinger: «Die Entwicklung von Dan Reisinger mit seiner aggressiven, kreativen Energie läuft sehr mit der von Israel parallel. Als wachsende Nation schuf das Land eine Atmosphäre, in der ein intelligenter und talentierter junger Mann seine Ideen mit Erfolg prakti-

Le conservateur Gaon de la section design du Musée d'Israël dit de Dan Reisinger: «L'évolution de Dan Reisinger, avec son énergie créatrice agressive, suit assez bien celle d'Israël. Cette nation en développement a créé une atmosphère où un intelligent et talentueux jeune homme pouvait mettre ses idées en pratique. C'est ce qu'a réussi Dan Reisinger.

At the age of fifteen he was a new immigrant from Yugoslavia earning his living as a house painter; his unique way of combining colour did not go unnoticed. He was recommended to the director of the Bezalel School of Arts and Design, and thus as a very young student was brought into a professional environment where he got the best training the country could offer. While other new immigrants added words to our spoken language, Dan Reisinger added colour and form to our visual language. He has often gone abroad, twice for further studies in London, where he also did work for the BBC and the General Post Office. He has consequently developed a keen ability to absorb international trends and translate them into his own idiom. His work — environmental, three-dimensional and graphic — defies identification with any specific style which would stamp or classify him. If anything, his trademark is colour.

The use of several languages forces him to find solutions for bringing logos of different alphabets into one style-image. In some cases he ingeniously unites them until the distinction between the English and Hebrew almost disappears.

Where has his colour trademark been carried to the ultimate? Is it in environmental graphics (Tel Aviv seashore, supermarkets and department stores) or in his rotating sculpture-paintings? In Tel Aviv he was asked to propose colours for the benches along the beach. He soon discovered that his benches would clash with the drab background of walls near the seashore, and so convinced the municipality to change the environment. The walls were painted brightly, according to his design, and

zieren konnte. Das genau tat Dan Reisinger.
Mit 15 Jahren, als neuer Immigrant aus Jugoslawien, verdiente er seinen Lebensunterhalt als Anstreicher von Häusern. Seine einmaligen Farbkombinationen blieben nicht unbemerkt. Er wurde dem Direktor der Bezalel School of Art and Design empfohlen und erhielt auf diese Weise die beste Ausbildung in einer professionellen Umgebung, die das Land ihm bieten konnte. Während andere Immigranten unserer gesprochenen Sprache neue Werte brachten, hat Dan Reisinger unserer visuellen Sprache neue Farben und Formen geschenkt. Er war öfter im Ausland, zweimal zum weiteren Studium in London, wo er auch für die BBC und die Post gearbeitet hat. Er hat dort seine besondere Begabung entwickelt, internationale Trends aufzuspüren und in seine eigene Sprache umzusetzen. Der gleichzeitige Gebrauch mehrerer Sprachen zwingt ihn zu Lösungen, in denen er Logos mehrerer Alphabete in einem einheitlichen Stil unterbringt. In manchen Fällen verbindet er sie in besonders genialer Weise, so dass Unterschiede zwischen Englisch und Hebräisch fast verschwinden. Wo hat er sein Warenzeichen ‹Farbe› wohl am stärksten eingesetzt, entweder in seinen Umweltgestaltungsaufgaben (Tel Aviv Seeküste, Supermärkte und Kaufhäuser) oder gar in seinen rotierenden, skulpturähnlichen Gemälden? In Tel Aviv wurde er um Farbgestaltungsvorschläge für die Strandbänke gebeten. Ihm wurde bald klar, dass diese Bänke nicht zu dem langweiligen Hintergrund der farblosen Wände am Ufer passen würden. Er gewann die Gemeinde für eine Neugestaltung der gesamten Umgebung. Die Wände wurden

Nouvel immigrant, arrivé de Yougoslavie à 15 ans, il gagnait sa vie à peindre les murs des maisons. Des combinaisons de couleurs originales n'ont pas tardé à attirer l'attention: recommandé au directeur de la Bezalel School of Art and Design, il y a reçu la meilleure formation, dans un milieu professionnel. Tout comme d'autres immigrants apportaient de nouvelles valeurs à notre parler, de même Dan Reisinger a donné à notre langage visuel des couleurs et des formes neuves. Il a été souvent à l'étranger, deux fois à Londres pour parfaire ses études. Dans la capitale britannique, il a travaillé entre autres pour la BBC et l'Office central des postes. A cette occasion, il a développé un don particulier pour saisir les tendances internationales et les traduire dans sa langue.

L'usage simultané de plusieurs langues l'oblige à des solutions regroupant dans un style homogène des logotypes de plusieurs alphabets. Bien souvent, il les relie avec un tel génie que les différences entre l'anglais et l'hébreu disparaissent pratiquement.

Où sa marque personnelle, la couleur, est-elle la plus forte? Est-ce dans ses œuvres environnementalistes (côtes de Tel Aviv, supermarchés et grands magasins) ou bien dans ses tableaux tournants à allures de sculptures? Tel Aviv lui a commandé des propositions de couleurs pour les bancs de la plage. Il a bien vite compris que ses bancs n'iraient pas avec les murs sans couleurs de la rive. Une fois les communes gagnées à l'idée de recomposer de tout l'environnement, les murs ont été recouverts de coloris très vifs. Deux rangées de bancs sont venus meubler cette vibrante tache de couleur.

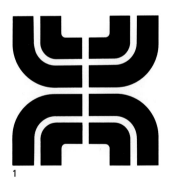

1

2

3

4

1
Habimah National Theatre; the Hebrew letter H (two curved lines) is combined four times to create the image of a "menorah", the emblem of the State of Israel.
2
"10 Fingers", a gallery for folk-art and craft
3
European Maccabi Games
4
"Lili", paper products; the design forms the word "Lili" both in English (left to right) and in Hebrew (right to left).

1
Habimah National Theatre; der hebräische Buchstabe H (zwei gebogene Linien) ist viermal so verbunden, dass er das Bild einer «Minorah» formt, das Symbol des Staates Israel.
2
«10 Finger», eine Galerie für Volkskunst
3
Europäische Maccabi-Spiele
4
«Lili», ein Papierhersteller; das Design erlaubt die Worte sowohl in Englisch von links nach rechts wie Hebräisch von rechts nach links zu lesen.

1
Théâtre national Habimah; la lettre hébraïque «H» (deux lignes courbes) est combinée quatre fois pour créer l'image de la «menorah», emblème de l'Etat d'Israël.
2
«10 doigts», galerie d'art populaire
3
Jeux européens de Maccabi
4
«Lili», produits en papier; le graphisme forme le mot «Lili» en anglais (de gauche à droite) et en hébreu (de droite à gauche).

the benches have become secondary to one of the most vibrant sights in town.

His experiments in combining colour led him to develop the sculpture-painting which give the possibility of forming an almost infinite number of patterns. They are composed of painted columns which rotate on vertical axes, and range in size from executive toys to entire wall-scale pieces."

Some personal comments: "I consider myself a craftsman carrying on a family tradition (4th generation) using paint and brush to enhance aesthetic order in the environment.

As for communication, I rely less on the verbal message — preferring the magic of visual directness.

As a student in Bezalel, I had the privilege to receive a very immediate influence of the Bauhaus via my teachers in painting and design; this I think encouraged my intuitive love for the minimal and the basic.

Originally I saw myself as a poster artist, greatly inspired by the British poster designers Games, Henrion, Eckersley and others. However, the fast-growing needs of a new country challenged my curiosity and motivated a personal ambition to take part in many aspects of design.

Perhaps my professional idealism coincided with the necessity to create a new reality."

nach seinen Vorschlägen in sehr bunten Farben gestrichen. Die Bänke wurden zweitrangig in diesem absolut vibrierenden und farbigsten Fleck der Stadt.

Sein Experimentieren mit Farbe führte ihn zur Entwicklung seiner skulpturellen Gemälde, bei denen eine unbegrenzte Anzahl von Figurationen entsteht. Sie setzen sich aus bemalten Säulen zusammen, die auf vertikalen Achsen rotieren. Ihre Grössen rangieren von Spielzeuggrösse bis zu wandhohen Versionen.»

Einige persönliche Kommentare: «Ich sehe mich selbst als Handwerker, der eine Familientradition in der vierten Generation weiterführt, nämlich Farbe und Pinsel zu benutzen, um die Umweltästhetik zu verbessern.

Was die Kommunikation anbelangt, verlasse ich mich weniger auf nüchterne, buchstäbliche Aussagen, indem ich den Zauber einer visuellen Direktheit vorziehe.

Als Student in Bezalel hatte ich das Glück, durch meine Lehrer einem direkten Bauhaus-Einfluss ausgesetzt zu sein sowohl in der Malerei wie im Design. Das scheint meine intuitive Neigung für das Minimale und das sehr Grundsätzliche bestärkt zu haben.

Ursprünglich sah ich mich als Plakat-Künstler stark beeinflusst von den britischen Plakat-Designern Games, Henrion, Eckersley und anderen. Die schnell wachsenden Bedürfnisse eines neuen Landes spornten meine Neugier und persönlichen Ehrgeiz an, mich in vielen Bereichen des Designs zu betätigen.

Vielleicht deckte sich mein beruflicher Idealismus mit dem Bedürfnis, eine neue Realität zu gestalten.

Ses expériences avec les couleurs l'ont amené à inventer ses tableaux sculpturaux, où naissent une variété infinie de figures. Ils se composent de colonnes peintes, pivotant sur des axes verticaux. Leur taille va du jouet à la paroi complète.»

Quelques commentaires personnels: «Je me considère comme un artisan poursuivant, à la quatrième génération, la tradition familiale d'améliorer l'esthétique environnante à grands coups de pinceaux et de couleurs.

Pour la communication, je me fie moins aux messages crus, littéraux, qu'au charme direct du visuel. Pendant mes études à Bezalel, j'ai eu la chance de subir, par mes maîtres, une influence directe du Bauhaus, tant en peinture qu'en design. Ma tendance intuitive vers le minimal et l'essentiel semble en être sortie renforcée.

Dans mes affiches, j'ai commencé par trahir la forte empreinte des designers britanniques, Games, Henrion, Eckersley et d'autres. Mais les besoins croissants d'un pays neuf ont aiguillonné ma curiosité et mon orgueil, me poussant dans de nombreux domaines du design.

Peut-être mon idéalisme professionnel recoupe-t-il la nécessité d'organiser une nouvelle réalité?»

3

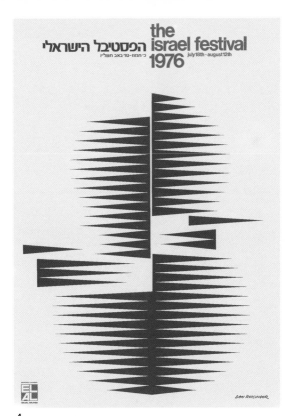

4

5

6

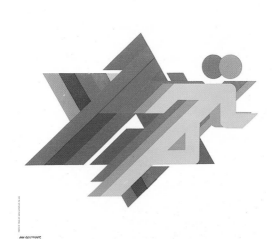

7

8

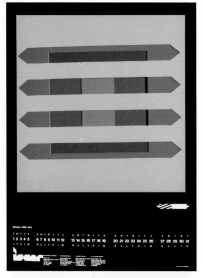

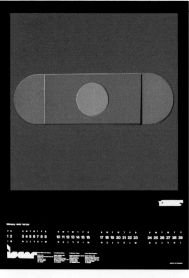

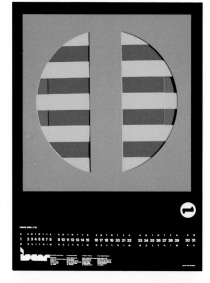

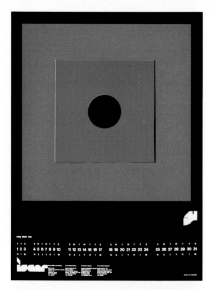

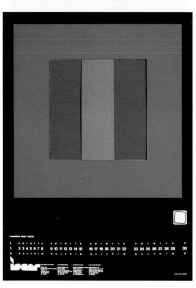

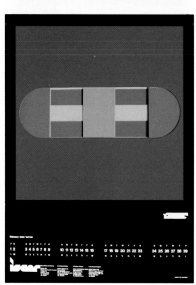

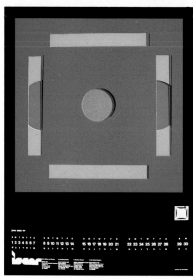

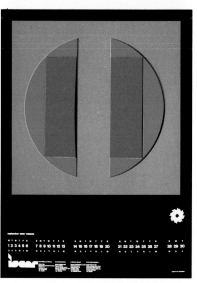

1980 Calendar for ISCAR, cutting-tool company; this calendar is composed of 6 independent sheets which hinge on to a thick cardboard background. The sheets are printed on both sides — one colour, one month, to each side. A different shape is cut out of each sheet; these shapes resemble items manufactured by ISCAR. By hanging the sheets in different order on to the background — leaving the relevant month on top — they create a variety of 43,000 different images.

Kalender 1980 für ISCAR, eine Stanzwerkzeuggesellschaft; dieser Kalender setzt sich aus sechs unabhängigen Blättern zusammen, die an einem dicken Papphintergrund mit Scharnieren befestigt sind. Die Blätter sind auf beiden Seiten bedruckt, jeweils eine Farbe für einen Monat. Aus jedem Blatt ist eine unterschiedliche Form ausgeschnitten. Diese Formen ähneln den von ISCAR hergestellten Gegenständen. Durch willkürliches Übereinanderhängen der einzelnen Blätter, mit dem jeweiligen Monatsblatt obendrauf, kann man eine Zahl von 43 000 verschiedenen Image-Kompositionen erreichen.

Calendrier 1980 pour ISCAR, entreprise de production d'outils tranchants; le calendrier se compose de 6 feuilles indépendantes, fixées sur un carton épais. Les feuilles sont imprimées des 2 côtés. Chaque côté, en une couleur déterminée, correspond à un mois du calendrier. Une forme différente est découpée dans chaque feuille. Ces formes ressemblent aux articles produits par ISCAR. En changeant la succession des feuilles par rapport au fond en carton et en gardant le mois correspondant au-dessus, une variété de 43 000 images différentes peut être obtenue.

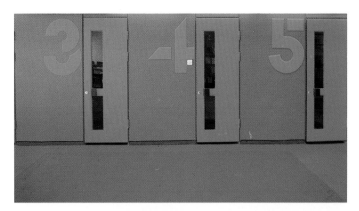

Haifa Medical School; a colour planning for total interior of building. Each floor is painted in the colour indicated on the main sign in the lobby. Library and study rooms are marked with large numbers for identification. Typography in "Milton Glazer Bold", a Hebrew type-face adapted accordingly. Background mural in lobby designed to reflect colour into white entrance hall.

Haifa Medical School; ein Farbplanungssystem für die gesamte Innenausstattung des Gebäudes. Jeder Flur erhielt die Farbe, mit der er auf dem Haupthinweiszeichen in der Eingangshalle gekennzeichnet ist. Die Bibliothek und Arbeitsräume erhalten aus Identifikationsgründen grosse Buchstaben. Typografie in «Milton Glazer Bold», einem hebräischen Alfabet, das entsprechend abgewandelt wurde. Den Hintergrund bildet ein Wandgemälde in der Lobby, das so entworfen wurde, dass es die Farben in die weisse Eingangshalle reflektiert.

Ecole de médecine de Haïfa; planifaction des couleurs pour l'aménagement intérieur de l'ensemble du bâtiment. Chaque étage est peint dans la couleur indiquée sur le tableau d'orientation du hall d'entrée. La bibliothèque et les salles d'étude sont marquées de grands numéros d'identification. Typographie en «Milton Glazer Bold», les caractères hébraïques sont adaptés en conséquence. Le mur de fond du hall d'entrée est conçu de manière à refléter les couleurs dans l'aire d'entrée entièrement blanche.

Supergraphics, Tel Aviv sea-shore promenade; these supergraphics provide the background for a four-page feature in "Time Magazine", promoting Tambour paints.

Supergraphics, Tel-Aviv-Strandpromenade; diese Supergraphics waren die Basis eines vierseitigen Artikels im «Time Magazine», einer Werbung für Tambour-Farben.

Supergraphiques, promenade sur la plage de Tel Aviv; ces supergraphiques constituent l'arrière-plan pour une annonce publicitaire sur quatre pages dans «Time Magazine» pour la promotion des couleurs Tambour.

Jacques Richez

1918	Born at Dieppe	1918	Geboren in Dieppe	1918	Né à Dieppe
1953	Invited to join the Alliance Graphique Internationale	1953	Zum Mitglied der Alliance Graphique Internationale ernannt	1953	Membre de l'Alliance Graphique Internationale
1957	2nd prize at the international poster competition for the XIe Triennale of Milan	1957	2. Preis des internationalen Plakat-Wettbewerbs der XI. Triennale, Mailand	1957	2e prix au concours international de l'affiche de la 11e Triennale de Milan
1958	Designed the official poster for the World Exhibition at Brussels	1958	Entwurf des offiziellen Plakates der Weltausstellung Brüssel	1958	Création de l'affiche officielle de l'Exposition universelle de Bruxelles
1967–69	Vice President of ICOGRADA	1967–69	Vizepräsident von ICOGRADA	1967–69	Vice-président du International Council of Graphic Design Associations (ICOGRADA)
1968–70	Vice President of AGI	1968–70	Vizepräsident der AGI		
1974–76	Vice President of AGI	1974–76	Vizepräsident der AGI	1968–70	Vice-président de l'AGI
1969	Prize for the best poster of the month in Poland	1969	Preis für das beste Plakat des Monats in Polen	1974–76	Vice-président de l'AGI, 2e mandat
1970	Jury member of the World Biennale of posters in Warsaw	1970	Jury-Mitglied der Welt-Biennale für Plakate in Warschau	1969	Prix pour la meilleure affiche du mois en Pologne
1972	Special honourable mention by the jury of the Warsaw poster Biennale; took part in the section "Experimental Graphics" at the Venice Biennale	1972	Ehrenauszeichnung durch die Jury der Warschauer Plakat-Biennale; Teilnahme an der Biennale Venedig im Bereich «Experimental Graphics»	1970	Membre du jury à la Biennale internationale de l'affiche à Varsovie
1973	Named by a US jury one of the significant people in photographic research (Time-Life Photography 1973)	1973	Besondere Anerkennung durch die US-Jury als einer der einflussreichsten Vertreter im Bereich der Photographie (Time-Life Photography 1973)	1972	Mention spéciale décernée par le jury de la Biennale de l'affiche à Varsovie; participe à la section «Graphisme expérimental» à la Biennale de Venise; fonde un groupe AGI en Belgique avec G. Fiszman, H. de Kempeneer, Michel Olyff
1974–76	Jury member of the "Institut Supérieur des Arts Graphiques", Paris	1974–76	Jury-Mitglied des «Institut Supérieur des Arts Graphiques», Paris	1973	Distinction spéciale par un jury américain pour sa contribution significative à la recherche photographique (Time-Life Photography 1973)
1975	Organised the exhibition "107 AGI Graphistes", Musées Royaux des Beaux-Arts, Brussels	1975	Zusammenstellung der Ausstellung «107 AGI Graphistes», Musées Royaux des Beaux-Arts, Brüssel	1974–76	Membre du jury de l'Institut Supérieur des Arts Graphiques, Paris
				1975	Organise l'exposition «107 graphistes AGI», Musées Royaux des Beaux-Arts, Bruxelles

Author of "Graphic Art applied to Communication" (1964); "Texts and Pretexts, 25 years of reflecting on Graphic Design" (1980).
Monographs in "16 European Graphic Designers", Tokyo and Fribourg; Graphis, Zürich; Novum Gebrauchsgraphik, Munich; Idea, Tokyo; Graphic Design, Tokyo; Linea Graphica, Milan; and many other publications.
One-man shows: 1948, 1958, 1974, 1977, 1979 and 1981 in Brussels; 1974 Gand, 1975 Milan, 1976 Anvers.
Posters in the Museums of: Warsaw, Washington, Milwaukee, Ontario, Essen, Paris, Brussels, Liège, Colorado and New York.

Autor von «Graphic Art applied to Communication» (1964), «Texts and Pretexts, 25 years of reflecting on Graphic Design» (1980).
Monographien in «16 European Graphic Designers», Tokio und Freiburg; Graphis, Zürich; Novum Gebrauchsgraphik, München; Idea, Tokio; Graphic Design, Tokio; Linea Graphica, Mailand; und viele andere Veröffentlichungen.
Einzelausstellungen: 1948, 1958, 1974, 1977, 1979 und 1981 in Brüssel; 1974 Gent, 1975 Mailand, 1976 Antwerpen.
Plakate in den Museen von:
Warschau, Washington, Milwaukee, Ontario, Essen, Paris, Brüssel, Liège, Colorado und New York.

Auteur de «L'art graphique appliqué à la communication» (1964), «Textes et Prétextes, 25 années de réflexions sur le graphisme design» (1980).
Monographies dans «16 European Graphic Designers», Tokyo et Fribourg; Graphic Design, Tokyo; Linea Graphica, Milan; ainsi que de nombreuses autres publications.
Expositions individuelles: 1948, 1958, 1974, 1977, 1979 et 1981 à Bruxelles; 1974 Gand, 1975 Milan, 1976 Anvers.

Jacques Richez demonstrates in his later work a fascinating inter-relationship between drawing, photography and design with quite amazing results. An established designer with a worldwide reputation, ever since his poster for the World Exhibition in Brussels in 1958, he produced a prodigious variety of posters, symbols, logotypes and exhibitions in his adopted Belgium (he was originally a Frenchman), where artistic sensibility of both client and public seems less appreciated than in his native France. Besides being a most gifted designer he is also an exquisite draughtsman (not all designers are) and an experimental photographer, both in black and white and colour where he has developed new techniques. In his recent work he creates a fascinating interface between life drawing and photography of the female body — often wrapped in complicated drapes. These juxtapositions of techniques in different and differing media make for a delicate and unexpected result — adding a new dimension both to photography and drawing in their inter-relationship, in their subtle difference and in their similarity.

He explains: "My philosophy? Very simple: reflection and responsibility. I have never accepted the wellknown notion which says the graphic designer is a transmitter of messages and is not personally responsible for what he transmits. In a profession where the final aim is to communicate, i.e. to influence opinion, it seems to me that the least is to

Jacques Richez zeigt in seinen späteren Arbeiten eine faszinierende Wechselbeziehung zwischen Zeichnung, Fotografie und Design mit erstaunlichen Ergebnissen. Als etablierter Designer von Weltruf (seit seinem Plakat für die Weltausstellung in Brüssel 1958) hat er eine gewaltige Vielzahl von verschiedenen Plakaten, Symbolen, Logotypen und Ausstellungen entworfen. All das für seine Wahlheimat Belgien (er ist in Frankreich geboren), wo man die künstlerische Sensibilität sowohl beim Kunden wie auch beim Publikum weniger schätzt als in seiner ursprünglichen Heimat. Abgesehen davon, dass er ein sehr begabter Designer ist, hat er ein ganz ausgefallenes handwerkliches Geschick (nicht alle Designer besitzen das). Er ist auch ein experimenteller Fotograf sowohl in Schwarzweiss wie in Farbe. In seinen jüngsten Arbeiten gestaltete er eine erstaunliche Zwischenbeziehung von Zeichnung und Fotografie des weiblichen Körpers, teilweise auf komplizierte Weise in Tüchern drapiert. Die Gegenüberstellung von Techniken in verschiedenen und in sich variierenden Medien führt zu delikaten ganz unerwarteten Ergebnissen. Sowohl die Fotografie wie auch die Zeichnung erhalten durch diese Zwischenbeziehung eine neue Dimension mit ihren feinen Unterschieden und ihrer Ähnlichkeit.

Er erklärt über sich: «Meine Philosophie? Ganz einfach: Reflexion und Verantwortung. Ich habe nie die wohlbekannte Haltung akzeptiert, dass ein De-

Dans ses créations étonnantes et subtiles, Jacques Richez exprime les fascinantes relations entre le dessin, la photographie et le graphisme. Graphiste de notoriété internationale depuis son affiche pour l'Exposition universelle à Bruxelles en 1958, il a réalisé un nombre prodigieux d'affiches, de symboles, de logotypes et d'expositions dans son pays adoptif, la Belgique, où la sensibilité artistique est moins appréciée, tant par le client que par le public, que dans son pays d'origine, la France. Tout en étant un graphiste remarquablement doué, il est également un dessinateur hors pair (ce qui n'est de loin pas le cas pour tous les graphistes). Il pratique aussi la photographie expérimentale, à la fois en noir et blanc et en couleur. Dans ses récents travaux, il a su établir un séduisant rapport entre le dessin et la photographie du corps féminin, parfois entouré de draperies compliquées. Cette juxtaposition des techniques dans des médias aussi différents que variables, aboutit à des créations subtiles souvent inattendues. La photographie et le dessin acquièrent ainsi une nouvelle dimension dans leurs relations mutuelles, que ce soit dans leurs subtiles différences ou dans leurs similitudes.

Il explique: «Ma philosophie? Très simple: réflexion et responsabilité. Je n'ai jamais accepté pour moi la notion bien connue selon laquelle le graphiste est un traducteur de messages et qu'il n'est pas personnellement responsable de ce qu'il transmet.

1

2

1, 2
Two photo montages out of series of 12 "The quarries of Carrara"

1, 2
Zwei Fotomontagen aus einer Serie von 12 «The Quarries of Carrara»

1, 2
Deux photomontages extraits d'une série de 12 sur «Les carrières de Carrara»

question the implications and consequences of our actions. This lead me, already some years ago, to distance myself from commercial advertising and to devote my work to a form of visual communication likely to be more useful to the community. What proved difficult—and still is today—is not the choice itself but the daily effort to reconcile my professional life with my ideas in a country where there is not a single example of an administration, of a public service department or a cultural organisation with a planned and cohesive design policy."

signer Botschaften überträgt, jedoch nicht persönlich für das, was er übermittelt, verantwortlich ist. In einem Beruf, dessen Hauptanliegen Kommunikation ist, dass heisst Meinungsbeeinflussung, scheint es unumgänglich, sich zu fragen, was für Folgen und Konsequenzen unsere Arbeiten bringen. Deshalb habe ich mich seit einigen Jahren von der kommerziellen Werbung distanziert und mich für eine Form der visuellen Kommunikation entschlossen, die der Gemeinde nützlicher sein kann. Was sich als schwierig erwies, und das ist heute noch das gleiche, ist nicht die Wahl an sich. Es ist vielmehr die tägliche Bemühung, mein Berufsleben mit meinen Ideen in Einklang zu bringen in einem Land, in dem es keine einzige Verwaltung, einen öffentlichen Dienst oder eine kulturelle Organisation mit einer geplanten, festen Design-Politik gibt.»

Dans un métier dont le but et la finalité est de communiquer – et donc d'influencer l'opinion – la moindre des choses, me semble-t-il, est de s'interroger sur les implications et les conséquences de notre action. Ceci m'a conduit, il y a pas mal d'années déjà, à prendre mes distances vis-à-vis de la publicité commerciale et à consacrer mon travail à une forme de communication visuelle plus utile à la collectivité. Ce qui a été difficile – et l'est encore – n'est pas le choix en lui-même, mais la volonté quotidienne de préserver l'accord entre la vie professionnelle et les idées, dans un pays où il n'est pas un seul exemple d'administration, de service public ou d'organisation culturelle qui ait choisi de mener une politique graphique réfléchie et cohérente.»

1–3
Photo-graphic research combining photography with delicate drawings of drapes and the human figure. In the motifs 1 and 2 only the darkest quarter of the circle is a photography. Sometimes both drawing and photographs are cut out and positioned at a distance of 1 cm from the background. As the backs of these cut-outs are coloured, these colours are subtly reflected as delicate shadows—hence the name "colour traps".

1–3
Foto-Grafik-Untersuchung, Kombinierung von Fotografie und feinen Zeichnungen von drapierten Tüchern um einen menschlichen Körper. In den Motiven 1 und 2 ist nur das dunkelste Viertel des Kreises eine Fotografie. Manchmal sind die Zeichnungen und die Fotografien ausgeschnitten und mit einem Abstand von 1 cm neu auf den Hintergrund montiert. Da die Rückseite dieser Ausschnitte farbig ist, reflektiert sie farbige delikate Schatten, daher der Name «colour traps».

1–3
Recherches photo-graphiques associant la photographie au dessin de délicates draperies et du corps humain. Dans les motifs 1 et 2, seul le quart de cercle le plus foncé est une photo. Parfois les dessins et photographies sont découpés et placés à 1 cm de l'arrière-plan. Le dos de ces parties découpées étant coloré, des ombres délicates sont projetées par réflexion sur le fond. Ces couleurs réfléchies irréelles expliquent le terme de «colour traps».

1

2

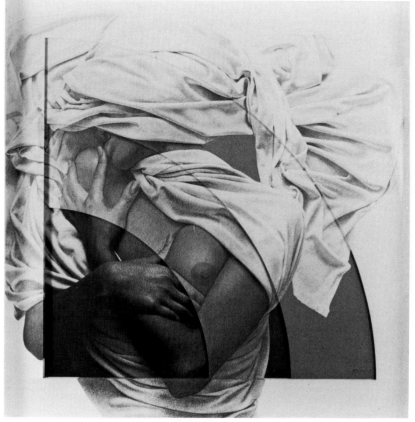

RICHEZ

1

2

3

4

5

1–5 Theatre posters
6 Poster motif for a play ''Ella''

1–5 Theaterplakate
6 Plakatmotiv für das Theaterstück «Ella»

1–5 Affiches de théâtre
6 Motif d'affiche pour la pièce «Ella»

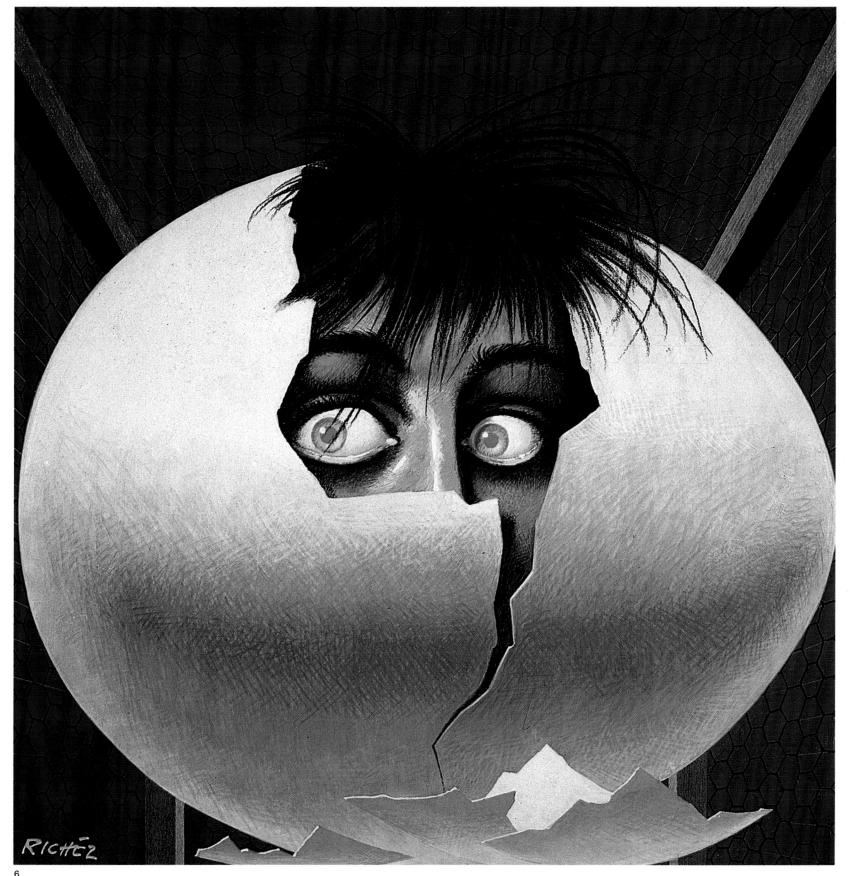

Two views of an exhibition "150 ans à la Une", a panorama of Belgian newspaper printing since 1830

Zwei Ansichten einer Ausstellung «150 ans à la Une», einer Gesamtschau des belgischen Zeitungsdrucks seit 1830

Deux vues de l'exposition «150 ans à la Une», présentant une vue d'ensemble de l'impression de journaux belges depuis 1830

Hainaut
vivant

EXPOSITION
DU 6 JUILLET
AU 21 AOUT 1977
DE 10 A 20 H.
ENTREE LIBRE

PASSAGE 44 / BD BOTANIQUE / BRUXELLES
CREDIT COMMUNAL DE BELGIQUE

RICHEZ

Poster and view of an exhibition "Hainaut vivant" showing the folklore, history, culture and economy of a Belgian province. View of the Folklore section with audio-visual display.

Plakat und Ansicht einer Ausstellung «Hainaut vivant» über Folklore, Geschichte, Kultur und Wirtschaft der belgischen Provinz. Ansicht der Folklore-Sektion mit audio-visuellem Display.

Affiche et vue de l'exposition «Hainaut vivant» présentant le folklore, l'histoire, la culture et l'économie d'une province belge. Vue de la section folklorique avec présentation audio-visuelle.

Henryk Tomaszewski

1914	Born in Warsaw	1914	Geboren in Warschau	1914	Né à Varsovie
1934–39	Studied painting at the Academy of Fine Arts in Warsaw	1934–39	Studium an der Akademie der bildenden Künste in Warschau	1934–39	Etudes de dessin à l'Académie des beaux-arts à Varsovie
1936	Published his first works	1936	Erste Veröffentlichung seiner Arbeiten	1936	Publication de ses premiers travaux
1939	1st Award for the design of the Polish Industrial Pavilion, World Exhibition New York	1939	Erster Preis für die Gestaltung des polnischen Industriepavillons auf der World Exhibition New York	1939	1er prix pour la conception du pavillon industriel polonais, Exposition mondiale à New York
1947	Polish entry in the International UN Competition	1947	Preis für den besten polnischen Beitrag zum internationalen UNO-Wettbewerb	1947	Prix pour la meilleure contribution polonaise au Concours international de l'ONU
1948	1st Prize at the International Poster Exhibition in Vienna	1948	Erster Preis der internationalen Plakatausstellung Wien	1948	1er prix à l'Exposition internationale de l'affiche à Vienne
1948	Award for the best Polish entry in the "Sports in Art" International Competition	1948	Preis für den besten polnischen Beitrag im internationalen Wettbewerb «Sports in Art»	1948	Prix pour la meilleure contribution polonaise au concours international «Les sports dans l'art»
1953	Polish Government National Award	1953	Verleihung des National-Preises durch die polnische Regierung	1953	Prix national du gouvernement polonais
1955	Award of the City of Vienna for the best poster	1955	Preis der Stadt Wien für das beste Plakat	1955	Prix de la Ville de Vienne pour la meilleure affiche
1958	Award of the Polish Prime Minister for illustrations of Children's books	1958	Preis des polnischen Premierministers für die Illustration eines Kinderbuches	1958	Prix du Premier Ministre polonais pour les illustrations d'un livre d'enfant
1958	Member of the Alliance Graphique Internationale	1958	Mitglied der Alliance Graphique Internationale	1958	Membre de l'Alliance Graphique Internationale
1960	Annual Award for satirical drawings	1960	Jahrespreis für Zeichnungen	1960	Prix annuel de dessins satiriques
1963	1st Prize at the 7th Biennale in São Paulo, Brazil	1963	Erster Preis der 7. Biennale in São Paulo, Brasilien	1963	1er prix à la 7e Biennale à São Paulo, Brésil
1965	Gold Medal in Leipzig	1965	Goldmedaille in Leipzig	1965	Médaille d'or à Leipzig
1966	Silver Medal International Poster Biennale in Warsaw	1966	Silbermedaille der internationalen Plakat-Biennale, Warschau	1966	Médaille d'argent à la Biennale internationale de l'affiche à Varsovie
1970	Gold Medal International Poster Biennale in Warsaw	1970	Goldmedaille der internationalen Plakat-Biennale, Warschau	1970	Médaille d'or à la Biennale internationale de l'affiche à Varsovie
1976	Honorary Royal Designer for Industry, Royal Society of Arts, London	1976	Ernennung zum «Honorary Royal Designer für Industry» durch die Royal Society of Arts, London	1976	Nomination comme «Honorary Royal Designer for Industry» par la «Royal Society of Arts», Londres
1979	1st Prize at the 3rd Poster Biennale, Finland	1979	Erster Preis der 3. Plakat-Biennale, Finnland	1979	1er prix à la 3e Biennale de l'affiche, Finlande

Represented in permanent collections of the Museums of: Warsaw; São Paulo; Modern Art, New York; Villa Hügel, Essen; Modern Art, Kamakura, Japan
Since 1952 Professor at the Academy of Fine Arts in Warsaw

Vertreten in folgenden Museumssammlungen: Warschau; São Paulo; Modern Art, New York; Villa Hügel, Essen; Modern Art, Kamakura, Japan
Seit 1952 Professor an der Akademie der bildenden Künste in Warschau

Représenté dans les collections permanentes des musées de: Varsovie; São Paulo; Modern Art, New York; Villa Hügel, Essen; Modern Art, Kamakura, Japon
Depuis 1952, professeur à l'Académie des beaux-arts de Varsovie

Tomaszewski's seemingly playful drawings and paintings, using often minimal means, are the result of deep, long and logically clear thoughts. His articulate verbal explanations and teachings have exercised a great influence on many students in Poland and from other countries during his many years as Professor at the Warsaw Academy. The small motif often rendered in what seems to be the manner of a small child is the result of the sublimated, deep study of an object or a theme which is gradually whittled down to a small significant detail, symbolic, for instance, of a most complex and involved theatrical play which it communicates on the final poster. The detail seen implies the many and varied facets which have been left out in a long and often painful process of elimination.

Tomaszewskis scheinbar spielerische Zeichnungen und Gemälde, oft sehr sparsam in der Verwendung von Ausdrucksmitteln, sind das Ergebnis langer, ausführlicher, logischer und klarer Gedankengänge. Seine artikulierten, verbalen Ausführungen wie sein Unterricht haben einen starken Einfluss auf viele polnische und ausländische Studenten während seiner langjährigen Tätigkeit als Professor der Warschauer Akademie ausgeübt. Ein kleines Motiv, oft den Eindruck gebend, als sei es von einem kleinem Kind ausgeführt, ist das Ergebnis einer vergeistigten, intensiven Studie eines Gegenstandes oder Themas. Dieses wird allmählich zu einem kleinen entscheidenden Detail reduziert, das z.B. symbolisch ein besonders kompliziertes und verworrenes Theaterstück auf dem endgültigen Plakat vermittelt.
Das dargestellte Detail beinhaltet die vielen verschiedenen Aspekte, die in einem langwierigen und schmerzhaften Prozess der Eliminierung ausgelassen wurden.

Les dessins et peintures de Tomaszewski, d'une simplicité enjouée et très souvent réalisées avec une grande sobriété dans les moyens d'expression, sont le résultat de réflexions profondes et logiques. Les considérations et l'enseignement de Tomaszewski comme professeur à l'Académie de Varsovie pendant de longues années ont trouvé un vaste écho auprès de nombreux étudiants polonais et étrangers. Un petit motif, rendu à la manière d'un enfant, est le résultat de l'étude intense et sublime d'un objet ou sujet que l'artiste épure graduellement, jusqu'à obtenir un petit détail expressif, qui prend valeur de symbole pour annoncer, par exemple, une pièce de théâtre hautement complexe et différenciée sur une affiche publicitaire. Le détail représenté implique les multiples facettes qui ont été élaguées dans le cours d'un long et pénible processus d'élimination.

1 Poster "Marionette"
2 Poster for Circus
3 Poster for Exhibition "Belgian Belle Epoque"

1 Plakat «Marionette»
2 Zirkusplakat
3 Ausstellungsplakat «Belgian Belle Epoque»

1 Affiche «Marionette»
2 Affiche pour «Le cirque»
3 Affiche pour l'exposition «La Belle Epoque belge»

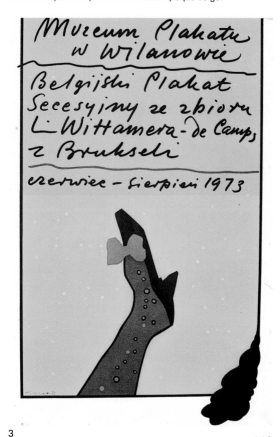

1

2

3

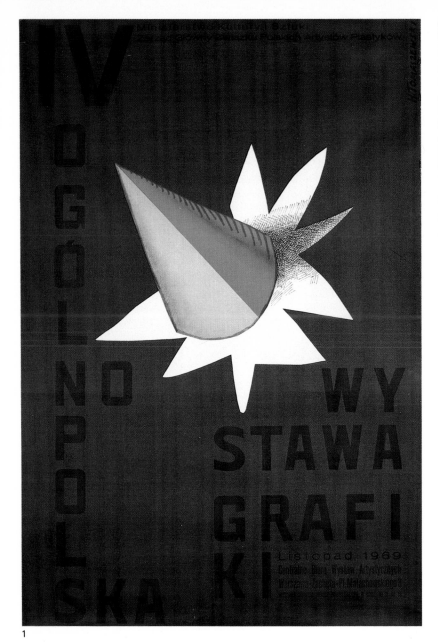

1 Poster "Wystawa Grafiki"
2 Poster "Jazz Jamboree"

1 Plakat «Wystawa Grafiki»
2 Plakat «Jazz Jamboree»

1 Affiche «Wystawa Grafiki»
2 Affiche «Jamboree de jazz»

144

3

4

3 Poster "Police"
4 Theatre poster "Pamietnik Szubrawca"

3 Plakat «Police»
4 Theaterplakat «Pamietnik Szubrawca»

3 Affiche «La police»
4 Affiche de théâtre «Pamietnik Szubrawca»

1

2

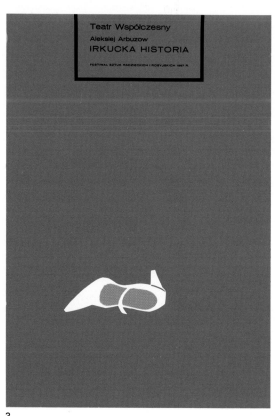

3

1 Theatre poster "Napoleon"
2 Theatre poster "Amadeus"
3 Theatre poster "The History of Irkutsk"

1 Theaterplakat «Napoleon»
2 Theaterplakat «Amadeus»
3 Theaterplakat «The History of Irkutsk»

1 Affiche de théâtre «Napoléon»
2 Affiche de théâtre «Amadeus»
3 Affiche de théâtre «L'histoire d'Irkoutsk»

1

2

1 Poster "Witkacy"
2 Theatre poster "Hadrian VII"

1 Plakat «Witkacy»
2 Theaterplakat für «Hadrian VII.»

1 Affiche «Witkacy»
2 Affiche de théâtre «Hadrian VII»

1

2

3

4

1 Poster "Johann Strauss"
2 Theatre poster "M. Gorki 'Barbars'"
3 Poster "Ladies and Hussars"
4 Poster for the Theater of Nations

1 Plakat «Johann Strauss»
2 Theaterplakat «M. Gorki ‹Barbars›»
3 Plakat «Damen und Husaren»
4 Plakat für das Theater der Nationen

1 Affiche «Johann Strauss»
2 Affiche de théâtre «M. Gorki ‹Barbars›»
3 Affiche «Dames et hussards»
4 Affiche pour le Théâtre des Nations

Theater poster "Julius Caesar"
Theaterplakat «Julius Caesar»
Affiche de théâtre «Julius Caesar»

Wolfgang Weingart

Born 1941. Apprenticed as typesetter. 1968 Instructor in typography at Kunstgewerbeschule, Basel, Switzerland. Collaborator on "Typographische Monatsblätter". Founder of Periodika "TM/communication". Lecturer in Switzerland and USA. Instructor in typography at Summer courses in Brissago. Articles in many international professional publications. 1980 "Projects", book published by Niggli on his teaching results at Basel. Prizes for book jackets and posters from Swiss Ministry of Interior. Weingart is a self taught educator and designer. He is a member of the "Alliance Graphique Internationale" (AGI).

One of his former students writes:
Wolfgang Weingart is part of a diminishing breed of graphic designers who have first been trained in the mechanics of their profession, before making it their art. It is his roots in the tradition and discipline of hand-set typography, which he learned as an apprentice, that have enabled him to successfully take on the challenge of the unruly world of millimeter grids and ultra-fast typesetting machines. Furthermore, few typographers have been able to combine the type case with the reproduction camera — the typographic with the photographic — as he has done. The careful observer will find even in Weingart's wildest and most explosive images an order, structure, and simplicity indicative of the skillful typographer. This combined with a boundless fantasy, the courage to do the unpredictable and unthinkable, and the craftsmanship to make it work, have resulted in the originality and richness of his work, making it impossible to imitate. What motivates him to push ideas to their limit is a strong aversion to inconsequent, unprofessional, and anemic design in the world. He never leaves anything to speculation or chance, and will pursue an idea until he is sure if it works or

Geboren 1941, lernte das Handwerk des Schriftsetzers. Seit 1968 Lehrer für Typografie an der Kunstgewerbeschule (Schule für Gestaltung) in Basel, Schweiz. Mitarbeiter der «Typographischen Monatsblätter» und Begründer der Periodika «TM/communication». Vorträge seiner Lehrmethodik in der Schweiz, BRD und den USA. Unterrichtet in den letzten Jahren das Fach Typografie während der Brissago-Sommerkurse. Veröffentlichungen in der internationalen Fachpresse. 1980 erschien im Arthur-Niggli-Verlag das Buch «Projekte» mit Ergebnissen aus dem Typografie-Unterricht in Basel. Seine Buchumschläge und Plakate wurden vom Eidgenössischen Departement des Innern in Bern ausgezeichnet. Weingart ist Mitglied der «Alliance Graphique Internationale» (AGI). Als Lehrer und Gestalter Autodidakt.

Einer seiner früheren Studenten schreibt:
Wolfgang Weingart gehört zu den wenigen Gestaltern, die erst in der Technik des Berufs ausgebildet wurden, den sie dann zu ihrer Kunst machten. Nachdem er als Lehrling die traditionelle Disziplin des Handsatzes erlernt hatte, war es ihm möglich, sich in der ungeordneten Welt des Millimeter-Rasters und der ultraschnellen Setzmaschine durchzusetzen. Wenigen Typografen gelang es wie ihm, den Setzkasten mit der Reproduktionskamera, Typografie und Fotografie, zu kombinieren. Selbst in den wildesten und explosivsten Bildern kann ein aufmerksamer Betrachter die Ordnung, Struktur und Einfachheit, so typisch für einen erfahrenen geschickten Typografen, erkennen. Diese Kombination von endloser Fantasie und dem Mut, Unvorhersehbares und Unerdenkbares zu wagen, wie auch die handwerkliche Fähigkeit, es zu realisieren, machen seine Arbeiten so vielseitig und originell und deswegen unnachahmbar. Seine Motivation, seine Ideen zur äussersten Grenze auszuarbeiten, ist bedingt durch seine Abneigung gegenüber allen inkonsequenten, nicht durchdachten, blassen Design-Lösungen in dieser Welt. Nichts überlässt er dem Zufall oder der Spekulation. Er verfolgt seine

Né en 1941. Apprentissage de compositeur. En 1968, enseignement en typographie à l'Ecole des arts et métiers de Bâle, Suisse. Collaborateur de la «Revue suisse de l'imprimerie». Fondateur du périodique «TM/communication». Chargé de cours en Suisse, Allemagne et aux Etats-Unis. Enseignement de la typographie dans des cours d'été à Brissago. Nombreuses publications dans la presse professionnelle internationale. En 1980, publication de «Projets» aux Editions Niggli sur son enseignement de la typographie à Bâle. Divers prix lui ont été décernés pour ses couvertures de livres et affiches par le Département fédéral de l'intérieur à Berne.

Un de ses anciens étudiants écrit:
Wolfgang Weingart appartient à cette minorité de dessinateurs qui ont reçu d'abord une formation technique, dont ils tirent ensuite leur art. Après avoir appris en Allemagne, pendant son apprentissage, la discipline traditionnelle de la composition manuelle, il a pu s'imposer dans le monde désordonné de la trame millimétrée et de la composeuse ultra-rapide. Peu de typographes ont su, comme lui, combiner la casse et la caméra, la typographie et la photographie. Même dans ses tableaux les plus violents et explosifs, l'observateur attentif reconnaîtra ordre, structure et simplicité, les caractéristiques d'un typographe habile et expérimenté. Ces mariages d'imagination débridée et de courage de l'imprévisible et de l'impensable avec la capacité manuelle de la réalisation rendent ses œuvres extrêmement variées et originales, donc inimitables. Sa motivation de développer ses idées jusqu'à la limite découle de son dégoût pour toutes les solutions graphiques de ce monde qui ne sont pas poussées jusqu'au bout de leur logique. Rien n'est laissé au hasard ou à la spéculation. Il s'attache à ses idées tant qu'il n'a pas découvert si elles sont réalisables ou non. Comme jadis Gutenberg, il réa-

not. Like Gutenberg, once did, Weingart realizes his publications or poster designs from beginning to end, by himself. He chooses to be involved in the entire process, from the concept through and including the preparation of the film montage for the printer. One reason for this is that he finds new directions by doing the work himself. When looking through the copy camera, or while developing film, new ideas and possibilities become evident. In this way, even mistakes open ways to other fascinating possibilities of visual expression. Another reason for working on his own is that he dislikes giving orders to other people, preferring instead to be in direct control and creatively involved each step of the way. To the dismay of printers, he will follow his work from the printing-room, to the cutting machine, to the bindery.

Fortunately, his clients are not "hard" clients because they do not dictate to the designer what they want. Instead, they come to him knowing what to expect; and expecting something special! Thus each new project is a challenge to his design reputation, as well as an opportunity for experimentation and learning. He takes the risk, makes the extra effort, and so far has continuously startled and surprised us with his typography. The leitmotif for Weingart the Designer, and Weingart the Teacher, is best expressed in his own words regarding his teaching activity at the School of Design Basel: "What we need today are personalities who, through their own personal effort, can influence the development of typography, and who, with fantasy and intelligence, can make responsible typographic contributions to the foundation of the environment."

The demands he places on his students and on himself in striving to produce quality typography are both frustrating and infuriating, yet at the same time admirable and invigorating. The reason for this being his constant reminder to us: "To make quality today is hard work."

Ideen, bis er herausgefunden hat, ob sie durchführbar sind oder nicht. Wie einst Gutenberg führt er seine Veröffentlichungen und Plakate immer selbst aus. Er zieht es vor, am ganzen Prozess beteiligt zu sein, vom Konzept bis zur Vorbereitung der Filmmontage für den Drucker. Ein Grund dafür ist, dass er bei eigener Ausführung oft auf neue Möglichkeiten stösst. Während er durch die Reprokamera blickt oder einen Film entwickelt, bieten sich ihm neue Ideen und Möglichkeiten. Auf diese Weise zeigen sogar Fehler manchmal neue Wege und faszinierende Möglichkeiten visuellen Ausdrucks. Ein weiterer Grund, alles selbst zu machen, ist seine Abneigung, anderen Anweisungen zu geben. Er zieht es vor, selbst alles zu kontrollieren und sich an jedem weiteren kreativen Schritt zu beteiligen. Zum Ärger aller Drucker verfolgt er seine Arbeiten von der Druckerei zur Schneidemaschine bis zur Buchbinderei. Glücklicherweise hat er keine schwierigen Kunden, die vorschreiben, was sie wollen. Sie kommen zu ihm, weil sie wissen, was sie von ihm erwarten, nämlich etwas Aussergewöhnliches. So ist jede neue Aufgabe sowohl eine Herausforderung an seinen Ruf als Gestalter wie auch eine Gelegenheit zum Experimentieren und Lernen. Er riskiert, gibt sich extra Mühe, und bisher hat er uns mit seiner Typografie laufend erstaunt und überrascht. Weingarts Leitmotiv als Gestalter und Lehrer ist am besten von ihm selbst an der Schule für Gestaltung Basel ausgedrückt worden: «Wir brauchen heute Individuen, die durch ihren persönlichen Einsatz die Entwicklung der Typografie beeinflussen können und mit Fantasie und Intelligenz verantwortungsvolle typografische Beiträge zur Umwelt leisten.» Die Anforderungen gegenüber sich und seinen Studenten für hohe Qualität in der Typografie sind sowohl frustrierend und irritierend, jedoch bewundernswert und erfrischend. Deshalb macht er uns auch ständig neu klar: «Qualität zu erreichen ist heutzutage harte Arbeit.»

lise toujours lui-même ses publications et ses affiches. Il préfère participer à toute l'élaboration, de la conception au montage du film pour l'imprimeur. L'une des raisons en est que, dans ce processus, il rencontre souvent de nouvelles possibilités. Pendant qu'il regarde à travers la caméra ou qu'il développe un film, de nouvelles perspectives se présentent à lui. Même les erreurs ouvrent ainsi parfois de nouvelles voies à une fascinante expression visuelle. Mais s'il fait tout lui-même, c'est encore parce qu'il n'aime pas donner des directives aux autres, préférant tout contrôler et effectuer chaque pas de la démarche créatrice. Au grand déplaisir des imprimeurs, il suit ses œuvres de l'impression à la coupe et à la reliure. Par bonheur, il n'a pas de clients difficiles, qui lui imposent leurs vues. Ils viennent à lui parce qu'ils savent ce qu'ils attendent de son talent: un produit sortant de l'ordinaire. Ainsi toute nouvelle commande est-elle à la fois un défi à sa réputation et une occasion d'expérimenter et d'apprendre. Il prend des risques et ne ménage pas sa peine; sa typographie nous étonne et nous surprend sans cesse. Sa démarche en tant que dessinateur et professeur, c'est lui-même qui l'a le mieux définie à l'Ecole des arts et métiers de Bâle: «Aujourd'hui, il nous faut des personnalités dont l'engagement puisse influencer l'évolution de la typographie, dont l'imagination et l'intelligence fournissent une contribution typographique en pleine responsabilité de l'environnement.» L'exigence d'une haute qualité typographique de la part de ses élèves et de soi-même est à la fois frustrante et irritante, mais aussi merveilleuse et rafraîchissante. Elle nous oblige à redécouvrir chaque jour que: «La recherche de la qualité est désormais une tâche ardue.»

Catalogue cover (page 1 and 4) "The Art of Writing" Kunstgewerbemuseum Zurich

Katalog-Umschlag (4. und 1. Seite) «Schreibkunst». Kunstgewerbemuseum Zürich

Couverture de catalogue (4e et 1re page) «Schreibkunst». Musée cantonal des beaux-arts et d'art appliqué Zurich

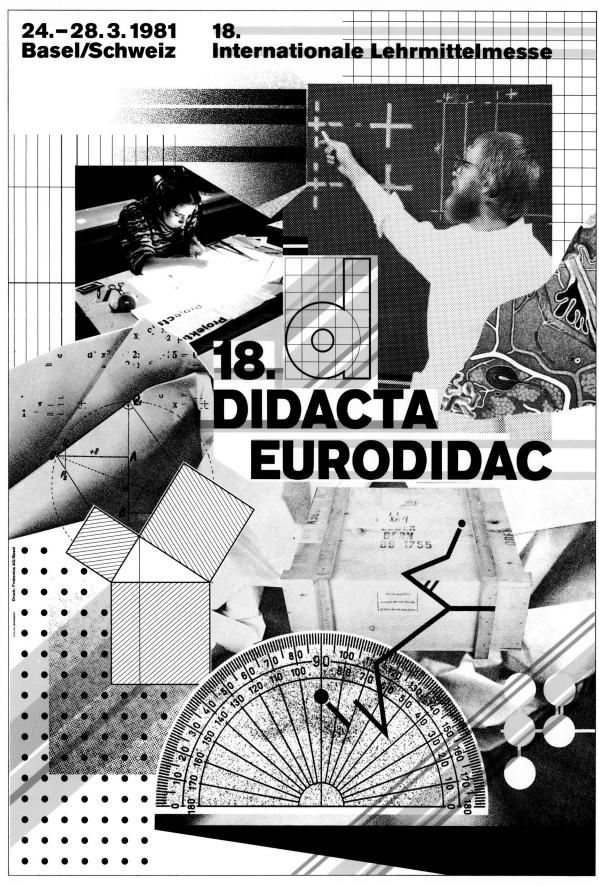

24.–28.3.1981
Basel/Schweiz

18.
Internationale Lehrmittelmesse

18.
d
DIDACTA
EURODIDAC

Druck: Frobenius AG/Basel

DESIGN WEINGART

Poster "Didacta/Eurodidac", the 18th international fair for Educational Media, held in connection with the Swiss Industries Fair Basle

Plakat «Didacta/Eurodidac». 18. Internationale Lehrmittelmesse in Verbindung mit der Schweizer Mustermesse Basel

Affiche «Didacta/Eurodidac». 18e Foire Internationale de Matériel Didactique en liaison avec la Foire Suisse d'Echantillons Bâle

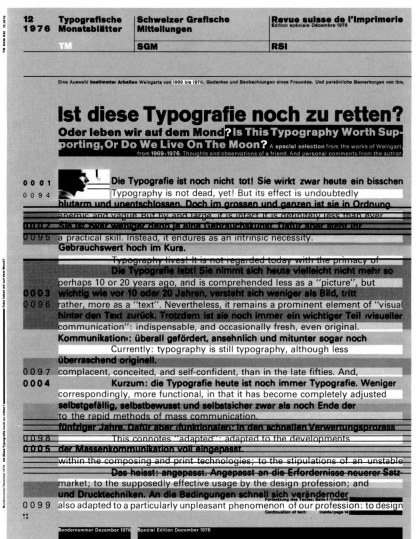

12 1976 Typografische Monatsblätter | Schweizer Grafische Mittelungen | Revue suisse de l'imprimerie Édition spéciale Décembre 1976

TM | SGM | RSI

Eine Auswahl bestimmter Arbeiten Weingarts von 1969 bis 1976. Gedanken und Beobachtungen eines Freundes. Und persönliche Bemerkungen von ihm.

Ist diese Typografie noch zu retten?

Oder leben wir auf dem Mond? Is This Typography Worth Supporting, Or Do We Live On The Moon? A special selection from the works of Weingart, from 1969-1976. Thoughts and observations of a friend. And personal comments from the author.

0001 | **Die Typografie ist noch nicht tot! Sie wirkt zwar heute ein bisschen**
0094 | Typography is not dead, yet! But its effect is undoubtedly
blutarm und unentschlossen. Doch im grossen und ganzen ist sie in Ordnung.
anemic and vague. But by and large, it is intact. It is definitely less than ever
0002 | Sie ist zwar weniger denn je eine Gebrauchskunst. Dafür aber steht ihr
0095 | a practical skill. Instead, it endures as an intrinsic necessity.
Gebrauchswert hoch im Kurs.
Typography lives! It is not regarded today with the primacy of
Die Typografie lebt! Sie nimmt sich heute vielleicht nicht mehr so
perhaps 10 or 20 years ago, and is comprehended less as a "picture", but
0003 | wichtig wie vor 10 oder 20 Jahren, versteht sich weniger als Bild, tritt
0096 | rather, more as a "text". Nevertheless, it remains a prominent element of "visual
hinter den Text zurück. Trotzdem ist sie noch immer ein wichtiger Teil «visueller
communication": indispensable, and occasionally fresh, even original.
Kommunikation»: überall gefördert, ansehnlich und mitunter sogar noch
Currently: typography is still typography, although less
überraschend originell.
0097 | complacent, conceited, and self-confident, than in the late fifties. And,
0004 | **Kurzum: die Typografie heute ist noch immer Typografie. Weniger**
correspondingly, more functional, in that it has become completely adjusted
selbstgefällig, selbstbewusst und selbstsicher zwar als noch Ende der
to the rapid methods of mass communication.
fünfziger Jahre. Dafür aber «funktionaler» in den schnellen Verwertungsprozess
0098 | This connotes "adapted": adapted to the developments
0005 | **der Massenkommunikation voll eingepasst.**
within the composing and print technologies; to the stipulations of an unstable
Das heisst: angepasst. Angepasst an die Erfordernisse neuerer Satz
market; to the supposedly effective usage by the design profession; and
und Drucktechniken. An die Bedingungen schnell sich verändernder
0099 | also adapted to a particularly unpleasant phenomenon of our profession: to design

Fortsetzung des Textes: Seite 4 /innenteil
Continuation of text: inside/page 14

Sondernummer Dezember 1976 Special Edition December 1976

1

2

1
Cover for the magazine "Typographische Monatsblätter", St. Gallen
2
Cover for "Idea" magazine; comments by Weingart:
"I have never been to Japan. I know it only from books and photographs. I know some excellent films from this land that is so mysterious to me. I know that there the sun rises earlier than here in Switzerland. I know that there exists a wonderful mountain whose top is powdered with snow and whose blossoms must be enchanting. And I know that these diligent people live with the constant threat of earthquakes. All this that I have said, I have tried to put on paper from fantasy which has perhaps nothing to do with the reality of this country."

1
Schutzumschlag für die Zeitschrift «Typographische Monatsblätter», St. Gallen
2
Schutzumschlag für die japanische Zeitschrift «Idea», Tokio.
Persönliche Bemerkungen von Wolfgang Weingart zum Schutzumschlag «Idea»: «Ich kenne Japan nur von Fotografien und aus hervorragenden Filmen. Ich weiss, dass die Sonne dort früher aufgeht als in der Schweiz. Und weiss, dass es dort einen wunderbaren Berg mit einem immer schneebedeckten Gipfel und bezaubernden Blüten gibt. Und dass dieses emsige Volk von Erdbeben bedroht wird. All diese Vorstellungen habe ich versucht aufs Papier zu bringen, und vielleicht haben diese persönlichen Vorstellungen gar nichts mehr mit der Wirklichkeit dieses Landes zu tun.»

1
Jaquette pour la «Revue suisse de l'imprimerie», St-Gall
2
Jaquette pour le magazine japonais «Idea», Tokyo.
Remarques personnelles de Wolfgang Weingart concernant la jaquette «Idea»: «Je n'ai jamais été au Japon. Je connais ce pays uniquement par les livres et les photographies. Je connais également quelques films de ce pays qui me paraît si mystérieux. Je sais que là-bas le soleil se lève plus tôt qu'en Suisse. Je sais qu'il y a une merveilleuse montagne au sommet saupoudré de neige, et des fleurs enchanteresses. Je sais aussi que ce peuple diligent vit dans la peur constante des tremblements de terre. Tout cela, j'ai essayé de le reproduire sur papier à partir des représentations puisées dans mon imagination: peut-être n'ont-elles rien de commun avec la réalité japonaise.»

Art 11'80
in den Hallen der Schweizer Mustermesse Basel/Schweiz

· **Die
internationale Kunstmesse**
Kunst des 20. Jahrhunderts, Kunstbücher

· **Le
Salon international d'Art**
Art du 20e siècle, livres d'art

· **The
international Art Fair**
20th Century Art, Art Books

12.–17. Juni
1980 · **La
Mostra internazionale d'Arte**
Arte del 20° secolo, libri d'arte

Basel/Schweiz

1

Register zum Inhalt	Contents' Register		Ausstellerverzeichnis **1**
Points de repère	Rubriche del contenuto		Répertoire des exposants
			Index of Exhibitors
			Elenco degli espositori
			Künstlerverzeichnis **2**
			Répertoire des artistes
			Index of Artists
			Elenco degli artisti
			Bildseiten **3**
			Pages illustrées
			Illustrated pages
			Pagine illustrate
			Nachtrag **4**
			Supplément
			Supplement
			Supplemento

2

| Ausstellerbeirat | Exhibitors' Advisory Board |
| Conseil consultatif des exposants | Comitato di espositori |

Titelseite	Schweizer Mustermesse Basel
Typografische Konzeption	W. Weingart/Basel
Layout Bildteil	Aldo Codoni/Basel
Photolithos	Schwitter AG/Basel
Satz und Druck	Gustav Glaser, Offsetdruck/Basel
Einband	Buchbinderei Grollimund AG/Reinach BL

Sekretariat
Internationale Kunstmesse Basel CH-4021 Basel
Art 11'80 Telefon 061-26 20 20
p.A. Schweizer Mustermesse Telex 62 685 fairs ch

Schweiz	Dr. Peter Lotz	Vorsitz	Basel
	Ernst Beyeler	Galerie Beyeler	Basel
	Trudl Bruckner	Galerie Riehentor	Basel
	Pablo Stähli	Galerie Stähli	Zürich
	Willy Jäggi (Bücher)	Buchhandlung Jäggi	Basel
Deutschland	Kenda Bargera	Galerie Bargera	Köln
	Folker Skulima	Galerie Skulima	Berlin
	Hartmut Stöcker	Galerie Art in Progress	München
Italien	Lucio Amelio	Modern Art Agency	Napoli
Spanien	Juana de Mordó	Galerie Juana de Mordó	Madrid
Frankreich	Denise René	Galerie Denise René	Paris
	Karl Flinker	Galerie Flinker	Paris
Holland	Will Hoogstraate	Galerie d'Eendt	Amsterdam
Belgien	Isy Brachot	Galerie Isy Brachot	Bruxelles
Grossbritannien	Annely Juda	Annely Juda Fine Art	London
Österreich	John Sailer	Galerie Ulysses	Wien
Amerika, Canada,	Robert Elkon	Robert Elkon Gallery	New York
Südamerika	Leo Castelli	Gallery Leo Castelli	New York
Israel	Herbert Goldman	Goldman's Art Gallery	Haifa
Korrespondierendes Mitglied	André Emmerich	Gimpel-Hanover & André Emmerich Galerien	Zürich, London, New York

Schadenersatz für fehlerhafte, unvollständige
oder nicht erfolgte Eintragungen und Anzeigen ist ausgeschlossen.
Für den Inhalt der Eintragungen und Anzeigen ist der Aussteller
als Auftraggeber verantwortlich.

© Art
Internationale Kunstmesse Basel

Dr. F. Walthard	Präsident Art 11'80 Generaldirektor Schweizer Mustermesse Basel	Basel
G. E. Kindhauser	Kaufmänischer Direktor Schweizer Mustermesse Basel	Basel
Dr. E. M. Bammatter	Vizedirektor Schweizer Mustermesse Basel	Basel
Anita Keagi	Sekretariat Art 11'80 Schweizer Mustermesse Basel	Basel

3

| Vorwort | Avant-propos | Foreword | Prefazione |

F. Walthard
Präsident der Art 11'80
Generaldirektor der Schweizer Mustermesse

F. Walthard
Président d'Art 11'80
Directeur général de la Foire Suisse d'Echantillons

F. Walthard
President of Art 11'80
Director General of the Swiss Industries Fair

F. Walthard
Presidente dell'Art 11'80
Direttore generale della Fiera Campionaria Svizzera

Mit der Art 11'80 hat für die Basler Kunstmesse
das zweite Jahrzehnt ihres Bestehens begonnen.
Voll Optimismus kann sie zusammen mit den
Ausstellern und dem weiten internationalen Kreis von
Kunstfreunden in die Zukunft blicken, denn sie hat
den inneren Schwung und die Beweglichkeit für notwendige Anpassungen bewahrt und so im Verlaufe der
Jahre dank der wachsenden Erfahrung und ihrem Erfolg
ständig an Anziehungskraft gewonnen. Besonders
erfreulich ist in diesem Jahr, dass neben den alteingesessenen Galerien – denen bei dieser Gelegenheit
für ihre langjährige Treue gedankt sei – auch viele ehemalige Aussteller den Weg wieder zurückgefunden
haben und dass zudem der anhaltend rege Andrang bei
den neuen Bewerbern eine besonders grosse Auswahl erstklassiger Galerien ermöglicht hat. Diese positive
Bilanz spiegelt die Bedeutung wider, die der Kunstmessen – allen voran der Art – heute ganz allgemein
beigemessen wird, sie zeigt aber auch, wie sehr es
dieser verhältnismässig jungen Form der Kunstvermittlung
gelungen ist, sich neben den traditionellen Trägern
durchzusetzen und von der Kunstwelt international anerkannt zu werden.
Zu Beginn des nun vor uns liegenden Jahrzehnts
tritt die Art mit umgestaltetem Plakat und Katalog
in äusserlich neuem Gewand in Erscheinung. Durch zahlreiche Ergänzungen und Hinweise hat der Katalog
an Übersichtlichkeit gewonnen, verschiedene grafische
Neuerungen erhöhen zudem seine Lesefreundlichkeit.
Damit steigt sein Wert, sei es als Nachschlagverzeichnis
der aktuellen Kunstszene, sei es zur Vorbereitung
der Messe oder als informativer Messebegleiter, oder
nicht zuletzt als gewichtiges Sammelstück des jährlichen Kunstereignisses in Basel. Wir wünschen ihm deshalb wie in vergangenen Jahren eine gute Aufnahme
und eine möglichst weite Verbreitung.

Avec Art 11'80, le Salon bâlois des arts entre
dans la seconde décennie de son existence.
Et c'est plein d'optimisme, qu'il peut tourner son
regard vers l'avenir, de même que les exposants et
le vaste cercle international des amis des arts, car il a su
conserver au cours des années son élan et sa capacité d'adaptation, grâce à l'expérience acquise, sa force
d'attraction ne cessant de croître avec son succès.
Il est particulièrement réjouissant de constater, cette
année, qu'en plus des galeries habituelles – que
nous tenons à remercier de leur longue fidélité – nombre
d'anciens exposants ont retrouvé le chemin de notre
manifestation, sans parler de tous les nouveaux venus
qui nous permettent de présenter un choix remarquablement élevé de galeries de premier ordre. Ce bilan
positif montre bien l'importance attribuée aujourd'hui
aux salons d'art – et spécialement à Art –, mais aussi
que cette forme de diffusion artistique encore relativement jeune est parvenue à s'affirmer à côté des manifestations traditionnelles et à se faire reconnaître,
à l'échelon international, par tout le monde des arts.
À l'aube de cette nouvelle décennie, Art se présente avec une affiche et un catalogue modifiés,
autrement dit sous un nouvel aspect. Le catalogue, grâce
à de nombreux compléments et à diverses innovations graphiques, est devenu plus clair et plus agréable
à consulter. Sa valeur a donc augmenté d'autant,
que ce soit comme rappel des tendances artistiques
actuelles, pour préparer et accompagner la visite
du Salon, et surtout comme pièce de collection rappelant
le grand événement artistique annuel de Bâle. Nous
lui souhaitons donc, comme ces dernières années, un
bon accueil et une large diffusion.

With Art 11'80, the second decade of existence
has begun for the Basle Art Fair. It can,
together with the exhibitors and the wide international circle of art lovers, look into the future
full of optimism, for it has retained its inner verve and
the flexibility for necessary adjustments, and over
the years its power of attraction has thus continuously
grown thanks to increased experience and to its
success. This year it is particularly gratifying that apart
from old-established galleries – to whom thanks are
given here for their many years of loyalty – many former
exhibitors have again found the way back, and
that in addition the continued lively interest from new
applicants has made a particularly large selection
of first-class galleries possible. This positive outcome
reflects the importance generally attached to the
art fairs – above all to Art – but it also shows just how
much this relatively young form of presentation
has succeeded in prevailing next to the traditional media,
and in becoming internationally recognized in the
art world.
At the start of the decade that lies before us, Art
is appearing in a new costume with a redesigned
poster and catalogue. With numerous supplements and
references, the catalogue has gained in clarity,
various graphic innovations also increase its readability.
Its value thus increases, either as a work of reference
for the contemporary art scene, or for preparing the Fair,
or as an informative guide to the Fair or, last but
not least, as an important compendium of the annual art
event in Basle. As in previous years, we therefore
hope that it will be well received and widely distributed.

Con l'Art 11'80 ha inizio per la Mostra d'arte di
Basilea il secondo decennio della sua esistenza.
Insieme agli espositori e alla vasta cerchia
internazionale di amici dell'arte, essa può guardare al
futuro piena d'ottimismo, avendo conservato integri
lo slancio interiore e le necessarie capacità di adattamento
ed avendo in tal modo nel corso degli anni accresciuto costantemente la sua forza d'attrazione grazie
all'esperienza accumulata e al continuo successo.
Quest'anno, motivo di particolare soddisfazione è dato
dal fatto che accanto alle gallerie che ormai sono
di casa – cogliamo l'occasione per rivolgere loro il nostro
ringraziamento per la loro lunga fedeltà - abbiano
ritrovato la strada per la Mostra molti espositori dei primi
tempi ed inoltre che la crescente richiesta di nuove
partecipazioni abbia reso possibile in particolare una
grande scelta di gallerie di prim'ordine. Questo
positivo bilancio non solo rispecchia l'importanza che
oggi vanno assumendo in generale le mostre d'arte
– prime tra tutte l'Art – ma fa vedere anche come a
questa relativamente giovane forma di mercato
d'arte sia riuscita ad imporsi in mezzo alle tradizionali
manifestazioni e ad avere il riconoscimento e l'apprezzamento in campo internazionale da parte del mondo
artistico.
All'inizio del nuovo decennio, con un diverso tipo
di manifesto e di catalogo l'Art si presenta in una
veste esteriore nuova. Il catalogo ha una forma più chiara
grazie alle numerose delucidazioni e integrazioni
apportate, mentre le diverse novità grafiche aumentano
il piacere della sua lettura. In tal modo cresce anche
il suo valore intrinseco, sia come opera di consultazione
in merito ai fatti artistici d'attualità, sia come preparazione alla visita della Mostra o come guida informativa durante la Mostra, o ancora come raccolta di
grande rilievo a testimonianza dell'annuale manifestazione
artistica di Basilea. Per questo ci auguriamo come
negli anni passati una buona accoglienza e una vasta
diffusione.

4

Official Information

L'autenticità l'originalità delle opere esposte sono garantite dall'espositore.

Informazioni generali

The exhibitor guarantees the exhibits are genuine works and by the artists to whom they are attributed.

Duration of the Fair	12-17 June 1980	Durata della Mostra	Dal 12 al 17 giugno 1980
Place	Halle 10-17, 20 of the Swiss Industries Fair, Basle	Luogo	Padiglioni 10-17, 20 della Fiera Campionaria Svizzera, Basilea
Opening hours	10 a.m. until 8 p.m.	Orario d'apertura	Tutti giorni dalle ore 10 alle 20
Entrance Tickets	Day ticket SFr. 6.- (one admission), day ticket SFr. 9.- (several admissions on one day and one admission into KAM), permanent pass SFr. 25.-, evening ticket from 5.00 p.m. SFr. 4.- (one admission), schoolchildren and students (on presentation of legitimation card) SFr. 4.- (one admission), guided school classes SFr. 2.- per person (one admission).	Biglietti d'ingresso	Biglietto giornaliero Fr. 6.- (un solo ingresso), biglietto giornaliero Fr. 9.- (più ingressi nello stesso giorno e un solo ingresso alla KAM), tessera permanente Fr. 25.-, biglietto serale a partire dalle ore 17.00 Fr. 4.- (un solo ingresso), scolari e studenti (dietro presentazione della carta d'identità) Fr. 4.- (un solo ingresso), visite guidate di scolaresche a persona Fr. 2.- (un solo ingresso).
Information	Hall 10, phone 061-26 20 20, telex 62 685 fairs ch	Informazioni	Padiglione 10, telefono 061-26 20 20, telex 62 685 fairs ch
Cloakroom	In front of Entrance hall 10	Guardaroba	Davanti del padiglione 10
Bank-Change	Swiss Bank Corporation, hall 10, phone 061-26 74 04	Banca-Cambio	Società di Banca Svizzera, padiglione 10, telefono 061-26 74 04
Air Travel Service	Swissair, Passengers flight reservation, phone 061-22 54 90 / Booking office at the fair, hall 10, phone 061-26 33 44	Servizio viaggi aerei	Swissair, Riservazione passaggeri unicamente, telefono 061-22 54 90 / Sportello alla fiera, padiglione 10, telefono 061-26 33 44
Rail-way Information	SBB, hall 24, phone 061-26 10 10	Corrispondenze ferroviarie	FFS, padiglione 24, telefono 061-26 10 10
Rent-a-Car Service	Avis Rent-a-Car, hall 10, Telefon 061-26 90 30	Noleggio auto	Avis Rent-a-Car, padiglione 10, telefono 061-26 90 30
Forwarding Agents	Danzas AG, Basle, hall 10, phone 061-26 50 35/36 / MAT Transport AG, Basle, hall 10, phone 061-26 74 01/02/03, telex 64 770 / Roba AG, Basle, hall 10, phone 061-26 74 05/06/07, telex 64 780	Spedizionieri	Danzas SA, Basilea, padiglione 10, telefono 061-26 50 35/36 / MAT Trasporti SA, Basilea, padiglione 10, telefono 061-26 74 01/02/03, telex 64 770 / Roba SA, Basilea, padiglione 10, telefono 061-26 74 05/06/07, telex 64 780
Customs Office	Hall 10, phone 061-26 77 24	Ufficio doganale	Padiglione 10, telefono 061-26 77 24
Accommodation	Central Accommodation Office Basle, CH-4021 Basle, phone 061-26 77 00, telex 62 982 fits ch / During the Fair in the Art Building	Alloggiamento	Ufficio centrale di alloggi, CH-4021 Basilea, telefono 061-26 77 00, telex 62 982 fits ch / Durante la Mostra nell'edificio d'Art
First-aid post	Hall 13, phone 061-26 20 20, int. 388	Servizio sanitario	Padiglione 13, telefono 061-26 20 20, int. 388
Post, telephone, telegraph, telex	Post Office Basle 21, Entrance from Fair Square, phone 061-26 30 30 and counter in hall 10 (also on Saturday/Sunday)	Posta, telefono, telegrafo, telex	Ufficio postale Basilea 21, ingresso piazzale della Fiera, telefono 061-26 30 30 E sportelli nel padiglione 10 (aperti anche sabato/domenica)
Kindergarten	Hall 20, open daily from 2 p.m.-6 p.m., phone 061-26 20 20	Giardino d'infanzia	Padiglione 20, aperto tutti giorni dalle ore 14 alle 18, telefono 061-26 20 20
Restaurants	Building C: / Treize Etoiles, hall 11, phone 061-26 72 71 / Art-Restaurant, hall 12, phone 061-26 73 05 / Coffee Shop, hall 16, phone 061-26 48 97 / Café Boulevard, court yard, phone 061-26 73 05 / Building A: / Mustermesse-Restaurant with Grillroom and Rôtisserie, phone 061-32 76 50	Ristoranti	Edificio C: / Treize Etoiles, padiglione 11, telefono 061-26 72 71 / Art-Ristorante, padiglione 12, telefono 061-26 73 05 / Caffè, padiglione 16, telefono 061-26 48 97 / Caffè Boulevard, cortile rotondo, telefono 061-26 73 05 / Edificio A: / Mustermesse-Ristorante con Grillroom e Rôtisserie, telefono 061-32 76 50
Glass and frame service	André Frey, hall 10, phone 061-26 84 29 / Shop: Altkircherstrasse 17, 4054 Basle, phone 061-38 72 96	Servizio vetro e incorniciatura	André Frey, padiglione 10, telefono 061-26 84 29 / Negozio: Altkircherstrasse 17, 4054 Basilea, telefono 061-38 72 96
Plan of the Halle	At the beginning of the catalogue	Pianta dei padiglioni	Vedi le prime pagine del catalogo

5

Österreich — Sonderausstellung — Halle 14

Autriche — Exposition spéciale — Halle 14

Austria — Special Exhibition — Hall 14

Austria — Esposizione speciale — Padiglione 14

6

Ausstellerverzeichnis — Index of Exhibitors

Répertoire des exposants — Elenco degli espositori

7

Künstlerverzeichnis — Index of Artists

Répertoire des artistes — Elenco degli artisti

8

5 Official notes
6 Advertisement "Special exhibition Austria"
7 List of exhibitors
8 List of artists

5 Offizielle Mitteilungen
6 Anzeige «Sonderausstellung Österreich»
7 Ausstellerverzeichnis
8 Künstlerverzeichnis

5 Informations générales
6 Annonce «Exposition spéciale Autriche»
7 Répertoire des exposants
8 Répertoire des artistes

Poster "The Art of Writing",
Kunstgewerbemuseum Zurich 1981

Plakat «Schreibkunst» Kunstgewerbemuseum
Zürich 1981

Affiche «Schreibkunst». Musée cantonal des
beaux-arts et d'art appliqué Zurich 1981

1

2

1 Poster "Art-aid". State art-aid Basle
1979

Plakat «Kunstkredit». Staatlicher Kunstkredit Basel-Stadt
1979

Affiche «Kunstkredit». Crédit d'art public Bâle-Ville
1979

2 Poster "Art-aid". State art-aid Basle
1981

Plakat «Kunstkredit». Staatlicher Kunstkredit Basel-Stadt
1981

Affiche «Kunstkredit». Crédit d'art public Bâle-Ville
1981

Impressum

Author
FHK Henrion

Translations
Andrew Bluhm, English
Denise Anne Schai, French

Graphic conception
Hans Rudolf Ziegler

Responsible for publication
Konrad Baumann

Color separations
Cliché + Litho AG, Zurich

Total production
Offset + Buchdruck AG, Zurich

© 1983 by ABC Verlag, Zurich
ISBN 3-85504-075-3
Printed in Switzerland

Impressum

Auto.
FHK Henrion

Übersetzungen
Andrew Bluhm, Englisch
Denise Anne Schai, Französisch

Grafische Gestaltung
Hans Rudolf Ziegler

Verlegerische Gesamtleitung
Konrad Baumann

Fotolithos
Cliché + Litho AG, Zürich

Gesamtherstellung
Offset + Buchdruck AG, Zürich

© 1983 by ABC Verlag, Zürich
ISBN 3-85504-075-3
Gedruckt in der Schweiz

Impressum

Auteur
FHK Henrion

Traductions
Andrew Bluhm, anglais
Denise Anne Schai, français

Conception graphique
Hans Rudolf Ziegler

Direction de l'ouvrage
Konrad Baumann

Photolithographies
Cliché + Litho AG, Zurich

Production générale
Offset + Buchdruck AG, Zurich

© 1983 by ABC Verlag, Zurich
ISBN 3-85504-075-3
Imprimé en Suisse